P9-AFJ-097

H. L. Mencken

OF BUNCOMBE

THE JOHNS HOPKINS PRESS, BALTIMORE

$$\frac{E}{742}$$
.M4

© 1956, The Johns Hopkins Press, Baltimore 18, Md.

Distributed in Great Britain by
Geoffrey Cumberlege, Oxford University Press, London

Printed in U.S.A. by the William Byrd Press, Richmond

Library of Congress Catalog Card No. 56–11658

556903

A CARNIVAL OF BUNCOMBE

A CARNIVAL

Edited by Malcolm Moos

Contents

Introduction

Politics, even before the television camera exposed the secret rites of the smoke-filled room, has long been recognized as first-class drama. Politics also involves many elements of a spectator sport, particularly at election time, when people choose sides to follow their teams and their favorite candidates from one dramatic crisis to another. Who, then, can be surprised that political reporting often assumes the forms of the entertainment world?

At this craft—political reporting as entertainment—H. L. Mencken excelled. For the "Sage of Baltimore" insisted upon regarding politics as fun. He "never giggled, seldom even chuckled; he roared with laughter."

Developing a style that combined in equal proportions the noise of a snorting volcano and the "language of the free lunch counter," Mencken shook politics and politicians for almost half a century.

In the egotistical trade of politics, of course, Mencken found high-grade ore for his very special gifts. He despised pretentiousness, bluster, and hypocrisy, and all were favorite targets. But while he could be merciless in exposing these traits in those who entered the boisterous currents of politics, he simultaneously managed to interpose a stream of belly laughs into his attacks that always made for gay copy. He delighted in using such words as "swinish" or "hoggish" and—to borrow his own phrase—in having at "the booboisie of the hinterland."

In amusing us with the antics of politicians at play he was very likely without peer.

> Has the art of politics no apparent utility? Does it appear to be unqualifiedly ratty, raffish, sordid, obscene, and low down, and its salient virtuosi a gang of unmitigated scoundrels? Then let us not forget its high capacity to soothe and tickle the midriff, its incomparable services as a maker of entertainment.

Several features contributed to the unique quality of Mencken's political reporting. He loved to exaggerate, and one who took many of his statements to heart did so at extreme peril. But if, as Ortega y Gasset reminds us, "to think is to exaggerate," perhaps Mencken felt fully justified in lacing his political coverage with a tall tale here and there. In any case exaggeration was a trademark of his reporting and gave his columns much of their heady flavor.

But on another level, Mencken's workmanship tends to follow quite a different pattern than one tradition commonly found in political reporting. Politics as a spectator sport has borrowed many figures of speech from the field of sports, and the columns of political reporting are stuffed with analogies between the world of competitive sports and the interplay of partisan politics. Moreover, the number of political writers who started as sports writers before making the transition to politics may suggest more than a chance coincidence. James Reston, the late Heywood Broun and Lloyd Lewis, and Westbrook Pegler, to name but a few, all began their newspaper careers as sports reporters. Other writers, of course, who never had anything to do with sports also interlard their political reporting with many comparisons from this field.

With Mencken, the approach was different. Much of his writing is seemingly unconcerned with the shape of political institutions, and the political settings in his columns are not staged in terms of two titanic forces locked in mortal combat to win "a point after touchdown" victory, or the dark horse who gallops out of the mist to win a presidential nomination. Yet the drama he gets across to his readers always packs a wallop.

How does he manage it? By one device at least which he himself credits to Theodore Roosevelt, in explaining the reason for TR's success: "Life fascinated him and he knew how to make his doings fascinating to others." But in addition Mencken knew where to spot the soft streaks in the individuals engaged in this most competitive of all games—the art of politics. And while he appears ruthless in his comments on the struggle that Disraeli once characterized as the "climb to the top of the greasy pole," there can be little doubt that Mencken knew how to raise a titter once he spotted a politico stealing a base from an opponent through a particular device or tactic. In a sense it involves the exploitation of human frailties which seem far more luminous in politics simply because there is far less cover than in the comfortable security of the professions and the business world.

No one was really ever indifferent to Mencken. That a man who had few rivals as a demolition expert should arouse the ire of many who felt deeply that Mencken was a cynic totally emptied of political idealism is, of course, in no way surprising, particularly if we look at his beliefs about what life ought to be like. For Mencken's musings and observations on political ideology are certainly filled with startling pronouncements—so much so that some would call them indescribably fearsome or would question whether Mencken really believed in them himself. But our concern here is not with Mencken as the theorist—the architect of thought—but rather with Mencken the reporter with sharp insights into the behavior and motivations of the politicians and figures who ply the precincts, caucus rooms, convention halls, political rostrums, and public offices of this happy land.

Of course the way he used the bludgeon to describe these men and their activities gives us a mighty dim view of our political substructure. Yet even here Mencken holds out hope by adding the very sensible comment that our government system must be far more competent than it looks.

> There are the leaders. . . . On the lower levels one encounters men so dreadful that it would be painful to describe them realistically. Nonetheless, the government goes on. There is some dis-

order, but not enough to be uncomfortable. A certain amount of money is wasted, but not enough to bankrupt us. The laws are dishonest and idiotic, but it is easy to imagine worse. How are we to account for this? I can conjure up but two plausible theories. One is to the effect that the country is actually under the special protection of God, as many clergymen allege every Fourth of July. The other is that the hated and reviled bureaucracy must be a great deal more competent than it looks.

Mencken was grossly irreverent in his columns, but he was by no means a cynic, intent only on smiting the "reigning clowns." And if he was "overrated in his day as a thinker,"as Alistair Cooke writes (which many will dispute), "he was vastly underrated as a humorist with one deadly sensible eye on the behavior of the human animal."

One difficulty in following Mencken's insights into politics is that his vivid violent style and his impulse for droll fakery tend to stipple the canvas—that is, they sometimes obscure or crowd an astute observation. But Mencken's judgment on the techniques of politics and politicians, as we shall examine later, were highly perceptive. These judgments, moreover, together with his ability to give us a prismatic picture of the most American of all our political institutions—the national nominating convention—have withstood the test of time. And they have done so despite attempts to pass them off as "transient journalism" by "book-writers with one foot already in obscurity."

Let no one forget that Mencken also had his serious constructive moments, particularly in his service to civic crusades at the local level of politics. In his own Baltimore bailiwick he performed yeoman duty by arousing readers to the serious problems that menaced public health, to the need for sanitary milk, to a pure water supply, and to the necessity of controlling diphtheria and typhoid.

That those unfamiliar with Mencken the man shall not misconceive him as a dragon slayer, poised with a cutlass in one hand and a three-ton blockbuster in the other, a word is in order about his personal temperament. Mencken was a warm-hearted person with a gently courteous consideration for others. True, he was not a man to suffer fools gladly, but everyone who knew him closely or saw him in action, even from afar, attests to his kindness. He was uncommonly thoughtful about paying visits to elderly people who were hospitalized, and no friend ever felt neglected while he was convalescing. On such occasions when he went to see a sick friend, the Mencken wit really blossomed; and a long-time associate, Hamilton Owens, tells us that doctors and nurses "invariably made excuses" to rush into the room to see him perform.

Mencken was also held in high esteem by members of his own guild, both as a writer and as a fascinating companion. "Newspapermen idolized him," reports Lee McCardell. "He was never aloof. He wrapped his legs around the stool of a small-town lunch counter with the most undistinguished reporters in the business. He had no side," and he always "shared the minutiae of good reporting with the gang, filling them in on first names and middle initials. And he talked about everything under the sun."

Mencken was born with his motor racing. And he kept it that way for 68 active years. My own first glimpse of this frolicsome terror of the twenties was in the winter of 1946 when E. W. Kenworthy and I were huddled over typewriters in an office of the old Sun building, whose ceiling and walls were being dismantled. Mencken, about to step into an elevator, paused a moment, cigar in hand, while he stared at the incongruous sight of two men encircled only by the wire mesh used to reinforce concrete, shivering with cold while plaster dust drifted down like snow. Then he turned to the elevator operator: "Barney," he said, "throw those men some raw meat."

H. L. Mencken was the oldest child of a family that included three sons and a daughter. Born in Baltimore, September 12, 1880, he was the son of the owner of a tobacco business (August Mencken) whose father had left Germany in the midst of the unhinged political uprisings of 1848.

At an early age Mencken became a boy wonder, but unlike many boy wonders he never permitted himself to rust into the status of boy wonder emeritus. Right down to the moment he was stricken with a cerebral thrombosis he continued to push out creative work at a furious pace.

As a boy Mencken developed a huge appetite for reading. He liked and showed some aptitude for music, and he was valedictorian of his class at Baltimore's Polytechnic Institute. That newspaper work beckoned enticingly as a career right from the beginning seems never to have been in doubt.

The week after his father's death, in 1899, he applied for his first post with the Baltimore *Morning Herald*. Turned down initially, he kept returning for a month until the editor finally gave him an assignment (covering a suburb struck by a blizzard which resulted in Mencken's first published five line story about a horse-stealing rumor), and the rest is history.

From that moment the Mencken career soared. He was city editor of the *Herald* by 1903, and soon he was demonstrating the inimitable invective style that became his trademark. And in addition to his newspaper stints he began a string of other projects. His first book appeared in 1905—*George Bernard Shaw: His Plays*—and his development as a literary critic soon connected him with *Smart Set* and began his long association with Publisher Alfred A. Knopf and George Jean Nathan, both of whom joined him in founding the *American Mercury* in 1924. The announced objective of this lively magazine is revealing:

> The editors are committed to nothing save this: to keep common sense as fast as they can, to belabor sham as agreeably as possible, to give civilized entertainment.

In 1906, Mencken joined the Baltimore *Sun* to manage the newly created Sunday edition. Thereafter he remained actively associated with the *Sunpapers* until his illness in the fall of 1948.

Long thought of as a confirmed bachelor, Mencken (then 50) surprised everyone in 1930 by his marriage to Sara Powell Haardt of Montgomery, Alabama, whom he met while lecturing at Goucher College on "How to Catch a Husband." Some years younger than Mencken, Miss Haardt, who was also a writer, died in 1935 at the age of 37. To escape from his grief, Mencken plunged into a history of the *Sunpapers,* which was published on the *Sun*'s hundredth anniversary in 1937.

From 1911 to 1915 Mencken wrote his Free Lance column for

the *Evening Sun* editorial page, which was widely quoted across the nation. This activity gave way to his regular Monday articles, and in this endeavor Mencken turned out the bulk of his writing for the *Sunpapers* during the twenties and thirties. (From time to time he would rewrite one of these Monday articles for republication in the *Smart Set* or the *American Mercury*, but these were not generally the political articles. Of the sixty-nine articles printed here, only two were ever published more than once.) Except for the early years before 1917, and a brief time in 1938, when he managed the editorial page of the *Evening Sun*, Mencken did not hold down any desk position on a newspaper.

Meanwhile his output burgeoned as books (nearly 20) and articles poured out on literature, language, manners, politics, women, ethics, prohibition, and religion. By his own estimate, Mencken's writings embrace some 5,000,000 words—an incredible production for a man, by the way, who never left a letter unanswered for more than twenty-four hours.

In 1919, perhaps Mencken's greatest contribution hit the book stalls—*The American Language*. This volume, subsequently followed by two supplements, one of which weighed in at twenty pounds when the typed manuscript was plumped on publisher Knopf's desk, was a monumental study on the effervescence of American speech. His preoccupation with the subtleties and changes in American speechways was no doubt of very considerable significance in carbonating his columns on political reporting. Mencken himself used to say that he was not a scholar "but a scout for scholars," but there is general agreement that his philological researches have marked an important forward step in the study of the American language.

By the end of 1943, Mencken had completed a three-volume autobiography—*Happy Days, Heathen Days,* and *Newspaper Days*—and still showed few signs of being winded. He continued to turn up at national presidential conventions, where now he was photographed almost as often as front running candidates and certainly more frequently than some favorite sons. He kept up a stream of correspondence (answering even Christmas cards, which he himself never sent) and enjoyed the steady comforts of life at home on Hollins Street, where he lived with his brother August and where a few old friends came for an evening's drink or two and good talk.

In November, 1948, Mencken suffered a cerebral thrombosis, but after a critical period in an oxygen tent rallied sufficiently to return home. He never fully recovered his flashing conversational repartee, and he found difficulty in organizing his thoughts and speech came slowly. For Mencken, no doubt, the shock that he was no longer able to read was even more of a blow. But he faced his affliction cheerfully, had a student from Johns Hopkins, Bob Dewar, read to him, took in the movies now and then, and seemed to enjoy many hours watching children play in the park. On Saturday evening, January 28, 1956, an old friend, Louis Cheslock of the Peabody Institute and a member of the famous Saturday Night Club, dropped in and visited awhile before the open fire. Mencken retired about 11 P.M. with the remark that he didn't feel too well. That night he passed away in his sleep from a coronary occlusion. He was 75.

Two features of Mencken's political writing surely stand out as we come to spread it on a broader canvas. First, his poor guesses on what would happen, and second his deep faith in the right of free expression.

In the realm of political prophecy, Mencken's judgment was anything but sure footed. (Franklin Roosevelt didn't have a Chinaman's chance of election in 1932, and Hoover's re-election was highly probable.) His classical blooper in guessing at the political future, as Mark Watson relates it, occurred at the scene of carnage at Madison Square Garden in the summer of 1924, when the Democratic Party was stalemated for 103 ballots before naming a presidential nominee.

Somewhere toward the clamorous close of this tense struggle, as the Democratic convention moved near the one-hundredth ballot, Mencken squatted down before his old portable Corona and struck off the following lead for a special piece to the *Sun*.

Everything is uncertain in this convention but one thing: John W. Davis will never be nominated.

Informed that Davis had been nominated for president a few seconds after filing his story, Mencken, stunned for the moment, quickly snapped back: "Why that's incredible! I've already sent off a story that it's impossible." Then as an afterthought: "I wonder if those idiots in Baltimore will know enough to strike out the negative."

Mencken the militant upholder of free speech is quite another matter. For the world has need of its Voltaires in all ages. And no one was around in the twenties who could draw a bead so unerringly on a Dixie demagogue, intolerant lawmaker, preacher, or political jackass. Whatever Mencken may have held dear or central in the way of a political philosophy, no belief had greater priority than that men should work and live unmuzzled. Here he met his opponents head on, scorching like a flame-thrower fueled with high octane.

Appropriately for a craftsman who stirred old embers every time he thought about the delights of a presidential nominating convention, the last series of articles that Mencken ever wrote dealt with this boisterous by-product of our constitutional system—that "colossal travesty of popular institutions" as an unkind critic once put it. And what a convention!

In late July, 1948, in the same Philadelphia auditorium where the Republicans nominated Tom Dewey and then the Democrats met to name Harry Truman as their candidate, the Progressive party gathered to nominate Henry Wallace and launch a third party.

Back at his old stand in the press box to watch the attempt "to heave Henry into the presidency of this great Republic," Mencken was in a carnival mood. His first piece bearing the Philadelphia dateline July 22 and the overline "Mencken and the Swami," carried the headline: MARX, LENIN, UNCLE JOE MISSING AT CONVENTION.

On successive days he covered familiar terrain—Women—"the ladies were chiefly bulky and unlovely, precisely like Republican and Democratic ladies but they did not run to the same gaudy and preposterous frocks and hats." And Wallace, he suspected, had acquired such a "semi-celestial character" that "if when he is nominated today he suddenly sprouts wings and begins flapping about the hall no one will be surprised."

On Sunday, July 25, Mencken rolled out two pieces for Monday's *Sun*. In one he correctly observed that "in the United States new parties do pretty well at the start, and then fade away." The other article dealt with a Wallace rally, but on the way back to his hotel from this affair, which was held in a baseball park, Mencken confided to a fellow newsman: "You know, I don't feel well. When I write, the words don't seem to come as readily as they used to." It may have been the first forewarning of the stroke that hit him three months later. It had been quite a spell of political reporting. Forty-nine years of attendance, in fact, upon what he liked to call "political, homilectical, and patrio-inspirational orgies."

Newspaper workers searching for old faces at new conventions can perhaps still see him "descending into the crypt below" the rostrum "to find a drink." Others not so fortunate will heartily agree with the *Manchester Guardian* that "in a long line that stretches from Benjamin Franklin and Mark Twain to Will Rogers, the 'Sage of Baltimore' stands high."

ACKNOWLEDGMENTS

The paternity of this volume owes much to The Johns Hopkins Press. In March, 1955, John Kyle, Editor of the Press, asked A. D. Emmart of the Baltimore *Evening Sun* editorial staff to sample some of the famous Monday articles Mencken wrote for the *Evening Sun* during the 1920's and 1930's to see if they were still of contemporary interest. Mr. Emmart did so and came back with an affirmative and enthusiastic answer. He also suggested that Huntington Cairns sift through the articles—some 700 in all—covering a wide variety of subjects ranging from literary criticism to politics.

Mr. Cairns viewed these articles on microfilm in his summer home at Kitty Hawk in the summer of 1955 and concluded that sixty-nine of the pieces be published with appropriate introductory and background comment. Since the content of these articles centered chiefly on politics, I was asked to prepare the latter—an undertaking I joyfully accepted both because of my belief that Mencken was a master craftsman in many aspects of political reporting and also because I came to admire him personally a great deal during the brief period I knew him while I worked for the Baltimore *Evening Sun*.

These articles run from 1920 into late 1936 and terminate there since Mencken stopped writing his Monday pieces at that time. In some of my introductory comments, however, I have quoted from other articles of Mencken covering specific campaigns and other political subjects that do not appear in this collection.

For biographical and anecdotal material on Mencken himself I am much in the debt of several of Mencken's colleagues on the *Sunpapers*: Hamilton Owens; Lee McCardell; A. D. Emmart; Mark Watson; and William Manchester; among others.

Very special thanks is due August Mencken, who probably knew his brother best, and who has been most generous in giving his time and advice to all of us engaged in bringing these articles before the public.

BALTIMORE, JULY 25, 1956   *Malcolm Moos*

A CARNIVAL OF BUNCOMBE

Normalcy

F EW EVENTS BROUGHT ABOUT MORE HEADY ENTHUSIASM
for H. L. Mencken than the whirling eddies of a national political convention. The cyclonic yells of the delegates, galleries,
horrifying harangues, sweating and pontificating politicians,
or the hopelessness of a convention stalled on dead center when
leaders were unable to bring about a congruence of forces that
would yield a nomination—these were all fair game for his
pixyish pen. "I confess," he wrote as he packed up his fourteen-
year-old portable Corona and prepared to embark for one of
those mammoth colosseums where presidential nominations are
born, "that national conventions always entertain me immensely." And even after the physical torments of 103 ballots
at Madison Square Garden during the Democratic Convention
of 1924, which, of course, was devoid of creature comforts like
air conditioning, he could still write that there was something
about a national convention "as fascinating as a revival or
hanging." It is vulgar, ugly, stupid and tedious, to be sure, he
thought, and yet there suddenly "comes a show so gaudy and
hilarious, so melodramatic and obscene, so unimaginably exhilarating and preposterous that one lives a gorgeous year in an

hour." Actually, even the speeches of aging politicians "plainly on furlough from some home for extinct volcanoes" could wring enthusiasm out of Mencken.

But if Mencken found the delights of a small boy attending his first circus in following successive conventions and presidential campaigns, any reader will be quick to sense that the space he devotes to convention capers is overlaid with some mighty perceptive and snappy judgments about politics and political leaders. For the irreverent Mr. Mencken, however incorrigible his impulses were to indulge in spoofery and to be jocund, was simultaneously wise in his insights into politics and the eccentric orbits in which men and politics move.

The politics of the early 1920's made a perfect foil for his superheated sallies into conventions and campaigns. John Barleycorn, officially demoted to the illicit haunts of the cellar and speakeasy by the proclamation of the Prohibition Amendment in August, 1920, was a prime target of Mencken. He even explained the lack of enthusiasm among delegates to the Republican National Convention by asking, "how could you wring anything properly describable as enthusiasm out of delegates whose carburetors were filled with lakewater." And later he wrote that the only chance of Democratic nominee Cox lay in denouncing the "Great Experiment," whereupon the wets in the great cities would embrace him and make his election a certainty.

Unceasing in his attack against the Eighteenth Amendment until that famous night years later—Midnight, April 7, 1933— when the taps were opened at Baltimore's Rennert Hotel and cheering onlookers watched him raise a seidel of beer, tilt his head back, and let gravity take over, Mencken threw his riotous reportorial skill against the drys on every possible occasion. Noting the innovation of a professional cheer leader "as a substitute for wines and liquors at the Republican Convention of 1920," Mencken almost seems to be forewarning us against the dreadfully synthetic institution into which this convention performer has since developed.

Amusingly, Harding's inaugural address, which Mencken tells us the President wrote himself, and cites as the worst prose one could possibly conceive (Harding's prose reminded him of a "string of wet sponges"), was not drafted by Harding at all but was actually written by one of his advisers—a professor of political economy at The Johns Hopkins University. This slip, of course, in no way dispels the correctness of Mencken's judgment about Harding's speeches. For Harding was given to making speeches that resembled a tossed salad of platitudes, bumbling phrases—"bloviating" as Harding himself liked to describe them—and new words not to be found in any dictionary. (Normalcy, the now famous word that appeared in Harding's inaugural address, was a coinage that resulted simply because the President misread the word "normality," which was in the draft prepared for him.)

Looking back here and there, Mencken frequently lets the flight of the years get in the way of some of his facts. He credits the nomination of Coolidge for vice-president to Henry Cabot Lodge, when it was actually Wallace McCamant. But these are matters of small moment, particularly when the bulk of his reporting is direct, on-the-scenes writing with the facts tumbling straight from the political bin to his portable typewriter.

While any attempt to quantify the political behavior of any man as unique in many ways as H. L. Mencken serves little useful purpose, his political loyalties as measured by his actual votes for presidential candidates from 1920 through 1936 are not without interest. Twice during these years he voted for Republicans—1920 and 1936; twice he supported Democratic candidates—1928 and 1932; and in 1924 his vote went to a third party candidate—the nominee of the Progressive party.

Several elements of the 1920 campaign made it a supermarket for Mencken's reportorial gifts this year. Foremost perhaps was the fact that for the first time since 1896 both major parties had new candidates in the field, each of whom was, by and large, quite unfamiliar to the national electorate. Both, in Mencken's judgment, had more than sufficient reason to be modest about their qualifications, and it caused him no little pain to admit that he felt compelled to vote for Harding.

Scattered here and there in the pieces that follow, the reader will soon discover that Mencken frequently reveals a talent for assessing leaders in capsular form even though the judgments may sound offensive to many because of his wide-swinging sarcasm. Thus he sees the California progressive Hiram Johnson as a "great lover of the plain people, but always stopping short of suicidal fondness." Or again showing insights that other writers have taken pages or even chapters to catch hold of firmly, he notes that "it was from Roosevelt that Johnson borrowed an excellent political formula: 'first scare Wall street half to death by stirring up the boobery, and then make convenient terms behind the door.' "

Convinced at the Republican convention of 1920 that "Liberalism was laid in the coffin," with the nomination of Harding, Mencken found little that Harding ever did to his liking even though he voted for him after a night on his knees in prayerful meditation. He approved of Harding's pardon for Eugene Debs, though he complains that the commutation was granted belatedly and "grudgingly."

Still smarting over his critical memory of Woodrow Wilson —"the Anglomaniacal Woodrow," as he called him—Mencken shows his strong streak of anti-British sentiments in voluble style as we come to the close of this first selection of his articles when he begins to assess the prospects for the 1924 election. But whatever he is doing and no matter if he enrages or amuses, his pieces always seem to radiate his own boisterous enjoyment—and gustily so.   M. M.

A CARNIVAL OF BUNCOMBE

February 9, 1920

All of the great patriots now engaged in edging and squirming their way toward the Presidency of the Republic run true to form. This is to say, they are all extremely wary, and all more or less palpable frauds. What they want, primarily, is the job; the necessary equipment of unescapable issues, immutable principles and soaring ideals can wait until it becomes more certain which way the mob will be whooping. Of the whole crowd at present in the ring, it is probable that only Hoover would make a respectable President. General Wood is a simple-minded old dodo with a delusion of persecution; Palmer is a political mountebank of the first water; Harding is a second-rate provincial; Johnson is allowing himself to be lost in the shuffle; Borah is steadily diminishing in size as he gets closer to the fight; Gerard and the rest are simply bad jokes. Only Hoover stands out as a man of any genuine sense or dignity. He lacks an intelligible platform and is even without a definite party, but he at least shows a strong personality and a great deal of elemental competence. But can he be elected? I doubt it.

What will fetch him in the end, it seems to me, is Knownothingism in all its new and lovely forms. He is altogether too much the foreigner to be swallowed by the great masses of the plain people. They will listen, for a while, to his sweet words; they will hear his protestations of undying loyalty to the flag and to the inspired maxims of Andrew Jackson; but in the long run they will remember that he fled from the republic as a youngster and became, to all intents and purposes, an Englishman, and they will remember, too, that his boom, in its early stages, showed a suspiciously English cast of countenance. Was it actually launched by Viscount Grey? Well, what are the odds?

The accusation will be quite as potent as the proof. In such matters one does not need convincing evidence; one merely needs an effective charge.

William Randolph Hearst, a politician of large and delicate gifts, has already raised the issue, and in his journals of public education, with their 5,000,000 circulation, he devotes himself daily to pumping it up. Hoover, it appears by these Hearstian blasts, is actually no more than a pussyfoot sent out by Lloyd George, Sir George Paish and company to insinuate himself into the confidence of innocent Americans, seduce them into voting for him, so hoist himself into the White House—and then hand over the country to the unholy English. His ultimate aim, like that of young Pulitzer, young Reid, the Pierpont Morgan partners, Ladies' Home Journal Curtis and other such Anglomaniacs, is to restore the United States to its old place as a loyal British colony, and unload upon it the goat's share of Great Britain's war debt.

Thus Hearst. The Irish-American weeklies go even further. The very mention of Hoover's name lifts them to frenzies. Imagine him President—and taking orders from the Colonial Office! It is a dream more terrible than that of the League of Nations. In all these fears, of course, one discerns a certain exaggeration. It is probably untrue that Dr. Hoover is being financed by English money, or that he'd rather be the Premier of a British colony than president of a free nation, or that he has visions of being promoted from the White House to the House of Lords. In such notions there is a pervasive unlikelihood. But under even the most grotesque of them there remains a sediment of sense, and this sediment of sense takes the form of the doctrine that the interests of England and of the United States, since the close of the war, have begun to diverge sharply, and that it would thus be somewhat unsafe to intrust the interests of the United States to a man so long schooled in promoting the interests of England.

This feeling, it seems to me, is growing very rapidly, and it will be strong enough in the end to eliminate Hoover. It shows itself in many current phenomena—for example, in the acrimonious newspaper duel now going on between the two countries and in the revival of the old sport of pulling the lion's tail on the floor of Congress. The English, usually so skillful at leading the Yankee by the nose, now show a distressing lack of form. Their papers begin to go on at a furious rate, denouncing everything American as dishonest and disgusting. The doctrine that Americans won the war—a very tender point—is laughed at. American rapacity is blamed for the present demoralization of exchange. There is more or less open talk of repudiating England's American debt. Even Lord Grey's very discreet letter has not much improved the situation, for what he has gained by his mollifying words he has lost by his blow to the extreme wing of League of Nations advocates, most of whom are more English than the English, and now feel themselves repudiated and deserted.

In brief, one begins to hear hymns of hate in the offing, and Dr. Hoover will be lucky indeed if they do not drown out his self-sacrificing offer to serve the state. If he speaks against them, then Hearst and the Irish will have all the proof that is needed, speaking politically, to convict him of being a British spy. And if he essays to join in, then even the persons who are now friendly to him will begin to suspect him of a dark and treacherous hypocrisy. The times, in other words, are unfavorable to a candidate bearing his marks. England and the United States are fast drifting apart and the inner causes of that separation will produce important effects upon American domestic politics. The thing that holds up the peace treaty is not any notion that it is dishonest and unjust, or any desire to kick the corpse of Woodrow. It is suspicion of England, pure and simple, as anyone may quickly discover by reading the debates in the Senate, and the harangues of the anti-treaty missionaries on the stump.

Palmer is even weaker than Hoover, if only because he is a

man of much inferior ability and of infinitely less intrinsic honesty. His mediæval attempts to get into the White House by pumping up the Bolshevik issue have had the actual effect of greatly diminishing his chances. The American people, as a general thing, enjoy the public pursuit of criminals. They esteem and respect a prosecuting officer who entertains them with gaudy raids and is on the first pages of the newspapers every morning. To provide such sport for them is the surest way to get on in politics; every intelligent district attorney prays every night for a Thaw, a Becker or an O'Leary, that he may follow in the illustrious footsteps of Folk, Heney, Whitman and Hughes. But Palmer went a bit too far. He carried the farce to such lengths that the plain people began to sympathize with his victims, nine-tenths of whom were palpably innocent of any worse crime than folly. Today he faces a public conviction that he is a silly fellow, despotic and without sense. That conviction does little violence to the truth.

Aside from his efforts to scare the boobery with Bolshevist bugaboos, Palmer seems to put most reliance in his fidelity to Dr. Wilson's so-called ideals. Here he simply straps himself to a cadaver. Those ideals, for two years the marvel of Christendom, are now seen to have been mere buncombe. Dr. Wilson himself never made any actual effort to give them force and effect. On the contrary, it is now evident, by the testimony of all who were privy to the facts, that he heaved them overboard as so much rubbish at the first opportunity. Palmer does not actually believe in them. He has probably done more than any other one man, save only Mr. Wilson himself, to break down democratic self-government in America and substitute a Cossack despotism, unintelligent and dishonest. His final appeal for votes is with the affecting slogan: "Equal rights for all; special privileges to none." And this from the creator of the Chemical Foundation!

In brief, the fellow is a hollow charlatan. Wood is more honest. He is the simple-minded dragoon, viewing all human phenomena

from the standpoint of the barrack-room. His remedy for all ills
and evils is force. Turn out the guard, and let them have a whiff
of grape! One somehow warms to the old boy. He is archaic, but
transparent. He indulges himself in no pishposh about ideals.
He has no opinions upon any public question save the primary
one of protecting property. His is a policeman's philosophy, and
hence a good deal more respectable than that of Palmer, which
is a detective's. But what chance has he got? I can't see much.
There is no emotional push in his candidacy. The Red issue is
dying fast; it will be forgotten before election. And the issue of
Americanism is being murdered by idiots. Day by day its exponents pile up proofs that to be an American, as they conceive
it, is to be a poltroon and an ass.

Two issues show some likelihood of surviving. One is the issue
of national independence—what is now visible as the anti-English
issue. The other is the issue of personal freedom. Between Wilson
and his brigades of informers, spies, volunteer detectives, per-
jurers and complaisant judges, and the Prohibitionists and their
messianic delusion, the liberty of the citizen has pretty well vanished in America. In two or three years, if the thing goes on,
every third American will be a spy upon his fellow-citizens. But
is it going on? I begin to doubt that it is. I begin to see signs
that, deep down in their hearts, the American people are growing
tired of government by fiat and denunciation. Once they reach
the limit of endurance, there will be a chance again for the sort
of Americanism that civilized men can be proud of, and that sort
of Americanism will make an issue a thousand times as vital as
the imitations put forward by the Prohibitionists, the Palmer
White Guard, the Wilson mail openers and the press agents of
the American Legion.

Well, imagine Hoover or Palmer nominated by the Democrats,
and Wood or some other glorified gendarme nominated by the
Republicans. What then? In the offing lurks William Jennings
Bryan. I have a suspicion that Bryan is a better politician than

any of them. He must see, as every impartial man must see, that both the great parties are sick unto death—that both are thinking in terms of 1914. And he must see, too, the vast body of miscellaneous malcontents in the middle ground, all sore, all eager to strike, all waiting to be led. There are, to begin with, probably a million Socialists; Palmerism in State and nation has been manufacturing them by whole brigades and army corps. There are I. W. W.'s and their like—extravagant fanatics, fools ready to believe anything, but hard used, evilly done out of their common rights. There are racial groups, each with its bitter grievances. There are the revolutionary yokels out in the Northwest, marching like the Bolsheviki. There are the Irish, ready to repudiate Tammany, and the blacks, eager to punish the Republican party. There are, finally, the growing thousands of plain men, who tire of government by Burlesons, Palmers, Lusk committees, profiteers and newspapers, and begin to long for a restoration of peace, freedom and common decency.

Jennings is an oily fellow, an adept opportunist. His specialty is capitalizing grievances. Prohibition, at the moment, rather handicaps him, but he will know how to get rid of it if necessary. He is at home where men groan under atrocities and are beset by devils. He has the soft words that soothe the fevered brow. He can weep. Already one of his legs is over the side of the democratic ark. Suppose he takes a bold header into the wild waters of miscellaneous radicalism? Suppose he sets out to round up all who have scalded necks, and despair in their hearts, and a great yearning to raise blue hell? The chance is there—and there, perhaps, stands the statesman foreordained—there stands the super-Debs, the white Toussaint L'Overture, Spartacus come back to earth. He, too, has suffered. He lost his job because he wasn't English enough. He can feel with the downtrodden. He is a laborer, a farmer, an Irish patriot, an oppressed war veteran, a poor coon.

Given his health, there is fun ahead for Jennings.

THE CLOWNS IN THE RING

May 12, 1920

The collapse of Dr. Hoover, predicted in a treatise printed in this place so long ago as February 9, now leaves it a combat *a quatre mains* between Johnson and the General, with the odds considerably in favor of Johnson.

Hoover's fate, despite the violent clapper-clawing of his backers, was plainly in sight from the start, and surely no great gift of prevision was necessary to see it. He carried, in his English connections, a handicap that would have broken the back of a candidate four times as strong. Worse, he quickly showed that he was almost completely destitute of practical political talents. There remained only his reputation as a competent and intelligent administrator—which is precisely the last thing that the endless hordes and herds of the common people ever give a thought to. His corpse now floats the black, black tide, anon rising out of the water with post-mortem pertinacity and reaching clumsily for this issue or that. But no one seems to care any longer what issues Hoover is for and what issues he is against. He has died for the true, the good and the beautiful.

No man ever went into a Presidential campaign with better preliminary support. He had almost unlimited money, he was viewed hospitably by Big Business, and there was a singularly "spontaneous" whooping up of his merits by newspapers north, east, south and west. At one extreme the *Saturday Evening Post* belabored the shoe-drummers, the lime and cement dealers, the remote farm wives and the admirers of Rex Beach and Douglas Fairbanks in his interest; at the other extreme his merits were hammered into the *intelligentsia* by the *New Republic*. But somehow or other it simply failed to come off. There was no very active opposition to him—certainly nothing that had yet become palpably damaging. But the proletariat, with other more talented mimes in the ring, turned to those others and so forgot him. Whenever he has carried a State he has carried it by grace of a very effective organization. The populace has never thrilled and glowed at the thought of him. The Busy Berthas of the Anglophobes have never had to be unlimbered against him.

Hoover's speeches, in the main, have been platitudinous and ineffective. The harangue he delivered before the Johns Hopkins was typical—the obvious in terms of the trivial—a pronunciamento well within the talents of any literate man. I have a suspicion that the syndics of the university will soon begin to regret wasting their learned degree. They gave it to a man who promised to be a grateful President of the United States. But the man who bears it now threatens to fade into the shadows. Let them be more careful hereafter. In particular let them put less faith in the *New Republic*.

Nothing could be plainer than the fact that General Wood is not inflaming the masses. He has been jammed through, in a number of States, by organization politicians fevered by the scent of his huge bar'l, but it surely would be absurd to say that he has made much appeal to the public imagination. Wood started out with the apparent notion that he could horn his way to the nomination and the election on the single issue of Bolshevism—a safe and sane bugaboo, promising much at that time. But since then the obscene clownings of Mitchell Palmer have reduced it to such a joke that even the most credulous right-thinkers laugh at it, and so the General has had to comb the dump for other issues. Of this enterprise he has made a palpable mess. No one knows precisely what he is in favor of—least of all himself. On the single issue of the standing army he has bawled for antagonistic schemes on successive days. If anything has become obvious, indeed, it is that the gallant old bloodletter is intrinsically a hollow and stupid fellow, and that if he were elected he would be little more than a dummy in the hands of the profiteers who are running him.

I say he is stupid, but I add at once that he seems to be perfectly honest. In truth, he is the only honest candidate yet heard of—perhaps the only absolutely honest candidate in American history. Even his ludicrous boggling of issues that he apparently cannot understand seems to be inspired by a genuine desire to find out what would be to the public interest, *i.e.*, to the public as he understands the word, *i.e.*, to the propertied classes and their kept idealists, of whom I have the honor to be one. What ails the General is simply this: that he is the perfect model of a heavy dragoon—faithful, unimaginative, childlike, unsuspicious, always somewhat wistfully humorous. He is the cavalryman incarnate, all heart and no brains. I haven't the slightest doubt that he believes his backers to be unselfish patriots, and that a glimpse of their private account book would shock him to death. He also believed in Roosevelt.

This leaves Johnson, a very shrewd and far-reaching fellow, with a very accurate understanding of the popular mind, politely so called, and a conscience with almost as much stretch in it as a wad of chewing gum. Johnson was one of Roosevelt's chief aides in the Progressive mountebankery of eight years ago and got a great deal more out of it than Theodore himself. He is an old-line politician turned forward-looker and right-thinker—a great lover of the plain people, but always stopping short of a suicidal fondness. From Roosevelt he borrowed an excellent political formula, to wit, first scare Wall street half to death by stirring up the boobery, and then make convenient terms behind the door. He has applied this formula with much greater success than Roosevelt, and I have a sneaking suspicion that it will come very near getting him the Republican nomination.

The Penroses, of course, now call upon God to witness that they will never accept him, and he himself calls upon God to support him in his pious determination to make no compromise with them. But all this is mere hocus-pocus. The oaths of politicians are not to be taken seriously. If Hiram arrives in Chicago

with enough votes to dispose of Wood, the Penroses will be willing enough to talk business with him, and there is not the slightest doubt that he will offer terms well within their conception of
the satisfactory, and even of the felicitous. He is, in fact, hot for
the nomination on any conceivable terms, and he has been most
careful in his canvass to commit himself to nothing that would
keep him outside the fold irrevocably. Nothing would delight him more than to go into the campaign with the Republican
organization behind him and nothing would delight the Republican organization more than to compromise with so discreet and
reasonable a second choice.

In brief, the man is anything but a last-ditcher. On the contrary, he is a professional politician and officeseeker of the very
highest skill and practicality and he is plainly trimming his sails
for compromise. Have you noticed how carefully he avoids all
really embarrassing issues—for example, prohibition? And how
he gives out the reassuring news that he is innocent of any anarchistic plan to form a third party? And how he issues a plain
warning that the Vice-Presidency will not content him? What
are all these things save delicate overtures? And what is all the
tall talk of Penrose and company save a plain warning that,
when he comes in, he must come in lock, stock and barrel?

My bets at the moment are on Johnson. Later on I may
hedge, but for the present I stand pat. I hope and expect to vote
for him. He is almost the ideal candidate—an accomplished
boob-bumper, full of the sough and gush of the tinhorn messiah,
and yet safely practical. He will give a good show if he is elected.
There will be surcease from the austere and incomprehensible
imbecilities of the incumbent. He will steer a reasonably safe
course between the anarchy of democracy and the anarchy of
plutocratic despotism. He will please the plain people and he will
please the interests. There is no more likely President in the ring.

BAYARD vs LIONHEART

July 26, 1920

One discerns in all the current discussion of MM. Harding and Cox a certain sour dismay. It seems to be quite impossible for any wholly literate man to pump up any genuine enthusiasm for either of them. Each, of course, is praised lavishly by the professional politicians of his own party, and compared to Lincoln, Jefferson and Cleveland by the surviving hacks of the party press, but in the middle ground, among men who care less for party success than for the national dignity, there is a gone feeling in the stomach, with shooting pains down the legs. The Liberals, in particular, seem to be suffering badly. They discover that Harding is simply a third-rate political wheel-horse, with the face of a moving-picture actor, the intelligence of a respectable agricultural implement dealer, and the imagination of a lodge joiner, and that Cox is no more than a provincial David Harum with a gift for bamboozling the boobs.

These verdicts, it seems to me, are substantially just. No one but an idiot would argue seriously that either candidate is a first-rate man, or even a creditable specimen of second-rate man. Any State in the Union, at least above the Potomac, could produce a thousand men quite as good, and many States could produce a thousand a great deal better. Harding, intellectually, seems to be merely a benign blank—a decent, harmless, laborious, hollow-headed mediocrity perhaps comparable to the late Harrington, of Maryland. Cox is quicker of wit, but a good deal less honest. He belongs to the cunning type; there is a touch of the shyster in him. His chicaneries in the matter of prohibition, both during the convention and since, show the kink in his mind. He is willing to do anything to cadge votes, and he includes in that anything the ready sacrifices of his good faith, of the national welfare, and of the hopes and confidence of those who honestly support him. Neither candidate reveals the slightest dignity of conviction. Neither cares a hoot for any discernible principle. Neither, in any intelligible sense, is a man of honor.

But it is one thing to yield to virtuous indignation against such individuals and quite another thing to devise any practicable scheme for booting them out of the synagogue. The weakness of those of us who take a gaudy satisfaction in our ideas, and battle for them violently, and face punishment for them willingly and even proudly, is that we forget the primary business of the man in politics, which is the snatching and safeguarding of his job. That business, it must be plain, concerns itself only occasionally with the defense and propagation of ideas, and even then it must confine itself to those that, to a reflective man, must usually appear to be insane. The first and last aim of the politician is to get votes, and the safest of all ways to get votes is to appear to the plain man to be a plain man like himself, which is to say, to appear to him to be happily free from any heretical treason to the body of accepted platitudes—to be filled to the brim with the flabby, banal, childish notions that challenge no prejudice and lay no burden of examination upon the mind.

It is not often, in these later days of the democratic enlightenment, that positive merit lands a man in elective office in the United States; much more often it is a negative merit that gets him there. That negative merit is simply disvulnerability. Of the two candidates, that one wins who least arouses the suspicions and distrusts of the great masses of simple men. Well, what are more likely to arouse those suspicions and distrusts than ideas, convictions, principles? The plain people are not hostile to shysterism, save it be gross and unsuccessful. They admire a Roosevelt for his bold stratagems and duplicities, his sacrifice of faith and principle to the main chance, his magnificent disdain of fairness and honor. But they shy instantly and inevitably from the man who comes before them with notions that they cannot immediately translate into terms of their everyday delusions; they fear the novel idea, and particularly the revolutionary idea, as they fear the devil. When Roosevelt, losing hold upon his cunning at last, embraced the vast hodgepodge of innovations, some idiotic but some sound enough, that went by the name of Progressivism, they jumped from under him in trembling, and he came down with a thump that left him on his back until death delivered him from all hope and caring.

It seems to me that this fear of ideas is a peculiarly democratic phenomenon, and that it is nowhere so horribly apparent as in the United States, perhaps the nearest approach to an actual democracy yet seen in the world. It was Americans who invented the curious doctrine that there is a body of doctrine in every department of thought that every good citizen is in duty bound to accept and cherish; it was Americans who invented the right-thinker. The fundamental concept, of course, was not original. The theologians embraced it centuries ago, and continue to embrace it to this day. It appeared on the political side in the Middle Ages, and survived in Russia into our time. But it is only in the United States that it has been extended to all departments of thought. It is only here that *any* novel idea, in any field of human relations, carries with it a burden of obnoxiousness, and is instantly challenged as mysteriously immoral by the great masses of right-thinking men. It is only here, so far as I have been able to make out, that there is a right way and a wrong way to think about the beverages one drinks with one's meals, and the way children ought to be taught in the schools, and the manner in which foreign alliances should be negotiated, and what ought to be done about the Bolsheviki.

In the face of this singular passion for conformity, this dread of novelty and originality, it is obvious that the man of vigorous mind and stout convictions is gradually shouldered out of public life. He may slide into office once or twice, but soon or late he is bound to be held up, examined and incontinently kicked out. This leaves the field to the intellectual jelly-fish and inner tubes. There is room for two sorts of them—first, the blank cartridge who has no convictions at all and is willing to accept anything to make votes, and, secondly, the mountebank who is willing to conceal and disguise what he actually believes, according as the wind blows hot or cold. Of the first sort, Harding is an excellent specimen; of the second sort, Cox.

Such tests arise inevitably out of democracy—the domination of unreflective and timorous men, moved in vast herds by mob emotions. In private life no man of sense would think of applying them. We do not estimate the integrity and ability of an acquaintance by his flabby willingness to accept our ideas; we estimate him by the honesty and effectiveness with which he maintains his own. All of us, if we are of reflective habit, like and admire men whose fundamental beliefs differ radically from our own. But when a candidate for public office faces the voters he does not face men of sense; he faces a mob of men whose chief distinguishing mark is the fact that they are quite incapable of weighing ideas, or even of comprehending any save the most elemental—men whose whole thinking is done in terms of emotion, and whose dominant emotion is dread of what they cannot understand. So confronted, the candidate must either bark with the pack, or count himself lost. His one aim is to disarm suspicion, to arouse confidence in his orthodoxy, to avoid challenge. If he is a man of convictions, of enthusiasm, of self-respect, it is cruelly hard. But if he is, like Harding, a numskull like the idiots he faces, or, like Cox, a pliant intellectual Jenkins, it is easy.

The larger the mob, the harder the test. In small areas, before small electorates, a first-rate man occasionally fights his way through, carrying even the mob with him by the force of his personality. But when the field is nationwide, and the fight must be waged chiefly at second and third hand, and the force of personality cannot so readily make itself felt, then all the odds are on the man who is, intrinsically, the most devious and mediocre

—the man who can most adeptly disperse the notion that his mind is a virtual vacuum.

The Presidency tends, year by year, to go to such men. As democracy is perfected, the office represents, more and more closely, the inner soul of the people. We move toward a lofty ideal. On some great and glorious day the plain folks of the land will reach their heart's desire at last, and the White House will be adorned by a downright moron.

CAMPAIGN NOTES

September 13, 1920

The Saturnine Cabot. The curious imbecility of Dr. Harding's speech of acceptance continues to engage speculation. The thing was not only nonsensical in content; it was also downright illiterate in form; even a professor of English seldom writes worse English. Moreover, the mystery is made blacker by the well-known fact that the Hon. Henry Cabot Lodge read and redacted the manuscript—Cabot the palladium of correctness, the super-grammarian, the Harvard exquisite. How did all those ghastly snarls and bubbles of speech elude his cultured eye? What had he been drinking to make him so anæsthetic to syntax?

My guess is that he had been drinking nothing above his usual allowance and that the snarls and bubbles did not elude him at all. My guess is that he passed all that balderdash knowingly and deliberately—that he thus gave a sly and saturnine signal perceptible only to cognoscenti, of his fathomless contempt for the poor stonehead thrown upon his hands.

To the Rescue. Since then Gamaliel has fallen into the hands of kindlier masters, and his English thus exhibits improvements. Some of his recent speeches have shown a good deal of clarity and vigor, and even some touch of style. By the time he gets to the White House he may pick up some faculty for writing himself—it is, after all, a trivial art, and well within the capacities of any normal adult with sufficient patience—and so carry on the literary tradition established by the present incumbent. I believe that a literary gift is very valuable to a politician, particularly if it take the form of a talent for mere words, as opposed to ideas. The public likes sonorous and juicy phrases. The less sense there is in them, the better it likes them. To it literature still appeals chiefly as poetry—that is, as something set in opposition to the bitter facts of life. When it reads it doesn't want to be instructed; it wants to be soothed.

  The Case of Cox. The current notion that Dr. Cox is a very clever, practical politician, with a great hand for tickling the boobs, is one that I find myself unable to accept. On the contrary, it seems to me that his politics shows a good deal of clumsiness. He began his errors at San Francisco by trying to sit on both sides of the prohibition fence. This maneuver almost cost him the nomination and greatly wabbled some of his strongest supporters. He could have been nominated with much less difficulty as a straightout wet, and he would have gone into the campaign with the active and eager support of many politicians who are now alienated by his trimming—for example, the Tammany crowd and the Brennan gang in Illinois. As it is, the genuine wets show little active interest in him, and are devoting their chief efforts to their local tickets, and meanwhile the drys are suspicious of him, knowing him to be a turncoat. Running as a wet, Cox would have carried every large city in the country, for in the cities the prohibition issue completely overshadows all other issues. More, he would have done serious execution upon Gamaliel in many a rural district—say in Pennsylvania and New England—for the yokels are growing weary of paying $17 a quart for two-day-old redeye, and are ready to go over to the devil.

Cox made his second capital error when he galloped to Washington immediately he was nominated. It was an act of grateful homage, but was it good politics? Who believes that it was? The heaviest burden that the Democratic party has to carry in this campaign is the burden of Dr. Wilson's unpopularity. He is disliked for a hundred and one different reasons, but here one reason is as good as another. It is months since I last encountered a genuine Wilson man. Even the old exponents of the divine inspiration idea seem to have become poisoned by doubts. Cox, by gallantly shouldering this weight of unpopularity probably lost himself a million votes. And he is certainly not regaining them by his speeches for the League of Nations. I do not believe that most Americans are positively against the League. But an enormous majority of them are violently against any further discussion of the League. They are tired of the whole vexatious question and eager to hear the end of it.

Cox's charges of corruption on the Republican side again show his defective political sense. Assuming that his allegations are all true, he obviously made them too soon. He should have let the Republicans collect the money, and then exposed their method of spending it. This is what Borah and Hiram Johnson did in their battle against Wood and Lowden—and the success of the device is history. But Cox shot off all his ammunition before the enemy was within range. It is easy for the Republicans to prove today that they have not actually collected the money, and that is quite enough for the public, which plainly regards the Cox charges as unproved. The public, remember, does not object to large campaign funds; all it objects to is the use of such funds for bribery and corruption. Cox has proved no such bribery and corruption. His sole accomplishment is to put the Republicans on their guard—to prevent the very crimes that he talks of so darkly, and that might have got him so many votes if he had only permitted the Republicans time to commit them.

The Left Wing. The Socialists are dying the death in the

campaign; they are worse off than they have been for years. On the one hand, Dr. Christensen will make away with hundreds of thousands of potential Socialist votes, not only in the West, but also in the East, and on the other hand the effort to run Dr. Debs as a martyr has fallen dismally flat. The plain truth is that the plain people have very little liking for martyrs, and are not actively opposed to the injustices and atrocities which make them. It is one of the hardest things in the world, indeed, to stir up public indignation against legal injustice, for the mob is always in favor of the man giving the show, and the more violently he flogs his victims the better it likes it and him. The high spots of Roosevelt's popularity always came just after he had made some particularly foul and dishonorable attack upon an enemy. It was when he tried to be fair and judicious that the great masses of God's favorites turned upon him. The sense of justice, like the sense of honor, is the exclusive possession of a small and usually miserable minority of men. Dr. Palmer came a good deal nearer being President of the United States than Dr. Debs will come. The one is deprived of his liberty cruelly, dishonestly and unjustly; the other is perhaps the most eminent living exponent of cruelty, dishonesty and injustice.

THE LAST ROUND

October 4, 1920

After meditation and prayer of excessive virulence for many days and consultation with all the chief political dowsers of the Republic, I conclude with melancholy that God lays upon me the revolting duty of voting for the numskull, Gamaliel, on the first Tuesday in November. It is surely no job to lift the blood pressure and fill the liver with hosannahs. Since I acquired the precious boon of the suffrage, in the year 1901, I have never had to cast my vote for a worse dub. The hon. gentleman is an almost perfect specimen of a 100% American right-thinker. The operations of his medulla oblongata (the organ, apparently, of his ratiocination) resemble the rattlings of a colossal linotype charged with rubber stamps. He invariably utters the expected, which is but another name for the not worth hearing. One half looks for him to abandon connected speech at any moment, and to start a mere chaotic babbling of stereotyped phrases: "Please remit," "Errors and omissions excepted," "For review only," "Polizeilich verboten," "Für Damen," "Apartment to let." "Oh, say, can you see," "Less than ½ of 1% of alcohol by volume," "Post no bills," "Tradesmen's entrance," "In God we trust."

Nevertheless, I shall make my crossmark for Gamaliel. And why not? It is not a choice between the succubi and the cherubim; it is a choice between two devils—nay, four. The *Nation*, a gazette I esteem highly, urges me to vote for Christensen or Debs, but I find it impossible to swallow either. Christensen is a lodge-joiner, and I detest lodge-joiners even more than I detest politicians. Debs is a Socialist, and my last word on the gallows will be a hoot at Socialism. I believe in capitalism, and hope it lasts, at all events, until I am safe in hell. Socialism would cost me even more than it costs me to be robbed by professional patriots. It would be an act of political hari-kari for me to vote for Debs. I simply refuse to do it, despite all the blather of the *Nation*. Or to vote for Christensen, the most worthy supreme archon. If I were a good enough American to believe in laws, I'd propose one making it a felony to be a most worthy supreme archon, punishable by knocking in the head with a footstick. The effect of such a fellow upon me is that of a horse doctor's dose of ipecacuanha, administered *per ora* at a pressure of ten atmospheres.

This leaves Gamaliel—and Jim.

Well, why not Jim? Here another prejudice rears its obscene

and horrendous mask. Next to lodge-joiners, Socialists (and, may I add, forward-lookers, Prohibitionists, evangelical clergymen, stock brokers, anti-vivisectionists, Y.M.C.A. secretaries, boomers, good business men, the judiciary, policemen, women under 30, authors, social pushers, golf players, spiritualists, labor leaders, Christian Scientists, bishops, professors of English, army officers, democrats, war veterans, Single Taxers, collectors for charity, professional Jews, professional patriots, Scotchmen, Armenians, Southerners, suffragettes, uplifters, osteopaths, commuters, children, idealists, motorcyclists, dogfanciers, horsey women, clarinetists, actors, poets and persons who borrow gin) I detest, beyond all other sentient creatures, the fellow who is fundamentally a fraud. Jim is such a fellow. There is in him an unescapable obliquity. His opinions are always fluent, but they always strike me as being 95% dishonest. I believe firmly that he would change all of them overnight if he thought that it would make votes for him. In brief, he is essentially a politician, and I regard a politician as a man able to preserve his honor only by dint (a) of an illimitable and pathetic naïveté or (b) of a quite extraordinary sapience. Jim is not sharp enough to be a Henry Cabot Lodge and not flat-headed enough to be a Gamaliel. He falls into the middle section. That is to say, he is a professional job-grabber of the standard and familiar type—resilient, sneaking, limber, oleaginous, hollow and disingenuous.

Between such a zig-zag contortionist and an honest oaf of the Gamaliel kidney, I am all in favor of the oaf. The latter at least has the capital merit of representing accurately the mentality of the great masses of the plain people—he may lack cunning, but he is at all events, 100% American. I do not believe in democracy, and am heartily glad that the late war darn nigh ruined it, but so long as the American people admire it they should get it. They will get more of it from Gamaliel, despite his obligation to the Interests, than they will ever get from Jim. Gamaliel is the

normal American of the better class—the more honest and reflective class. His thoughts are muddled, but profound. He
speaks bad English, but he has a heart. He is the archetype of
the *Homo boobus*. Put him into the White House and you will
put every president of every Chamber of Commerce into the
White House, and every chairman of every Y.M.C.A. boob-
squeezing drive, and every sales manager of every shoe-factory,
and every reader of the *Saturday Evening Post* and every ab-
horrer of the Bolsheviki, and every Prominent Baltimorean.

The issues do not interest me. The only one that is of any
actual force and weight is the issue of poor Woodrow's astounding unpopularity. Curiously enough, no one has ever thought to
inquire into the origins and nature of that unpopularity. I am
by profession an explorer of the popular mind, and yet I am
as much in the dark about it as the crowd in the nearest cigar-
store. Some time ago I wrote an article on the subject, perhaps
the only full-length effort ever made to penetrate the problem;
it was actually all windy theorizing and ended upon an unre-
solved dissonance. All that seems to be established is that
Woodrow came home from Paris ranking with the master-minds
of the ages, and that he is now regarded by everyone save a
despairing band of last-ditch fanatics as a devious and foolish
fellow, of whom the nation will be well rid on March 4. It seems
unjust, but there it is. For crimes equally obscure Socrates was
hemlocked in a far more civilized land. The public, I suspect, is
an ass.

The League issue is pumped-up and of no horse-power. What
is chiefly aiding Gamaliel is the fact that the plain people are
tired of hearing about it. He promises to scrap it, and so they
are in favor of him, save where idealism still flourishes, as in the
far West, or where every third white voter has a job that he
wants to keep, as in the South. Here in the East the agitation
for it is mainly carried on (a) by financial gentlemen who believe that it would safeguard their loot, (b) by politicians who

YEARY LIBRARY
LAREDO JR. COLLEGE
LAREDO, TEXAS

took to good works when the plain people canned them at the polls, *e.g.*, Dr. Taft, Dr. Root and Dr. Marburg, (c) by theorizing professors with their eyes on college presidencies and Oxford LL.D.'s, and (d) by social pushers who are in favor of it because it is English, just as they are in favor of the poetry of Alfred Noyes. The rest is silence. I travel around a good deal and keep my ears open, but it is months since I have met anyone, not belonging to or obviously influenced by one or other of these groups, who was visibly hot for the League. Its chief advocates are all of such character that their advocacy loses ten votes for it to every one gained.

Personally, I am in favor of the League—not that I am under any delusion about its intents and purposes, but precisely because I regard it as thumpingly dishonest. Like democracy, it deserves to be tried. Five years of it will see all the principal members engaged in trying to slaughter one another. In other words, it will make for wars—and I have acquired an evil taste for wars. Don't blame it on any intrinsic depravity. There was a time when I cooed for peace with the best of them, but all the present whoopers for peace insisted upon war, and after viewing war for six years I found that it was better than a revival or a leg-show—nay, even better than a hanging.

Such unspeakable appetites, however, ought to be hidden in the cellar, and not spoken of in public. Moreover, a man is a scoundrel who puts his private yearnings above the honest desires and obvious well-being of the great majority of his fellow citizens. In the present case, that majority is plainly in favor of keeping out of the mess. The bonus agitation has alarmed the taxpayer. In every community there is a one-legged soldier. Another war means another Palmer. Let the heart of the world bust if it will! Let Turk eat Armenian, and Armenian eat Kurd! Let the Poles steal what they can grab, and keep what they can hold! Let the Russians try genuine democracy if they want to! Let the French lift everything that is not nailed down and the English take what is left! Let Europe, Asia and Africa be damned!

Such is *vox populi* as I hear it in the deep silence of these equinoxial nights. The duty of a patriot is clear. I shall vote for Gamaliel. The Binet-Simon test, true enough, may show that he is backward. But even though the indicator runs clear off the gauge on the minus side, he will be born on March 4, 1921.

IN PRAISE OF GAMALIEL

October 18, 1920

The learned *Freeman* calls attention to something that must have long since wrung the hearts of right-thinking Republicans, to wit, the fact that the candidates and fuglemen of their party are strangely silent about certain great moral issues that lie temptingly under their noses. For example, the Hog Island issue: who hears anything about the herculean stealing that went on down there during the war? Again, the Debs-O'Hare issue: what Republican boob-bumper has ever sobbed and bellowed over the continued caging of dear old Gene? Yet again: the Hard-Boiled Smith issue: who of the Grand Old Party lifts his voice against the mad riot of courts-martial that went on during the war? Several months ago Hard-Boiled himself was paroled after serving half of his light sentence; meanwhile, the military dungeons are still full of boys jailed under the Zulu-esque system that he adorned. But does Gamaliel moan and beat his breast? He does not.

The *Freeman* hints that he is silent because every blast of indignation would come back, boomerang-like, and singe his own withers. All such great moral enterprises, in fact, were managed

upon a strictly bi-partisan basis. Every time a Democratic
patriot, whether capitalist or honest toiler, got an easy dollar
at Hog Island, a Republican patriot was given another dollar.
Every time a German factory was sold at 10 cents on the dollar
to a deserving Democrat, a German mill was sold at 11 cents on
the dollar to a Republican full of exalted rage against the Hun.
And every time a Democratic judge and a Democratic state's
attorney railroaded a Socialist to jail, or a Democratic judge
advocate demanded 30 years for some bewildered doughboy accused of failing to salute a major in the Quartermaster's Department, a Republican judge and state's attorney railroaded
two Socialists and a Dunkard, and a Republican judge advocate demanded 100 years for some doughboy accused of sticking
out his tongue at a lithograph of General Pershing. In brief,
it was a brotherly and amicable business, and the Republicans
had a fair whack at the loot and the fun. If Gamaliel and his
whoopers went into the matter, the matter would explode in their
hands. They must let it alone, as the committees of investigation appointed by a Republican House of Representatives had
to let it alone. It is far safer to set up a din about the League
of Nations, which is fortunately unintelligible, and hence not
loaded. The worst that can happen is that Woodrow calls someone a liar, and someone calls Woodrow another.

So far the estimable *Freeman*. Unluckily, it too has to be a
bit wary—it too has to avoid monkeying with a buzzsaw. That
buzzsaw is its naïve and charming belief in the intrinsic integrity and passion for justice of the great masses of plain men—
its laudable superstition that an unveiling of the facts would
send them into tantrums of indignation, and so cause them to
set down both Cox and Gamaliel as agents of the devil, and to
cast their virtuous votes for Debs, and if not for Debs, then for
Christensen, the grand worthy exalted supreme archon. This
belief, as I say, is charming and laudable, but that is all I care
to say in favor of it at the present time. To argue that it is

sound, it seems to me, is to spit boorishly into the very eye of
the facts.

In other words, there is actually no such nobility in the public
breast, and not all the yelling and tear-squeezing of Gamaliel,
imagining him reckless enough to take a chance, would suffice to
plant it there. No loud demand for light upon all those gaudy
satanries has ever issued from the awful depths of the boob conscience. There has come, once or twice, a demand for the hides
of the scoundrels who put up the price of sugar, flour, potatoes
and hog-meat, and there will come anon an even more raucous
demand for the hides of those who prepare to sell a mixture of
10% anthracite and 90% cobblestone at $20 a ton, but there
has never been any authentic rage against the merry men who
robbed, not the consumer, but the Government and the enemy.
It is not a crime, by American ethics, to rob the Government,
either in peace or in war. On the contrary, it is an evidence of
normalcy, the act of an intelligent and patriotic man. All of the
chief operators at Hog Island were eminent patriots, and for
two long years anyone who attacked them stood in danger of
getting 10 years under the Espionage Act.

Nor is there any settled public horror of cruel and unusual
punishments, as in the case of Debs and company and that of
the victims of Hard-Boiled Smith. The only persons who demand that Debs be released today are (a) Socialists, and (b)
a few sentimental Liberals, of whom I am surely not one. The
plain fact is that the great masses of the plain people, in all
such melodramatic affairs, are almost unanimously on the side
of the prosecution, and that it is impossible to interest them in
the case of the defense, save by turning it into a super-prosecu-
tion. This was not done in Hard-Boiled's case for obvious
reasons, and so he has been released without protest, and no one
bawls about his poor victims. The mob likes a cruel and bloody
show; the prosecution gives the show. Every intelligent district
attorney with an eye upon the Federal bench prays nightly that

God will deliver a Debs, a Leary or a Kate O'Hare into his hands. Nearly half of the eminent men mentioned for the Presidency during the past eight or ten years became eminent by trying to get some conspicuous victim or victims into jail. I name a few: Hughes, Folk, Palmer, Whitman, Heney, Johnson, Wood.

Thus Gamaliel is silent about all the atrocities mentioned by the *Freeman*. On the one hand, he knows that agitation of the matter would hurt him as much as it aided him, and on the other hand he knows that public interest in it would be feeble and transient. In brief, he is a sound politician, a man with a talent for boob-bumping. But has he anything else? Is there any further reason for voting for him? There is. Gamaliel has the very rare virtue (in American politics) of being relatively honest—of being almost as honest, in fact, as the average porch-climber, detective or seller of Mexican oil stock. He pulls the noses of the plain people in little ways, for they like to have their noses pulled, but when it comes to the capital issues he exposes himself in the altogether. He does not pretend falsely to be a Progressive when everyone knows that he is not. He does not say one thing to the wets and another thing to the drys. He does not fill the air with a babble about brummagem ideals that he doesn't believe in, and is secretly preparing to drop down the nearest sewer. He does not bawl for liberty, and make ready to stuff more jails with Debses. He doesn't take money from his millionaire backers, and then caress the proletariat with vague and windy libels upon capitalism. He does not blow hot and think cold. He doesn't seek votes by false pretenses.

It seems to be that here is sufficient reason to vote for him— that here is the reason the overwhelming majority of Americans are going to vote for him. They tire, after twenty years, of a steady diet of white protestations and black acts; they are weary of hearing highfalutin and meaningless words; they sicken of an idealism that is oblique, confusing, dishonest and ferocious. The thing began under Roosevelt, the bogus Progressive. It has continued *ad nauseam* under Wilson, the bogus Liberal. Today no sane American believes in any official statement of national policy, whether foreign or domestic. He has been fooled too often, and too callously and impudently. Every idea that has aroused him to sentimental enthusiasm and filled his breast with the holiest of passions has been dragged down into the mud by its propounders, and made to seem evil and disgusting. He wants a change. He wants a renaissance of honesty —even of ordinary, celluloid politician's honesty. Tired to death of intellectual charlatanry, he turns despairingly to honest imbecility.

But all this, you may say, is a reason for voting for Debs, not for the Marion stonehead. Such is the eloquent argument of the Hon. Jesse Lee Bennett, my suffering colleague. But *is* it? I think not. Debs is honest too, but his notions are hopeless. His whole case is predicated upon the theory that capitalism is sick unto death, and will presently give way to something new and worse. This theory is nonsense, at all events in America. Capitalism may be down with salaam convulsions in Russia, it may show an appalling albuminuria in Italy, and it may be covered with urticaria in England and Germany, but in the United States it was never more vigorous. It will outlive you and me, fair friends. The war did not weaken it; the war enormously strengthened it. We'll live under capitalism until we die, and on the whole we'll be reasonably comfortable. Gamaliel represents this capitalism, openly and unashamed. He is not a fraudulent Progressive like Cox, but a frank reactionary. Well, if we are to have reaction, why not have it willingly and without any attempt to disguise it? Why not hand over the conduct of the state to an honest reactionary? Why take on more idealism in place of the idealism that we are getting rid of? Why try to cure fraud with more fraud?

THE LAST GASP

November 1, 1920

Tomorrow the dirty job. I shall be on my knees all night, praying for strength to vote for Gamaliel. What ass first let loose the doctrine that the suffrage is a high boon and voting a noble privilege? Looking back over 19 years I can recall few times when I voted with anything approaching exhilaration— maybe the two times I voted for the late Major-General Roosevelt, a fellow who always delighted me—the mountebank inordinate and almost fabulous, the great *reductio ad absurdum* of democracy, and even of civilization. Tomorrow my one cross mark with joy in it will go to the account of the Hon. W. Ashbie Hawkins, candidate for the United States Senate. This Mr. Hawkins I do not know, and have never knowingly witnessed. My decision to vote for him has been reached by pure reason. He at least has an intelligible platform: justice and self-determination for our fellow-Christians of the darker side of the moon. What is John Walter's platform? I have yet to hear it. In the Senate he has raised protective coloration to the height of a grand passion. As for the Hon. Old Man Weller, I shall desert him for the Moor because he is a pussyfooter. His supporters go about whispering that he is as wet as the Hon. Sam Appleby or the Hon. Bob Crain, but he seems to lack the courage to say so himself. As between such a *pianissimo* wet and a frank and honest dry, I am in favor of the dry. The Hon. Mr. Hawkins, I assume, is wet. If not, then a curse upon him.

In my Congressional district, the number of which I forget, the candidates are the Hon. J. Charles Linthicum, the Hon. William O. Atwood and Dr. med. Knickman. The Hon. Mr. Atwood I have known for many years and hold in high esteem. He is honest and intelligent and full of the milk of human kindness. Unluckily, he is dry, and so I am forced to hatchet him, and even to speak against him. Remember this Mr. Atwood. If you are dry, vote for him; if you are wet, *pass auf!* He is no pussy-footer. This leaves Charlie and the doctor. Charlie I have nothing against, save that I am tired of voting for him. I shall cast my ballot for the doctor. He is as wet as the Hon. Mr. Atwood is dry. My agents tell me, indeed, that he is the wettest candidate ever heard of; compared to him, even Sam Appleby is dry. It seems impossible, but I simply tell you what I hear.

The loans, I suppose, will all go through. It is very seldom that a loan is defeated at the polls. The argument that its rejection will mean an increase in direct taxation is very potent with the small householders, who are chronically oppressed by extortionate taxation. The taxes on an average two-story house are now at least twice as much as they ought to be; many a poor man, having struggled for years to pay for one, now finds himself scarcely able to keep it up. The honest working man is also always in favor of loans; they bring him jobs. The net effect of a public improvement loan, in fact, despite the enthusiasm of the small householders, is to take money away from the haves and hand it over to the have-nots. It is simply a device to mortgage thrift. The more money a man saves, the larger his relative share of the ultimate cost. Borrowed money is always freely spent.

In the present case, the loans are also vigorously supported on boomiferous grounds. The argument is that they will attract more capital and population to Baltimore and so cause the city to go on increasing in size. This argument, so far, has failed to penetrate my native skepticism. I am far from convinced that the doubling of the city's population would accomplish any intelligible good. The boomers crow every time they bring a new factory to Baltimore, and the newspapers diligently applaud. But the more one ponders upon it, the more nonsensical it seems. Consider, for example, the great coup lately hymned: the capture of a huge oil refinery for Highlandtown, the second largest

in the world. Imagine this refinery in full operation. It will convert a whole section of the new city into one vast stench; it will
ruin a vast tract for all other purposes; worse, it will bring in a
horde of low-grade laborers and so diminish the general social
and intellectual level of the town, already low enough, God
knows. You and I will be taxed to pay cops to club and murder
those wild Slovaks and Slovenes and to pay firemen to put out
the weekly fire at the refinery, and to pave streets to reach it.
True enough, the refinery will also pay taxes, but it will not pay
enough to cover the communal cost of maintaining it. What
benefit will it bring to any civilized Baltimorean?

Here, of course, I preach treason. The principle that every
new factory is a boon to civilization is a settled one in American
thinking. This principle deserves a more scientific examination
than it has ever got. If you regard it as beyond cavil, then I
advise you to read a small book by Ralph Adams Cram, entitled
"Walled Towns." Mr. Cram is not scientific, but he is at least
eloquent. He is the same Cram who designed St. Thomas'
Church in New York. An artist, and hence an idiot. I apologize
for mentioning him, and for seeming to approve him. I shall be
glad to make amends by writing a poem in praise of the new
Highlandtown refinery when it is opened at last and its pall of
imperial smoke begins to settle over East Baltimore. Let us
have, not merely one such new factory, but a dozen. Out in the
slums of Southwest Baltimore, where I have lived for years,
there are factories which exhale an odor of decaying proteids.
A few whiffs of the more volatile mineral oils would give me some
relief. Across the street from my house is a city square and in
the next block is a convent. I advocate donating the square to a
guano factory, and dispossessing the holy nuns in favor of a
slaughter-house. The squeal of the pigs as their throats were
slit would certainly give more thrills to a forward-looking man
than the present somewhat melancholy tolling of the convent
bell. Every squeal would represent so many dollars—so much

more on the weekly bank statement, so many more workers to
patronize the movies and buy phonograph records, so much
more work for labor leaders.

But this takes us far from Gamaliel, and the eve of his annun-
ciation. Unless all signs fail, he will be elected tomorrow by a
collossal plurality. The solemn and holy referendum will thrust
upon us, certainly for four years and maybe for eight, a ruler
with the high ideals of a lodge joiner and the general intellectual
lift and punch of a mackerel. *Vox populi, vox Dei.* Maybe so.
But—*quam incomprehensibilia sunt judicia ejus, et investi-
gabiles viae ejus!* Let us hold our noses, and do our duty. . . .
But wouldn't Jim be less painful, less rasping to the higher
cerebral centers, less horribly ipecacuanhaistic? Alas, if Gamaliel is an oil refinery, then Jim is a soap factory! . . . A sweet
choice indeed. Oh, long may it wave!

OPTIMISTIC NOTE

November 29, 1920

The Gamalian plurality in the late plebiscite was so huge
that contemplation of it has distracted the public attention
from all subsidiary phenomena. One gapes at it as a yokel gapes
at a blood-sweating hippopotamus; its astounding vastness
makes it seem somehow indecent, as a very fat man always
seems somehow indecent. Nevertheless, other shows went on
on the fatal day, and some of them were diverting and instructive. There was, for example, the collapse of the third-party
movement, save in isolated *enclaves* among the hog, saleratus
and total immersion States. And there was, again, the failure of
the Socialists to roll up the 3,000,000 votes that they counted

on, or to carry any big city, or to elect more than their one lonesome Congressman.

The third-party movers saw their defeat in advance and many of them threw up the sponge back in July, but the Socialists went to the shambles full of fire and confidence, and so their great failure surprised and dashed them. Their whole campaign revolved around the Debs issue. They nominated Eugene because of his handiness and natural talents as a martyr, and they counted upon inflaming vast hordes of the boobery with the tale of his sufferings. But the boobery simply refused to be inflamed in New York by the double expulsion of the Socialist assemblymen. On the contrary, it apparently decided that Debs had better stay in jail, whether innocent or guilty. There he sits to this day, and there he will probably sit for a good while to come, for Woodrow is far too vindictive to turn him loose and Gamaliel shows signs of being far too shrewd.

Gamaliel, indeed, is probably a more sagacious fellow than some of us thought. His inability to speak intelligible English is so striking that it conceals what is no doubt a very tolerable gift for practical politics. Examine the history of the campaign, and you will find that he made none of the costly blunders that Cox made. Cox attempted two grand gestures, and each cost him more than a million votes. First he went to Washington, closeted himself with Woodrow, and then announced that he and the White House were at one on the League of Nations. Secondly, he tried to bamboozle the drys, and so managed to scare off the wets, who had nominated him. Neither gesture, of course, was honest, but that was no objection to them. What ailed them was that neither was wise.

Gamaliel indulged himself in no such colossal imbecilities. In general, he confined himself to mellifluous and meaningless phrases, knowing very well that the plain people are used to them, understand them in their way, and like them. And whenever he had to be specific he said what warmed the popular heart.

For instance, in the matter of poor Gene. Various enemies, including the lodge-joiner, Christensen, tried to inveigle him into promising to liberate Gene on March 5. A less astute man would have succumbed. It seemed a good chance to play to the public generosity, and to cast a handy brick at the bitter and tyrannical Woodrow. But Gamaliel refused to promise anything of the sort; on the contrary, he delivered himself of harsh words on the subject of traitors. Here his instinct was profoundly sound. He knew that the American people are never in favor of turning anyone out of jail—that their sympathies are always with the prosecution and against the defense. I have no doubt whatever that keeping Debs in jail saved Woodrow from an even worse drubbing than the one he got. Had he emptied the jails of all the men, women and children locked up for flouting him in the days of his divine inspiration, the plurality of Gamaliel would probably have been a million larger.

These phenomena hook up; the collapse of all the radical movements, and the general sentiment against emptying the jails. The United States has never developed a true proletariat, which often shows fine generosities and chivalries. Instead, it has simply developed two bourgeoisies, an upper and a lower. Both are narrow, selfish, corrupt, timorous, docile and ignoble; both fear ideas as they fear the plague; both are in favor of "law and order," *i.e.*, of harsh laws, unintelligently administered. The viewpoint of each is precisely that of a corner groceryman. There is, on the one hand, none of the fine fury and frenzy, the romantic daring, the gaudy imagination of the true proletarian, and on the other hand, there is none of the tolerance and serenity of the true aristocrat.

Think of how poltroonishly the upper bourgeoisie reacted to the mere hint of radicalism two years ago! Great captains of industry trembled and blubbered like children; the whole government ran amock; thousands of innocent persons were pursued like horse-thieves. And all to put down a movement that was never clearly organized, and had no efficient leaders and no money, and was without the slightest public support! The boobs, in fact were against it as violently as the trembling captains. They always are, and for a reason lately plainly stated by Secretary Colby; they hope to rise and believe that they *will* rise—they want the loot protected so that it will be still there when they come to collect their share of it. Until this universal belief in prosperity around the corner dies out in the American people, there can be no serious radical movement in the republic. Now and then—as after 1893—there may be a few growls, but that is as far as the thing will go. Nor can there ever be any genuine passion for liberty, or any organized movement against harsh laws, or any effective punishment of profiteers. Such things, to the bourgeoisie, are not evils; they are goods; upon them the whole structure of bourgeois society rests.

Only one thing will ever seriously damage that structure: unsuccessful war. The day the United States is beaten on land and sea, and the unbroken hope of 144 years suddenly blows up—that day it will be high time to look for the birth of radicalism. Until then, let us snooze at peace. We are all safe. All we have gobbled we may keep.

GAMALIELESE

March 7, 1921

On the question of the logical content of Dr. Harding's harangue of last Friday I do not presume to have views. The matter has been debated at great length by the editorial writers of the Republic, all of them experts in logic; moreover, I confess to being prejudiced. When a man arises publicly to argue that the United States entered the late war because of a "concern for preserved civilization," I can only snicker in a superior way and wonder why he isn't holding down the chair of history in some American university. When he says that the United States has "never sought territorial aggrandizement through force," the snicker arises to the virulence of a chuckle, and I turn to the first volume of General Grant's memoirs. And when, gaining momentum, he gravely informs the boobery that "ours is a constitutional freedom where the popular will is supreme, and minorities are sacredly protected," then I abandon myself to a mirth that transcends, perhaps, the seemly, and send picture postcards of A. Mitchell Palmer and the Atlanta Penitentiary to all of my enemies who happen to be Socialists.

But when it comes to the style of a great man's discourse, I can speak with a great deal less prejudices, and maybe with somewhat more competence, for I have earned most of my livelihood for twenty years past by translating the bad English of a multitude of authors into measurably better English. Thus qualified professionally, I rise to pay my small tribute to Dr. Harding. Setting aside a college professor or two and half a dozen dipsomaniacal newspaper reporters, he takes the first place in my Valhalla of literati. That is to say, he writes the worst English that I have ever encountered. It reminds me of a string of wet sponges; it reminds me of tattered washing on the line; it reminds me of stale bean-soup, of college yells, of dogs barking idiotically through endless nights. It is so bad that a sort of grandeur creeps into it. It drags itself out of the dark abysm (I was about to write abscess!) of pish, and crawls insanely up the topmost pinnacle of posh. It is rumble and bumble. It is flap and doodle. It is balder and dash.

But I grow lyrical. More scientifically, what is the matter with it? Why does it seem so flabby, so banal, so confused and childish, so stupidly at war with sense? If you first read the inaugural address and then heard it intoned, as I did (at least in part), then you will perhaps arrive at an answer. That answer is very simple. When Dr. Harding prepares a speech he does not think it out in terms of an educated reader locked up in jail, but in terms of a great horde of stoneheads gathered around a stand. That is to say, the thing is always a stump speech; it is conceived as a stump speech and written as a stump speech. More, it is a stump speech addressed primarily to the sort of audience that the speaker has been used to all his life, to wit, an audience of small town yokels, of low political serfs, or morons scarcely able to understand a word of more than two syllables, and wholly unable to pursue a logical idea for more than two centimeters.

Such imbeciles do not want ideas—that is, new ideas, ideas that are unfamiliar, ideas that challenge their attention. What they want is simply a gaudy series of platitudes, of threadbare phrases terrifically repeated, of sonorous nonsense driven home with gestures. As I say, they can't understand many words of more than two syllables, but that is not saying that they do not esteem such words. On the contrary, they like them and demand them. The roll of incomprehensible polysyllables enchants them. They like phrases which thunder like salvos of artillery. Let that thunder sound, and they take all the rest on trust. If a sentence begins furiously and then peters out into fatuity, they are still satified. If a phrase has a punch in it, they do not ask that it also have a meaning. If a word slides off the tongue like a ship going down the ways, they are content and applaud it an wait for the next.

Brought up amid such hinds, trained by long practice to engage and delight them, Dr. Harding carries over his stump manner into everything he writes. He is, perhaps, too old to learn a better way. He is, more likely, too discreet to experiment. The stump speech, put into cold type, maketh the judicious to grieve. But roared from an actual stump, with arms flying and eyes flashing and the old flag overhead, it is certainly and brilliantly effective. Read the inaugural address, and it will gag

you. But hear it recited through a sound-magnifier, with grand
gestures to ram home its periods, and you will begin to understand it.

Let us turn to a specific example. I exhume a sentence from
the latter half of the eminent orator's discourse:

> I would like government to do all it can to mitigate, then, in
> understanding, in mutuality of interest, in concern for the com-
> mon good, our tasks will be solved.

I assume that you have read it. I also assume that you set it
down as idiotic—a series of words without sense. You are quite
right; it is. But now imagine it intoned as it was designed to be
intoned. Imagine the slow tempo of a public speech. Imagine
the stately unrolling of the first clause, the delicate pause upon
the word "then"— and then the loud discharge of the phrase
"in understanding," "in mutuality of interest," "in concern for
the common good," each with its attendant glare and roll of
the eyes, each with its sublime heave, each with its gesture of a
blacksmith bringing down his sledge upon an egg—imagine all
this, and then ask yourself where you have got. You have got,
in brief, to a point where you don't know what it is all about.
You hear and applaud the phrases, but their connection has
already escaped you. And so, when in violation of all sequence
and logic, the final phrase, "our tasks will be solved," assaults
you, you do not notice its disharmony—all you notice is that,
if this or that, already forgotten, is done, "our tasks will be
solved." Whereupon, glad of the assurance and thrilled by the
vast gestures that drive it home, you give a cheer.

That is, if you are the sort of man who goes to political meetings, which is to say, if you are the sort of man that Dr. Harding is used to talking to, which is to say, if you are a jackass.

The whole inaugural address reeked with just such nonsense.
The thing started off with an error in English in its very first
sentence—the confusion of pronouns in the *one-he* combination,

so beloved of bad newspaper reporters. It bristled with words misused: *Civic* for *civil, luring* for *alluring, womanhood* for *women, referendum* for *reference,* even *task* for *problem.* "The *task* is to be *solved*"—what could be worse? Yet I find it twice. "The expressed views of world opinion"—what irritating tautology! "The expressed conscience of progress"—what on earth does it mean? "This is not selfishness, it is sanctity"—what intelligible idea do you get out of that? "I know that Congress and the administration will favor every wise government policy to aid the resumption and encourage continued progress"—the resumption of what? "Service is the supreme *commitment* of life"— *ach, du heiliger!*

But is such bosh out of place in a stump speech? Obviously not. It is precisely and thoroughly in place in a stump speech. A tight fabric of ideas would weary and exasperate the audience; what it wants is simply a loud burble of words, a procession of phrases that roar, a series of whoops. This is what it got in the inaugural address of the Hon. Warren Gamaliel Harding. And this is what it will get for four long years—unless God sends a miracle and the corruptible puts on incorruption. . . . Almost I long for the sweeter song, the rubber-stamps of more familiar design, the gentler and more seemly bosh of the late Woodrow.

GAMALIELESE AGAIN

September 9, 1921

The learned New York *Times,* in the course of a somewhat waspish counterblast to all the current criticism of the literary style of Dr. Harding (including especially my own modest observations), has this to say:

Mr. Harding's official style is excellent. Its merits are obvious. In the first place, it is a style that looks Presidential. It contains the long sentences and big words that are expected. . . . Furthermore, the President's style is one that radiates hopefulness and aspiration, and is a fit vehicle for sentiment of the kind dear to a million American firesides. . . . It is complained that the President is too verbose and too vague. But this is . . . to miss entirely the point of popular acceptance. In the President's misty language the great majority see a reflection of their own indeterminate thoughts.

In other words, bosh is the right medicine for boobs. The doctrine, alas, is not new. I began preaching it at least six years ago, when the late Dr. Wilson loosed his first evangelical dithyrambs upon the world; it was plainly stated in the very treatise upon Gamalielese that the *Times* complains of. What ails the style of Dr. Harding, in brief, is precisely the fact that he has spent his whole life addressing persons devoid of intelligence, and hence afraid of ideas. His normal hearer, down to the time he became a candidate for the Presidency, was an Ohio yokel whose notions of a lofty and satisfactory rhetoric were derived from reading the Marion *Star* (or Cox's paper, or some other of the sort), and from listening to speeches by visiting fraternal-order magnates, harangues in the Chautauquas upon "Christian Idealism" and "The Glorious Future of the Republic," stump oratory by Ohio Congressmen, and sermons by ecclesiastical morons trying to imitate Gypsy Smith and Billy Sunday. Addressing such simians, the learned doctor acquired a gift for the sort of discourse that is to their taste. It is a kind of baby-talk, a puerile and wind-blown gibberish. In sound it is like a rehearsal by a country band, with only the bass-drummer keeping time. In content it is a vacuum.

No need for the *Times* to argue that such a style is grateful to the mob. What the mob wants is the mere sough and burble of words; add a solemn mien and some transparent monkeyshines, and it is willing to listen and believe. But it is surely a novel doctrine that the merchanting of such slush is the whole, or even the chief business of a President of the United States— that he has explained his ideas sufficiently when the plain people see in them "a reflection of their own indeterminate thoughts," *i.e.*, of their own vague and blowsy delusions. To argue so much is to argue further that the ideal President would be a complete idiot.

Nay, there is more to the job than that. A President is theoretically (and ought to be actually) the President of the whole nation—of the more or less intelligent minority as well as of the vast herd of human blanks. For him to address himself exclusively to the blanks, leaving the minority quite unable to comprehend him—this is carrying democracy a bit too far. I do not argue that he should accept the ideas of the minority, or even that he should manufacture ideas agreeable to it; all I argue is that he should state his ideas, whatever their character, in such terms that educated men can understand, weigh and discuss them. If he doesn't, then they are never discussed at all, for the blanks never discuss anything; they merely poll-parrot phrases. Certainly, the *Times* doesn't maintain that a President's ideas should not be discussed at all. To do so would be to accept the final implication of democracy, to wit, that the worst clown procurable should reign, and that the doctrines of the reigning clown should be wholly beyond challenge.

What Dr. Harding obviously needs is active contact with superior minds. His own mind is not superior, and, to do him justice, he seems to be well aware of it. It would mellow and improve him to exchange ideas with men who know more than he knows, and have lived in more civilized surroundings, and are more accustomed to ratiocination. But how is there ever going to be any such exchange if he continues to garb his notions in such phrases that men accustomed to ratiocination can only stand aghast and flabbergasted before them, as before the

blood-sweating behemoth of Holy Writ? The louder the boobs
yell, the colder the sweat upon the intelligentsia.

My private suspicion, perhaps contumacious, is that the
eminent gentleman has done his thinking in terms of the stump
and the chautauqua for so many years that the jargon that
goes therewith has become second nature to him, and that he
couldn't express his ideas in clearer and more seemly terms if
he would. Either he has always been of the mob himself, or he
has talked himself into incurable identity with it. If this guess
is correct, then no amount of pleading will ever induce him to
say his say in plain English, and he will go down into history
shrouded in the "misty language" that the *Times* praises. The
consummation might be conceivably a good deal more sour.
After all, the ideas emitted by Presidents of the United States
during the past thirty or forty years have not been of such a
character that the sum of human knowledge has been appreciably enriched by them. On the contrary, most of these great
men have discharged little save piffle, and some of them have
discharged so much of it that the world still gags whenever it
thinks of them. If, now, we are to have a President who gets
through his whole term without setting off a single intelligible
idea, good or bad, the fact perhaps may be credited thankfully
to the inscrutable wisdom of God. Harding in his mist is bad
enough, but Harding crystal-clear might be a great deal worse.

But this consolation is not altogether soothing. The mind
inevitably cherishes a yearning for a President who would be
less esoteric, and hence more entertaining. We are all used to
more active performers. The show is often obscene, but it is
usually very amusing. Mere snickering at the snarls and whorls
of Gamalielese will soon pall; it will presently irritate, and then
it will bore. Far better a Roosevelt with his daily mountebankery
or a Wilson with his weekly appendix to the Revelation of St.
John the Divine. These boys kept the ball in the air. It was a
pleasure, in their days, to read the newspaper. But all Gamaliel

promises is a few more laughs, and then an illimitable tedium.

His acts, unluckily, are almost as obscure as his speeches. A neutral grayness hangs over all his official activities. There were those who hoped that he would select a Cabinet vastly better than that of the late Woodrow, and there were those who hoped that he would select one much worse. He did neither. Instead, he got together a gang of master-minds almost exactly equivalent, in intelligence, ability and common decency, to the gang that went out on March 4. No one can make out whether he is in favor of a League of Nations or against it. No one knows what his notions are regarding Mexico. No one can say whether he is an irreconcilable high-tariff man or a high-tariff man with reservations. No one knows what he is going to do about anything.

This past week I have been looking through some foreign papers, all post-dating the inaugural address. I find in them no echo of the *Times'* delight in the "misty language" of that historic harangue. On the contrary, all of them seem to regard it uneasily, and a bit askance. They seem to be unimpressed by the fact that it shows "a style that looks Presidential"; what they apparently hoped for was a style that would let them know what to expect from the United States. It may be, for all I know, a good thing to keep them guessing; it may work to our advantage to puzzle them and fool them. But how badly they take it! How ill-naturedly they protest that it is an offense against them to deluge them with balderdash! How pointedly they hint that plain English would help them to believe more in the sound sense and good intentions of the United States!

WHO'S LOONY NOW?

December 27, 1921

Dr. Harding's belated and grudging commutation of the prison sentence of the Hon. Eugene Debs leaves all the honors on the side of Debs. He has, according to his lights, fought a good fight; he has run a good race; he has kept the faith. He comes out of his cell without any compromise of his dignity and with nothing to apologize for.

Unquestionably wrong, both in his naive belief in the Marxian rumble-bumble and in his sentimental opposition to war, he has nevertheless maintained both varieties of his wrongness in a decent, courageous and civilized manner. Such a man, however wrong he may be, is of enormous value to a democracy, if only as a shining example to the ignoble masses of his fellow-citizens. The usual method of propagating ideas under a democracy is that of lying and evasion, bullying and bluster; Debs is fair and polite.

The average citizen of a democracy is a goose-stepping ignoramus and poltroon: Debs is independent and brave. The average democratic politician, of whatever party, is a scoundrel and a swine: Debs is honest and a gentleman. Is the old fellow disliked by right-thinkers and 100-percenters? Is his release denounced by the New York *Times*, the Rotary Clubs, and the idiots who seem to run the American Legion? Then it is precisely because he is fair, polite, independent, brave, honest and a gentleman.

Turn now to Harding. He had a chance to release Debs promptly, gracefully, with an air. He might have shown a fine and creditable generosity to a defeated antagonist—an old and ill man, no longer capable of any serious damage to anyone or anything. The instincts of a man of decent feelings, of gentle traditions, of civilized training and environment, would have been on the side of doing it. But the instincts of a bounder pulled the other way. They counseled delay, bargaining, petty vengefulness and spitefulness, childish meanness. Debs was offered his liberty if he would recant, turn his coat, shame the thousands who had loyally followed him. He was told that he might get out of prison if he would grovel and dissemble, *i.e.*, if he would do what Dr. Harding did to get into the White House. He refused. At last he has been turned loose. There is no honor in the transaction for anyone save Debs.

Least of all is there any honor in it for Daugherty, the Attorney-General, a fifth-rate political lawyer, apparently as ignorant of the elementary principles of law as he is of the punctilio. His harangue before the last annual meeting of the American Bar Association was extraordinarily silly, even for that forum. What he maintained, in brief, was that there could be no genuine distinction between political crime and ordinary crime—that a man who risked his liberty, not for his private gain but for what he conceived to be the public good, was on exactly the same footing as a man who risked his liberty in order to snatch a purse, and that he ought to be punished in exactly the same way.

The imbecility of the doctrine is so obvious that it is hard to imagine even an audience of lawyers listening to its exposition without bombarding its father with dead cats. So far as I know, it has never been enunciated in any other civilized country: the United States has a clear monopoly on it, without the aid of tariff walls.

Even in Russia, in the palmy days of the czar, no reputable lawyer would have argued that the two sorts of crime were identical; he might have conceivably argued that political crime was worse than ordinary crime, but he would not have risked derision by seeking to confuse one with the other. In all other countries, including England, from which our law comes, the distinction is never questioned. The Englishmen who committed precisely the same crime for which Debs was imprisoned were all released long ago, and so were the Frenchmen, Italians, Belgians and Germans.

Ordinary crime—that is, above the grade of simple misdemeanor—always shows two characters. First, its anti-social nature is obvious to all normal men, including the criminal himself: even a highwayman, unless he be insane, never actually believes that holding up a victim is a moral and proper act. Secondly, ordinary crime is forbidden by laws that, in theory at least, are permanent: it is not forbidden today and allowed tomorrow, but forbidden all the time. The act that Debs committed, and for committing which he was imprisoned, met neither condition. Debs committed it with a free conscience, believing honestly that he was performing a public service—and it ceased to be a crime at all long before his prison sentence was completed. Today anyone might commit it with absolute impunity. In large part, in fact, it has been committed over and over again by statesmen at the Disarmament Conference, and even by Harding himself.

Thus the argument of Daugherty was pure nonsense—in brief, exactly the sort of balderdash that one might reasonably expect to issue from a so-called lawyer of his peculiar training and talents. It fills one with a patriotic glow to reflect that this preposterous paralogist, with his legal absurdities that a child would laugh at, fills the place once adorned by William Pinkney, William Wirt, Roger B. Taney, Reverdy Johnson, William M. Evarts and Richard Olney. But that, of course, was long ago. His immediate predecessors were McReynolds, Gregory and Palmer—a great descent here, and brilliantly progressive. Who will follow Daugherty? I nominate that other great Ulster jurisconsult—I forget his name—who tried to have Fatty Arbuckle indicted for murder in the first degree.

Debs can afford to laugh at the Daugherty pishposh. He conducted his end of the combat with the greatest skill. He offered no plea and made no concession of principle. He let it be known publicly that the so-called ideas he discharged in the speech that jailed him were ideas that he still cherished, and that he would hold himself absolutely free to discharge them again on his release. He refused to take back anything, or to promise anything. This left Daugherty and Harding in a very uncomfortable position. On the one hand, they were bombarded with demands—a great many of them from persons notoriously opposed to Debs' notions—that the old boy, in common decency, be released; on the other hand, they were filled with the usual fears of stupid men that, once out, he would do or say something embarrassing to them. They compromised, as I say, by letting him out grudgingly, boorishly, with ill grace. As a final touch, they managed to make it impossible for him to get home for his Christmas dinner. An instructive and stimulating episode. A lesson in honor and good taste for young Americans.

But Debs' deliverance, however disgusting the surrounding circumstances, will at least give some comfort to his political opponents, particularly after he regains the full use of his legs and glottis, and is once more touring the country as a Socialist evangelist. While he was in jail it was clearly impossible for any self-respecting anti-Socialist to tackle him, for he was unable to defend himself. Worse, most of his more plausible aides and confederates were in the same boat, or, at all events, so beset by district attorneys, professional war veterans, and other such hoodlums that it was impossible for them to meet an attack. But now Dr. Harding is beginning to release them and in not a few states they begin to enjoy once more the common right to free speech, and so the pursuit of them becomes fair sport again.

I believe that in a stand-up combat under decent rules it should be easily possible to dispose of them—that their fundamental ideas are all hollow and feeble—that Socialism is a delusion, and its advocates boozy dreamers. Even their arguments against war, now so popular everywhere, will not stand analysis

—that is, so long as nationalism seems virtuous to mankind. Great states are made by conquest, not by passing resolutions, and it is necessary to conquest that large numbers of individuals be butchered. Sentimentalists always overestimate the value of these individuals, and their sufferings. Is it a fact of no significance that the overwhelming majority of men who have actually experienced war are in favor of it? These men know that it is by no means as black as it is painted—that for men, as for nations, it is often a great deal more pleasant than hard work, and that the forms of death it presents are vastly more appetizing than those which commonly overtake a farmer, a policeman or a delicatessen dealer, not to mention poets and philosophers, and their horrible final struggles with general paralysis. . . .

But of this, more anon.

MAKING READY FOR 1924

April 2, 1923

The Hon. Mr. Daugherty's announcement that Dr. Harding will be a candidate for reëlection next year is certainly not news. The plain fact is that Dr. Harding became an active candidate for a second term at 12.01 P.M. on March 4, 1921, exactly one minute after he had taken his oath of office. The history of his public career since then has been a history of incessant vacillations between what he has honestly conceived to be his duty as President and his varying notions of expediency as a candidate. His ludicrous wobbling over the issue of the bonus may well serve to exhibit the difficulties that have beset him. It was his manifest duty as President to oppose this bold and shameless effort to loot the public treasury for the benefit of professional heroes of the war, three-fourths of whom never heard a shot fired in anger. But it was wise for him, as candidate, to remember the voting strength of these grafters. Thus he blew hot one day and cold the next. First, if I remember rightly, he tried to line up the American Legion by advocating the bonus; then, hearing a yell from the taxpayers of the land, he turned against it; then he began, somewhat gingerly, to advocate it again; then, confronted by a depressing Treasury statement, he was against it again.

Just how he stands on the question today I do not know, and neither, I daresay, does he. He will be in favor of the bonus if his political advisers, led by the patriotic Daugherty, convince him that favoring it will get him more votes than opposing it. He will be against it if they come to the opposite conclusion. No other consideration will enter into their secluded debate of the matter. From this day forth, as an active candidate for renomination and reëlection, Dr. Harding will frankly subordinate every national interest, however grave, to his private interest. He is no longer President of the United States, save by a sort of legal fiction; he is simply a candidate for the Presidency. If Daugherty were convinced tomorrow that votes could be made by advocating the Ku Klux Klan or even the I.W.W., Harding would begin to advocate it day after tomorrow.

The spectacle is surely not one to exhilarate the reflective citizen of the Republic, but it is useless to mourn over it, for it goes inevitably with democracy. One of the greatest defects of democracy is that it forces every candidate for office, even the highest, into frauds and chicaneries that are wholly incompatible with the most elementary decency and honor. In proportion as he is intelligent and honest, his candidacy is hopeless. Facing a mob whose members invest their money in 10 per cent a month swindles, get converted at Billy Sunday revivals, believe in labor leaders and swallow patent medicines or go to osteopaths when they are ill, he is compelled, willy-nilly, to adapt his views to their changeable and illogical superstitions and delusions. Worse, he is compelled to fit these views, at the same time, into the prejudices of the professional politicians of his party, and into the notions of self-interest of the rich rogues who stand behind them. It is thus no wonder if his platform, like Roosevelt's in 1912, resembles words scrawled on a wall by feeble-minded children, or if, like Wilson's in 1916, it is as dishonest as the prospectus of a Texas oil promoter.

It seems to me that monarchy, even of the most absolute and intransigent kind, is appreciably superior to democracy here. A monarch elected and inaugurated by God, having no need to play the clown to the mob, can devote himself whole-heartedly to the business of his office, and no matter how stupid he may be he is at least in a better position to give effective service than a President who is likely to be quite as stupid as he is, and certain to be ten times as dishonest. It is not to the monarch's self-interest to be dishonest; he is more comfortable, like any other man, when he does what he genuinely wants to do. Moreover, the subordinate officers of the state, working under him, share his advantages. They do not have to grimace and cavort before the mob in order to get and hold their offices; the only person they have to please is the monarch himself, who is, at all events, a relatively educated man, with some notion of family honor and tradition in him, and uncorrupted by the habit of abasement.

But let us put this last consideration aside—that is, the matters of the superior early training, and, above all, the vastly superior heredity, of kings. Let us turn from such specially bred men to the sort of fellows who constitute the common run of Presidents under democracy—the Franklin Pierces, Tafts, Eberts, Poincarés, Chester A. Arthurs, Benjamin Harrisons, John Tylers, Rutherford B. Hayeses and so on—mainly ninth-rate politicians, petty and puerile men, strangers to anything resembling honor. It is my contention that even such preposterous worms, if they were turned into kings, would make relatively honest and competent administrators—that, at worst, they would be better than any Presidents save a miraculous few. I go further. I believe that even Harding, though he probably stands very near the bottom of the list, would make a very fair king—that if he mounted the throne, government under him would be very much cheaper and infinitely more honest and intelligent than it is today.

This is by no means mere rhetoric. I could point to many events of his Administration, even under the handicaps that beset him, that support the notion, and many obvious traits of his character that support it still more. Harding is an extremely ignorant man, and his long career as a newspaper publisher in a small town pretty well purged him of courage and self-respect, but it must be plain that he shows the good traits of the yokel as well as the bad, among them simplicity, diligence, economy and a strong sense of order. I believe that he was absolutely sincere when he promised, in his campaign, to cut down public expenses if elected, and I believe that the futility of his efforts to do so has given him a great deal of concern. He has been defeated by forces beyond him—partly lying in the very nature of democratic government, which is always extravagant and dishonest, and partly lying in the exigencies of his campaign for reëlection. Whenever he has been able to do so without risk, he has actually cut off unnecessary public expenditures— as in the matter, for example, of the outrageous Civil War pension bill he lately vetoed. That he is opposed, in his heart, to the American Legion bonus must be patent to everyone; his celebrated attack upon it was clearly sincere, and if he is for it today it is simply because he believes he can make votes thereby.

I could multiply examples, but they are not necessary: the occasional emergence of the hon. gentleman's good qualities, bursting through his political necessities, has won him many friends, even among his political foes. The point is that these good qualities are now under constant adverse pressure—that they can be given free play only by heroic efforts, too often beyond the man's strength. If he were absolutely free, as the responsible head of a great state ought to be—if he could devote his whole energies to administering the government according to his best skill and judgment, instead of spending nine-tenths of his time engaging in obscene devices to enchant the mob or humiliating bargainings with villainous politicians— then the chances are that he would run the state quite as competently as he used to run his newspaper, and so give us government a great deal better than any democracy deserves, or will ever get. His job does not require genius; it requires only industry, honesty, courage and common sense. But how can a man harbor such qualities and at the same time make votes? What chance has he got against the nearest mountebank?

As it is, Harding seems likely to yield to the system whole-heartedly, and so make a campaign of almost unprecedented imbecility and dishonesty. According to hints dropped by Daugherty, he will run as a dry—in political terms, on a platform of "law enforcement." Is he, then, a convert to the Prohibitionist buncombe? He is not. He is, in fact, no more a Prohibitionist, either in theory or in practice, than I am. But the Anti-Saloon League controls the Republican party in Ohio, and in order to get a renomination he must go to the Republican National Convention with the votes of his own State. Hence the Daughertean gabble about "law enforcement"! . . . Such is honor among the great officers of state under democracy!

NEXT YEAR'S STRUGGLE

June 11, 1923

Whatever may be said against Dr. Harding, either as a statesman or as a man, it must always be added in justice to him that he has the courage of his hypocrisies. Having been forced by the situation in his home State of Ohio, where the Anti-Saloon League has its national headquarters and runs the State organization of the Republican party, to declare himself unequivocably for Prohibition, he has now launched himself boldly into an active campaign for that great peruna, and will undoubtedly run upon the issue next year. No one, of course, believes that he is actually a Prohibitionist, and neither does anyone believe that he will be able to enforce Prohibition if he is reelected as one. But his advisers, headed by the learned and patriotic Daugherty, have obviously decided that he is in for slaughter unless he can tap some great well of Crô-Magnon emotion, and so they have counseled him to put on the white chemise of a dry, and he is, in fact, already in it, and posturing obscenely before the great masses of the plain people.

No doubt the ominous fizzling out of the World Court issue helped Daugherty and company to formulate this counsel, and Gamaliel himself to accept it. What influences brought about his sudden enthusiasm for a World Court, after he had been elected on a specific promise to keep the United States out of it, I do not know, but can at least guess. When he was in the Senate Dr. Harding was known as a Standard Oil Senator—and Standard Oil, as everyone knows, was strongly against our going into the League of Nations, chiefly because England would run the league and be in a position to keep Americans out of the new oil fields in the Near East. The Morgans and their pawnbroker allies, of course, were equally strong for going in, since getting Uncle Sam under the English hoof would ma-

terially protect their English and other foreign investments.
Thus the issue joined, and on the Tuesday following the first
Monday of November, 1920, the Morgans, after six years of
superb *Geschäft* under the Anglomaniacal Woodrow, got a bad
beating.

Such great master-minds, when they get a bad beating, do
not fight on; they try to come to terms with the foe. This is
what the sagacious Morgans did in that case, and at the Lau-
sanne conference their chance came. Two major results flowed
out of that historic assemblage of eminent diplomatists: (a) the
English agreed to let the Standard Oil crowd in on the oil-fields
of the Levant, and (b) the Hon. J. P. Morgan II paid a visit to
Dr. Harding at the White House. And out of that visit, in turn,
two other results flowed: (a) the English were permitted to
compromise their debt to the United States by agreeing to pay
about 50 cents on the dollar, and (b) Dr. Harding began to
hear a voice from the burning bush counseling him to disregard
the prejudice of the voters who elected him and to edge the
United States into a Grand International Court of Justice, *i.e.*,
the League of Nations in a new falseface, with the Union Jack
concealed beneath the undershirt.

Unluckily, the *booboisie* did not take kindly to this astounding *volte face*. They were still under the impression that they
had saved the Republic from the League of Nations in 1920.
So murmurs began to come in from the desolate reaches of the
prairie and forest, and these murmurs, impinging upon the ears
of certain great statesmen of Dr. Harding's own party, caused
them to sweat uneasily, and finally to exclaim, "Hey? What's
that?" The rest is history. It quickly became obvious that the
World Court scheme would cause turmoil in the Republican
party, and perhaps a schism in the face of the enemy. The
Morgans, alarmed, sent for Lord Robert Cecil to assault this
opposition with his title, and instructed their Liberals to round
up all idealists and men of vision. But the rebels continued in

rebellion, supported by an ever-increasing horde of plain people, and so it became necessary to put the World Court on ice and to cast about for a more likely issue. The situation in Ohio pointed to Prohibition, and Prohibition it seems likely to be.

The obvious thing for the Democrats to do, it would appear at first glance, would be to seek out some absolutely wet wet, put him up against Gamaliel, and so meet the issue squarely, and gallop home to a well-earned victory. The chances are, indeed, that if he were unobjectionable otherwise such a dripping and unchallengeable wet would win by a plurality approaching the fabulous, for not only would he have the nation-wide revulsion against the Prohibition buffoonery to help him, but also the deep-seated and growing unpopularity of Gamaliel himself, as a stupid, devious and trashy fellow.

But in politics, particularly when it comes to major strategy, the obvious is not always the practicable. What ails the poor Democrats is the plain fact that they have no such standard-bearer in sight. There are plenty of aspirants who are indubitably and incurably wet, and there are plenty who are unobjectionable otherwise, but there is none who is both. The name of the Hon. Al Smith will instantly occur to the judicious. Al, despite his hesitation over the Mullen-Gage repealer, is so wet that even Tammany trusts him; he would thus be sure to carry all the States north of the Mason and Dixon Line and east of the Ohio by majorities so large that they would have to be reckoned in blocks of 100,000. But he is also a Roman Catholic—and south of the Potomac it is a cardinal article of faith of every Democrat in good standing that every Catholic in the land is *particeps criminis* to a conspiracy to abrogate the Constitution, turn all the public schools over to the Jesuits, massacre the Baptist clergy and put a wop into the White House. Personally, I doubt that any such conspiracy exists; nevertheless, all the Southern Democrats believe in it, and not only the rank and file of them, but also their Governors, Congressmen and United States Senators. To deny the doctrine in Georgia or Alabama would be as hazardous as to deny that a madstone will cure hydrophobia, that salvation is impossible without total immersion, or that the Kaiser caused the war. One cannot flout lightly the basic faiths of men. Al would flout this one.

Thus this master wet appears to be eliminated from the race, and his admirers mourn. No other Democratic wet seems gaudy enough to have a chance. There remains the late Crown Prince, the Hon. Mr. McAdoo—but McAdoo, like Gamaliel, is a bogus dry; worse, he is a violent Anglomaniac, and hot for the League of Nations. If he were nominated, there would be no contest at all; both candidates would stand on the same platform.

Well, why not? If the thing actually came to pass, it would at least save a lot of useless jawing, most of it wholly hypocritical. Moreover, it would bring us one step nearer, and in a frank and refreshing manner, to the goal toward which American politics has been moving for years past: the amalgamation of the two great parties. Both have lost their old vitality, all their old reality; neither, as it stands today, is anything more than a huge and clumsy machine for cadging jobs. They do not carry living principles into their successive campaigns; they simply grab up anything that seems likely to make votes. The old distinctions between them have all faded out, and are now almost indiscernible. The Democrats are just as hot for centralization as the Republicans, and just as friendly toward a protective tariff; they stand together on the money question: there is no choice between them on the question of foreign policy; they are both wet and both dry.

The only reality that remains is their division on sectional lines. In the South the morons still vote the straight Democratic ticket. But even this brand begins to wear off. We have seen Maryland and Tennessee take to the fence; we have even seen some wobbling in Virginia and Texas. The time may come, and it may be soon, when the solid South will fall to pieces. Out of the wreck, I venture to believe, a new alignment of parties will come, and it will be based, not upon outworn traditions and shibboleths, but upon genuine differences of opinion. What those differences of opinion will be I do not risk prophesying, but it would not surprise me at all if one great party advocated the inspection and control of bootleggers by rigid Federal legislation, and the other, clinging to the tattered remains of local self-government, advocated licensing them by the commune.

2

Calvinism

On MARCH 3, 1929, WHILE CALVIN COOLIDGE WAS TIDYING up his office and marking time until his successor Herbert Hoover took over the presidency the following day, Mr. Mencken sucked in his breath and pronounced a final word on "Silent Cal's" White House tenancy. "It would be difficult," he wrote, "to imagine a more obscure and unimportant man." Behind this remark lies a judgment that Mencken applied steadily to Coolidge almost from the moment the Vermonter from Plymouth Notch took the oath of office by the light of a kerosene lamp on August 3, 1923, until his death early in January of 1933.

These were strange days during Mr. Coolidge's ten-year trek across the stage of national politics. "And the nights were a mite peculiar too," as Indiana's Jim Watson liked to remark later, when the fun-filled mood of the twenties gave way to the despair and troublesome times of the early thirties. Across these busy years whose political pages were dotted with off-beat movements like the moonbeams, goo-goos, single-taxers, and vegetarians, Mencken dealt with all variety of what he called "political muckers." Meanwhile, of course, he continued his duel with prohibition, prejudice, and the "preposterous bladders" who poked into major party politics.

The takeoff piece for this period of Mencken's writing—
September 3, 1923—was published just a month to the day
after Calvin Coolidge was sworn in as president by his own
father. Not entirely clear at the time was whether Coolidge
would be able to shake off the scandals of the Harding administration, or indeed whether he would be able to consolidate his
own position sufficiently within his party to assure his own nomination in 1924. But despite the scandals that had overtaken the
Harding regime, Coolidge was triumphantly elected in 1924
(Mr. Mencken's explanation for voter indifference to corruption is that people "are not in favor of stealing *per se* but stealing from the government somehow seems less reprehensible than
other kinds"). The overriding factors in the Coolidge victory,
however, were climbing prosperity, and a Democratic party
greatly weakened by a convention stalemate that required 103
ballots to break, and a bitter fight over whether the Ku Klux
Klan should be denounced in the party platform. The physical
rigors alone of the Democratic convention ordeal are playfully
recaptured for us in Mencken's "Post-Mortem" piece of July
14, 1924.

Again in this election year, both candidates—Democratic
nominee John W. Davis and his Republican opponent, Calvin
Coolidge—were making debuts as presidential contestants. But
the presidential sweepstake of 1924 became a tricornered affair
when a third candidate entered the lists. The challenger in this
canvass was Robert Marion LaFollette, the longtime Republican progressive from Wisconsin who now headed the Progressive
party ticket. And it was to this man, despite whispers that his
pockets "were stuffed with Soviet gold," that Mencken gave his
vote "unhesitatingly," for a "plain reason: he is the best man in
the running *as a man*."

In his appraisals of Coolidge—a life "as placid as that of a
man in a convent"—Mencken correctly conceived the President
as a master mechanic of politics, and far shrewder in these arts

than Harding. He also saw that Coolidge, even more than Harding, was unwilling to impress his views on Congress, and that he believed the presidency should not be active and reformist but rather an office to protect the established order of things. But a far more important matter which Mencken seems clearly to have understood was that the administration of Coolidge would lead to a firmer entrenchment of conservative elements of business leadership than the policies of the Harding years. Though tagging Harding as an "ignoramus," Mencken credits him with having social impulses which he felt Coolidge did not possess. And right after the election of 1924 he tells us that the Coolidge administration in the long run would drive us to worse consequences than Harding's because it would "manufacture radicalism in a wholesale manner"—radicalism that would be "far more dangerous to legitimate business than the mild stuff Dr. LaFollette now has on tap." If businessmen thought LaFollette looked dangerous in 1924, he wondered if they had really thought about the sort of radicalism that would be afoot "after four more years of Coolidge."

Here again, Mencken seems to be expressing in another way a thought of Eugene Debs, the Socialist who had been recently released from imprisonment by a pardon from President Harding. What disturbed him particularly, Debs used to say, was not the opposition to his views, but the indiscriminate attacks levelled at radicalism. When the day arrived that a really dangerous authoritarian leftist movement was about to imperil American institutions, argued Debs, people might fail to recognize the true nature of the threat because they had been misled about radicalism and because they were tired of hearing about its alleged evils.

In the celebrated conjecture over whether Coolidge really desired renomination and re-election in 1928, Mencken readily took sides. "He intrigued for a third term" [actually if it had come about it would not have been a third term in the real sense since Coolidge had served only one full term] "until it became obvious he couldn't get it without a fight." If Coolidge earnestly desired a third term, as many historians now believe, no doubt the anti-third-term resolution which Mr. Mencken obviously had in mind here, had a most discouraging effect on Coolidge's ambition. Introduced into the Senate by Robert M. LaFollette, Jr., and passed on February 10, 1928, this resolution declared that failure to observe the anti-third-term tradition would constitute a precedent "unwise, unpatriotic, and fraught with peril to our free institutions."

While Mencken's peppery pokes at Mr. Coolidge continue even after the Vermonter left office, a word of praise slips in here and there. He admits that Coolidge "knew how to write clear English," even though he was about as original as a "Rotarian," and he also commends him because "he writes as a man who lets himself go." And finally in his own image of gentleness which those who worked with him knew so well, he closes the Coolidge chapter on a kind note after Coolidge fooled the "amateur actuaries" by dying so suddenly in 1933. Perhaps with a mellow glance over his shoulder at the past, Mencken was prompted to see Coolidge in a new light when he wrote that the nation suffers most "when the White House busts with ideas," and that in retrospect Mr. Coolidge begins to seem "an extremely comfortable and praiseworthy citizen." But to the end Mencken remained immovably convinced that in accounting for the Coolidge career "the heavenly hierarchy seemed to be in a conspiracy to protect him and help him along," and that there were "massive evidences of celestial intervention at every step of it." On this there will be few dissents.   M. M.

CALVINISM (SECULAR)

September 3, 1923

The first important act of Dr. Coolidge, after the crown settled over his ears, was to appoint the Hon. C. Bascom Slemp, of Virginia, as his chief secretary. In other words, the first important act of his administration was the launching of a scheme for his nomination and reëlection next year. Certainly no Coolidgista, however fond, can attach any other significance to that most singular affront to the decencies. The Hon. Mr. Slemp, whatever his merits as husband and father, is surely no statesman; he is a politician pure and simple, and he has specialized for years in the herding of Republican jobholders in the South. His appointment thus indicates a plain effort to line up these cattle for 1924. Dr. Coolidge sees trouble ahead in the North and West, but in the South, by the artful aid of the Hon. Mr. Slemp, he may be sure of his delegates.

I gather from the newspapers that this haste to get down to what will be the principal and perhaps only genuine business of the Coolidge Administration has caused a painful impression in certain delicate quarters. The prevailing notion seems to be that a President thrust into the purple by divine intervention should go about the thing less eagerly and shamelessly. There should be a period, it appears, of mourning for his predecessor. and then a period of painful study of the great problems of state. Not until after that should the beneficiary of Heaven think of his own fortunes. I report the doctrine that is whispered about, but do not defend it. On the contrary, I denounce it as rubbish. It seems to me, indeed, that Dr. Coolidge waited quite as long as was necessary. His predecessor, Dr. Harding, was inaugurated at noon on March 4, 1921, and began to run for reëlection not later than 12.20 P.M. of the same day. Coolidge at least let a week slip by before he spat upon his hands and got down to *Geschäft*. He is a very scrupulous fellow.

The indecency that he is accused of, in truth, inheres in his office, and it is as unjust and useless to blame him for it as it would be to blame a dog for having fleas. It is certainly not always accurate to say that a President's obscene efforts to get himself reëlected are due to mere hollow vanity—to a bald desire to keep before the biggest spotlight of them all, and prance before his lieges. What moves him quite as often, I believe, is the far more seemly and excusable desire to have his conduct in office ratified—his quite natural yearning to go into the school histories as a President who was virtuous and approved. Unluckily, our system of government offers him no means of attaining to that desire save by the process of running for reëlection. If, at the end of his four years, he quietly returns to private life, then the morons who write the school histories will inevitably hint that he was kicked out of office for grave crimes and misdemeanors. In brief, he must run again or confess himself a failure—and if he must run again, then it is surely not unnatural for him to employ every lawful means to win.

The trading of jobs for votes in the South is a perfectly lawful means. No statute of the United States prohibits it, and it is not in contravention of the *mores* of the Republic. A President who handed out jobs down there without tying strings to them would not only get no public praise; he would be widely suspected of insanity. The custom of years stands behind the practice; every President since Washington, including the sainted Lincoln, has pursued it. The Southerners, being extreme realists in politics, accept it without question. The only sort of politician they can imagine is one who is trying to get or keep a job, and they assume quite accurately that a President of the United States is exactly like all the rest. Thus, when Dr. Slemp sends for them and whispers into their ears, they will receive his tidings with unaffected hosannas, and when the time comes to count noses in the Republican National Convention it will be found that every delegate and alternate, white and black, is a jobholder, and that every jobholder is thoroughly convinced that Cal is the greatest President the nation has seen since the Hon. Jefferson Davis.

Various publicists, chiefly Liberals of a visionary kind, have offered plans for doing away with this lamentable spectacle, and most such plans include lengthening the term of the President and making him ineligible for reëlection. But it is very likely that this lengthening would bring on quite as many disadvantages as benefits. To begin with, it would probably fail of its chief purpose, for even if a President could not run against himself he would seek to have his administration ratified by electing a successor of his own choosing, and we have already seen, in the cases of Roosevelt and Wilson, what follies this desire may lead him into. But even assuming it to work in this respect, there would still remain the disadvantage that an incompetent President, once thrust into office by accident, could not be got rid of until he had wrecked the country—above all, that his failure could not be brought home to him, quickly and impressively.

Suppose Dr. Taft had been in office, not for four years only, but for eight or ten years? In so long a time, with no fear of defeat and rebuke to keep him alert, his native laziness and shiftlessness would have sufficed to paralyze the government. Ballingerism would have been ten times as bad as it was. The primeval dollar-a-year men of that era, not content with what they got, would have put the Treasury on wheels and run away with it. The one bright moment in the Taft Administration, in fact, came when Dr. Taft was given his drubbing in November, 1912. Turning out such gross incompetents, to be sure, does very little practical good, for they are commonly followed by successors who are almost as bad, but it at least gives the voters a chance to register their disgust, and so it keeps them reasonably contented, and turns their thoughts away from the barricade and the bomb. Democracy, of course, does not work, but it is a capital anæsthetic.

Dr. Harding's premature death, I notice, is widely ascribed to the intolerable cares and burdens of the Presidential office. Such profound thinkers as Ambassador Herrick, indeed, came forward with proposals that some of the responsibility now resting upon the President be taken from him and cast upon other jobholders. There may be, for all I know, some sense in all this, but I hope the fact will not be overlooked that Dr. Harding, at the time he collapsed, was not actually engaged upon his Presidential duties; he was engaged upon his canvass for renomination and reëlection. In so far as he discussed the problems of his office on his tour, he discussed them with a sole eye to their effect upon the voters next year. On at least one capital matter—the question of American intervention in the affairs of Europe—he shifted his ground at least twice as the tides of public opinion seemed to shift. Here, in brief, he was not only not ruining his health solving a great problem; he was deliberately dodging its solution, and leaving the decision to the mob.

Nevertheless, it is probably true that concern about that decision gave him severely to think, and that this insalubrious exercise helped to destroy his health. I believe that Dr. Coolidge will bear up under the same strain a great deal better. He is, to begin with, a younger and healthier man; he is, above all, a far more cunning and realistic politician. He will, I venture, pursue an extremely *pianissimo* course, despite occasional small shows for the benefit of the Washington correspondents. There will be no vain and vexatious gabble about World Courts and other such scare-yokels. The Government will function in a silent and inoffensive manner. Congress, when it reassembles, will not be belabored with denunciations and beseechings. The time is short, and hay must be made. The Hon. C. Bascom Slemp will make it in the lovely Southland, and other adept professors will ply the rake in the North, East and West. Delegate after delegate will march up and dive into the tank. The Hon. Hiram Johnson, the California *Citrus aurantifolia*, will sweat more and more citric acid. The Feather Duster will gradually shed his gaudy plumage. All the other aspirants will fade and deliquesce. In the end it will be found that the voice of the Republican commonalty of the land, North and South, male and female, white and black, is substantially unanimously for the renomination and reëlection of the rightful heir of Lincoln, McKinley and Roosevelt, the Hon. J. Calvin Coolidge, of Massachusetts.

THE IMPENDING PLEBISCITE

October 22, 1923

The connoisseur of the higher political mountebankery cannot fail to yield his veneration to the great talents of the Hon. J. Calvin Coolidge, the present First Chief of the Republic. How much shrewder he is than his illustrious predecessor, the Martyr Harding! Harding, at the time the Reds did him to death, was rocking his own boat so violently that many of his most faithful partisans were coming down with *mal de mer*. The more he searched and felt about for issues, publicly and clumsily, the more he alarmed the great masses of the plain people. No less than three times he tried to heat them up with his unintelligible scheme for a World Court in which the leading burglars should sit upon the bench, and no less than three times he saw them blanch, tremble and go cold. If, at the time he fell a victim to his patriotism, he was gradually abandoning all such disturbing issues and concentrating his passion for Service upon Prohibition, then it was surely not due to any interior vision, but simply to the force of events. With the Ohio Anti-Saloon League pushing and the plain people themselves pulling, he had to go that way or blow up altogether.

Dr. Coolidge is far more adept and realistic. He sees very clearly that, in the struggle ahead of him, issues that are perplexing can only do him damage, and so he is avoiding them with magnificent assiduity. No more is heard about World Courts. There will be no economic conference. The coal strike was shoved off on Pinchot, who will remain a hero until the coal bills come in; *i.e.*, until about the time the Coolidge campaign really gets under weigh. Harding, given the word to recognize Mexico, would have tried to 'rouse the rabble over it; Coolidge performed the business *pianissimo*, well knowing that Mexico, if talked of too much, could only lose him votes. His whole appeal, it appears, will be based upon a clarion demand for law enforcement and respect for the Constitution, which is to say, for Prohibition. The issue will be clear, single, simple and familiar. More, it will win.

But it is a fact, then, that a majority of the people of the United States are still in favor of Prohibition? I doubt that anyone knows; I doubt, indeed, that anyone can say with assurance that a majority of them were *ever* in favor of it. But that is not the point. The point is that Dr. Coolidge doesn't have to convince a majority of the voters in order to be reëlected; all he has to do is to convince such a number as, added to the horde of jobholders and other safe men, will make a majority. It seems to me that it will be enormously easier for him to do this by embracing prohibition, a tried and well-understood issue with a great body of organized opinion already behind it, than it would be by endeavoring, like the late Harding, to manufacture a new issue, and so run the risk, like Harding again, of arousing only suspicion and alarm.

By declaring for moonshine and Christian Endeavor the learned and distinguished candidate will not only solidify the rural Methodists of the North and West, most of whom are Republicans anyhow; he will also stand a good chance of making even further inroads upon the rural and Methodist South than Harding made. The South, of course, was never wetter than it is today, but whoever believes that the great geysers of bad booze now spouting down there indicate that the low-caste Confederates have lost their enthusiasm for Prohibition is surely an unpracticed student of the Methodist-Baptist, or Ku Klux mind. The very fact, indeed, that the sub-Potomac yokels have plenty to drink themselves only augments their yearning to make the Jews, Catholics, fugitive Moors and other Reds of the big cities dry. Lynching is their sport; not suicide. They are Democrats, true enough, but before they are Democrats they are Christian idealists—and Dr. Coolidge, with great skill and delicacy, has got a strangle hold upon the best keg of Christian idealism ever on tap. They will vote for a Democrat if he is as dry as or drier than Coolidge, but——

Here, indeed, is where the eminent candidate reveals the full horse-power of his sagacity; by jumping aboard the water-wagon so early in the race he leaves the Democrats almost helpless. If they could find a safe and incurable wet of national reputation and had the courage to nominate him boldly and make the campaign on a beer-wagon, they might have a chance to win; certainly they would carry all of the big cities and most of the so-called key States almost unanimously. But they have neither the candidate nor the courage. The Hon. Al Smith is obviously hopeless; the day he was nominated the Methodist Ku Kluxers of every State south of the Potomac would begin building forts along the coast to repel the Pope. To make the attempt with any other leader would be still worse; he could be jammed through the convention only by nailing the Southern delegates to the floor, and the whole gang would go home as despondent as the gang which nominated Cox at San Francisco.

Thus the Democrats, lacking a candidate of any heft or beam

and facing an issue forced upon them, will have to do either one of two things: they will have to swallow the issue themselves and so reduce the contest to a mere sham battle, or they will have to pussyfoot. If they do the latter, both wets and drys will suspect them, and Dr. Coolidge will have a walk-over. And if they do the former he will have a walk-over almost as easy, for their cowardice will lose them all the wet States of the North without gaining them anything save the Ku Klux States of the South, most of which are bound to stick to them anyhow. In politics, the first candidate who grabs an issue always gets the best of it. The plain people distrust the trailer, particularly if his vacillations have been public, and their distrust has a sound instinct under it. Whoever is nominated by the Democrats will be a palpable fraud. No even half-honest man has any more chance of getting the nomination than a Chinaman.

The dangers of trailing in matters of statecraft are well exemplified by the current Gubernatorial campaign in Maryland. Both the Hon. Mr. Ritchie and the Hon. Mr. Armstrong, being convinced that a large majority of Marylanders are now wet, have announced that they are horrified by the corruptions bred by the Volstead act, and it is highly probable that the two are equally sincere—that is, that the conscience of neither would permit him to be shaken from this position unless he became convinced that the majority of Marylanders had suddenly become dry. Nevertheless, it must be plain to any observer that the wetness of Dr. Ritchie is believed in with a calmer and more childlike faith than the wetness of Dr. Armstrong. Both wets and drys believe that the former will remain wet if he is re-elected, and both suspect, the one crowd fearing and the other hoping, that the latter, if he is elected, will gradually dry out.

The reason is simple enough. Dr. Ritchie, seeing the way the wind was blowing, became an active wet long ago, whereas Dr. Armstrong's wetness was not publicly bruited about until the last minute, and seemed a sort of afterthought even then. A great many drys, in fact, confidently expected him to declare for Prohibition, and in some of the counties, especially on the Eastern Shore, the Methodist Ku Kluxers were organized to aid him on that understanding. His last-minute emergence with hop-leaves in his hair left these worthy Christians flabbergasted, and they were forced to seek a new issue. Unless my agents lie, it takes the form of whispers in the bucolic Little Bethels that Ritchie is not only a theoretical wet but also a personal connois-seur of champagne, Scotch, chianti, Danziger Goldwasser, vodka, Swedish punch, Bass' ale, Pilsner and all the other lux-urious and hellish guzzles of city folk—in brief that he prac-tices what he preaches and thus violates a fundamental principle of evangelical ethics.

But all this nocturnal buzzing in the rustic churchyards, it seems to me, will get the Hon. Mr. Armstrong nowhere, for, as I say, the rural Methodists can convince themselves that he is white only by painting the Hon. Mr. Ritchie blacker than black —and meanwhile I have yet to hear of a single city wet who trusts him fully, as his opponent is trusted. In the national campaign, the shoe, so to speak, will be on the other foot. There the Hon. Mr. Coolidge will have every advantage that Dr. Ritchie now has in Maryland, and many more besides. If the democrats had a political colossus hidden in their cellar—some superb and almost fabulous rabble-rouser, half Bryan and half Billy Sunday, with flashing eyes, a voice of brass and a heart as big as a wash-basket—if they could find such a superman and had the courage to turn him loose in a 10,000-horsepower touring car stocked with light wines and beer—then they might have some chance of mowing down Cal's jobholders and Ku Kluxers. But with a bogus dry on their spavined mule, feebly mouthing Calvinism at second-hand, they are doomed, I judge, to a bad beating.

THE CLOWNS MARCH IN

June 2, 1924

At first blush, the Republican National Convention at Cleveland next week promises to be a very dull show, for the Hon. Mr. Coolidge will be nominated without serious opposition and there are no issues of enough vitality to make a fight over the platform. The whole proceedings, in fact, will be largely formal. Some dreadful mountebank in a long-tailed coat will open them with a windy speech; then another mountebank will repeat the same rubbish in other words; then a half dozen windjammers will hymn good Cal as a combination of Pericles, Frederick the Great, Washington, Lincoln, Roosevelt and John the Baptist; then there will be an hour or two of idiotic whooping, and then the boys will go home. The LaFollette heretics, if they are heard of at all, will not be heard of for long; they will be shoved aside even more swiftly than they were shoved aside when Harding was nominated. And the battle for the Vice-Presidency will not be fought out in the hall, but somewhere in one of the hotels, behind locked doors and over a jug or two of bootleg Scotch.

A stupid business, indeed. Nevertheless, not without its charms to connoisseurs of the obscene. What, in truth, could more beautifully display the essential dishonesty and imbecility of the entire democratic process. Here will be assembled all the great heroes and master-minds of the majority party in the greatest free nation ever seen on earth, and the job before them will be the austere and solemn one of choosing the head of the state, the heir of Lincoln and Washington, the peer of Cæsar and Charlemagne. And here, after three or four days of bombarding the welkin and calling upon God for help, they will choose unanimously a man whom they regard unanimously as a cheap and puerile fellow!

I don't think I exaggerate. Before the end of the campaign,

of course, many of them will probably convince themselves that
Cal is actually a man of powerful intellect and lofty character,
and even, perhaps, a gentleman. But I doubt seriously that a
single Republican leader of any intelligence believes it today.
Do you think that Henry Cabot Lodge does? Or Smoot? Or
any of the Pennsylvania bosses? Or Borah? Or Hiram Johnson?
Or Moses? Or our own Weller? These men are not idiots. They
have eyes in their heads. They have seen Cal at close range. . . .
But they will all whoop for him in Cleveland.

In such whooping lies the very soul and essence of humor.
Nothing imaginable could be more solidly mirthful. Nor will
there be any lack of jocosity in the details of the farce: the imbecile paralogy of the speeches; the almost inconceivable nonsense of the platform; the low buffooneries of the Southern
delegates, white and black; the swindling of the visitors by the
local apostles of Service; the bootlegging and boozing; the
gaudy scenes in the hall. National conventions are almost
always held in uncomfortable and filthy places; the one at San
Francisco, four years ago, is the only decent one I have ever
heard of. The decorations are carried out by the sort of morons
who arrange street fairs. The hotels are crowded to suffocation.
The food is bad and expensive. Everyone present is robbed,
and everyone goes home exhausted and sore.

My agents in Cleveland report that elaborate preparations
are under way there to slack the thirst of the visitors, which
is always powerful at national conventions. The town is very
well supplied with bootleggers, and regular lines of rum ships
run into it from Canadian ports. Ohio has a State Volstead
act and a large force of spies and snoopers, many of them
former jail-birds. These agents of the Only True Christianity,
no doubt, will all concentrate in Cleveland, and dispute with
the national Prohibition blacklegs for the graft. I venture
the guess that bad Scotch will sell for $15 a bottle in the
hotels and at the convention hall, and that more than one

delegate will go home in the baggage car, a victim to methyl alcohol.

Ohio is run by the Anti-Saloon League, and so the city of Cleveland will be unable to imitate the charming hospitality of the city of San Francisco, four years ago. The municipality there ordered 60 barrels of excellent Bourbon for the entertainment of the delegates and alternates, and charged them to the local smallpox hospital. After the convention the Methodist mullahs of the town exposed the transaction, and proved that there had not been a patient in the hospital for four years. But the city officials who were responsible, when they came up for reëlection soon afterward, were re-elected by immense majorities. Despite Prohibition, the people of San Francisco are still civilized, and know the difference between entertaining human beings and entertaining horned cattle.

The managers of the Hon. Mr. Coolidge's campaign are apparently well aware that the nomination of the Hon. Al Smith by the Democrats would plunge them into a very bitter and serious fight, and so they are trying to weaken Al by weakening Tammany Hall. One of the principal arguments used to bring the Democratic convention to New York was that Tammany would see that the delegates and alternates got enough sound drinks at reasonable prices to keep pleasantly jingled —an unbroken tradition at Democratic national conventions since the days of Andrew Jackson. Now the Coolidge managers have hurled hundreds of Prohibition agents into Manhattan, and a desperate effort is under way to make the town bone-dry. The Dogberries of the Federal bench, as usual, lend themselves willingly to the buffoonery: dozens of injunctions issue from their mills every day, and some of the principal saloons of the Broadway region are now padlocked.

But all the New Yorkers that I know are still optimistic. There are, indeed, so many saloons in the town that all the Federal judges east of the Mississippi, working in eight-hour shifts like coal miners, could not close them completely in the month remaining before the convention opens. Every time one saloon is closed two open. Meanwhile, the 12-mile treaty with England seems to have failed absolutely to discourage boot-legging from the Bahamas. On the contrary, the price of Scotch has declined steadily since it was signed, and the stuff now coming in is of very excellent quality. It is my belief that the theory that it is heavily adulterated is spread by Prohibition-ists, who are certainly not noted for veracity. I have not only encountered no bad Scotch in New York for a year past; I have never heard of any. All the standard brands are obtain-able in unlimited quantities, and at prices, roughly speaking, about half those of a year ago.

Moreover, very good beer is everywhere on sale, and nine-tenths of the Italian restaurants, of which there must be at least two thousand in the town, are selling cocktails and wine. Along Broadway the difficulty of concealing so bulky a drink as beer and the high tolls demanded by the Prohibition en-forcement officers make the price somewhat high, but in the side streets it is now only 60 per cent above what it was in the days before the Volstead act. The last time I went into a beer-house in New York, two or three weeks ago, the *Wirt* greeted me with the news that he had just reduced the price 10 cents a *Seidel*. His place was packed to the doors.

I am thus inclined to believe that the efforts of M. Coolidge's partisans to employ the Eighteenth Amendment against M. Smith will fail. When the white, Protestant, Nordic delegates from the Christian Endeavor regions of the South and Middle West arrive in the big town, their tongues hanging out, they will get what they have dreamed of all these months. It will cost them somewhat more than the dreadful corn liquor of their native steppes, but they will quickly get too much aboard to bother about money. In brief, I formally prophesy that the Democratic National Convention will be as wet as Democratic national conventions have always been, and that the Prohibitionist delegates, as always, will do more than their fair share of the guzzling. The soberest men in the hall, no doubt, will be the Tammany delegates and their brethren from the other big cities of the East. To these cockneys drinking has vastly less fascination than it has for the hinds of the hinterland; decent drinks are always under their noses, and so they are not tortured by the pathological thirst of the rural Ku Kluxers. Moreover, they will have a serious job in hand, and so they will avoid the jug. That job will be to get the bucolic Baptists drunk, and shove Al down their gullets before they recognize the flavor.

POST-MORTEM

July 14, 1924

On the morning after the final adjournment of the late Democratic National Convention, as I snored in the Biltmore Hotel, dreaming of this and that, a colleague of the *Sunpaper* came in and shook me. My eyes, as I opened them, were half blinded by the flash of sunlight from his bald head. Under his union suit rolled the lovely curves of his matronly but still heroic form. His aspect was stern. Obviously, he was agog.

"What I want you to do," he said, "is to take down my words. Wake up Hyde. I want two witnesses."

I woke up Hyde, and besought him to proceed. He plunged at once into the oath laid down in the Maryland statutes: "In the presence of Almighty God, I do solemnly promise and declare"— But what? Simply that he was done with national conventions forever—that he would never attend another one in this life—that if, by any chance, I ever caught him at one

or within a hundred miles of one, I should be free to knock him
in the head, boil him down, and sell his bones to a dice factory.

I have never seen a more earnest man. His eyes flashed blue
and awful flames. His whole hide glowed scarlet through his
union suit. Had there been any hair on his head it would have
bristled like the *vibrissæ* of a Tom cat. In one long and indignant sentence he recited a great catalogue of hardships—
meals bolted suicidally or missed altogether, nights spent in
pursuing elusive and infamous politicians, hours wasted upon
the writing of dispatches that were overtaken by fresh news
before they could get into the *Sunpaper*, dreadful alarm and
surprises at 3 o'clock in the morning, all the horrors of war
without any of its glory. Twice he swore his oath, and then,
for good measure, he damned the whole universe.

But Hyde and I were not impressed. We had heard such
high talk before. We knew that the deponent was an honest
man, but we also knew that he was mistaken. We knew that he
would be on hand for the next great show, as he had been on
hand for this one and for all others in his time—that, for all
his protestations and high resolves, he could no more break
himself of the convention habit than he could break himself
of the habit of breakfasting on five fried eggs and two Manhattan cocktails. The fellow was doomed, as we were ourselves,
and if he didn't know it, it was simply because he was not himself.

For there is something about a national convention that makes
it as fascinating as a revival or a hanging. It is vulgar, it is
ugly, it is stupid, it is tedious, it is hard upon both the higher
cerebral centers and the *gluteus maximus*, and yet it is somehow
charming. One sits through long sessions wishing heartily that
all the delegates and alternates were dead and in hell—and then
suddenly there comes a show so gaudy and hilarious, so melodramatic and obscene, so unimaginably exhilarating and preposterous that one lives a gorgeous year in an hour.

There were three such supreme shows in the late Democratic convention—one given by the Hon. Homer Cummings when he begged for more time for the resolutions committee, one supplied by the Ku Kluxers and their enemies when they had their great combat on the floor, and the last furnished by the whole company when it went crazy in ten seconds and nominated the Hon. Mr. Davis. I missed all of these shows. I was asleep during the first and second, and during the third I was hard at work in *The Evening Sun* office under the stand, writing an article proving that Dr. Davis could never be nominated.

Nevertheless, I had my fair share of the fun—enough, at all events, to take me back in 1928—if God spares me, and I can still walk with two sticks. Hyde will be there too, slaving away in the press-stand for hot hour after hot hour, wearing out lead pencils by the box, with one eye up and one eye down. And somewhere not far away, tracking down the master-minds, will be John Owens, with his noble dome and his bloody oaths.

But what does the general public get out of it? The general public gets precisely the same show—a bit diluted, perhaps, by distance, but still incomparably humorous and thrilling. Herein, indeed, lies the chief merit of democracy, when all is said and done: it may be clumsy, it may be swinish, it may be unutterably incompetent and dishonest, but it is never dismal—its processes, even when they irritate, never actually bore.

The Coolidge convention at Cleveland came nearer doing it than any other convention that I can recall, but even the Coolidge convention, as dull as it was, was redeemed by the revolt of the La Follette husbandmen. The thing, as planned, was to be infinitely decorous—a musicale in the afternoon. Into the drawing-room stomped the prairie peasants in their muddy boots, and at once the musicale was converted into a dog-fight. A mere farce, tawdry and degrading? Not at all. There was also some genuine drama in it. The dogs were all caught and dispatched in the end, but not until they had done thrilling execution among the dog-catchers.

The New York convention was riotous from end to end. Even during the long days of balloting there was always melodrama under the surface. The volcano slept, but ever and anon it sent up a warning wisp of smoke. When it belched actual fire the show was superb. The battle that went on between the Ku Kluxers and their enemies was certainly no sham battle. There were deep and implacable hatreds in it. Each side was resolutely determined to butcher the other. In the end, both were butchered—and a discreet bystander made off with the prize.

It seems to me that the essence of comedy was here. And a moral lesson no less, to wit, the lesson that it is dangerous, in politics, to be too honest. The Hon. Mr. Davis won the nomination by dodging every issue that really stirred the convention. The two factions lost everything that they had fought for. It was as if Germany and France, after warring over Alsace-Lorraine for centuries, should hand it over to England.

The judicious will not fail to extract other lessons from the two conventions. For example, the lesson that politicians, in the main, are poor hands at practical politics—that their professional competence is very slight. Very few of them, indeed, show any sign of ordinary good sense. Their tricks are transparent and deceive no one, not even other politicians. When they accomplish anything, it is usually by accident.

Consider some of the master-minds on exhibition in New York. Tom Taggart, McAdoo and William Jennings Bryan are typical. It would be hard to think of three men who, while the sessions lasted, were talked of more, or with greater fear. Every rumor dealt with them. Every scheme took account of them. Taggart, it was whispered, was playing both ends against the middle; when the crash came he would grab everything for

himself. McAdoo was too astute and too desperate to be
beaten: if he could not actually win, he would at least break
up the convention and ruin the Democratic party. As for
Bryan, he had sworn a mighty oath to prevent the nomination
of Davis, and every time he rose on the floor the Davis men
trembled.

Well, what happened to all these great professors? In brief,
all of them came to ridiculous ends. Taggart managed his
machinations so badly that he got exactly nothing; his candidate, Ralston, had blown up long before the final struggle began. And McAdoo? McAdoo, on the day of fate, saw even his
Ku Kluxers deserting him: he stood on the burning deck alone,
and when he leaped into the water and swam ashore there was
no one left to give him a cheer. Bryan fared even worse. They
not only shoved his arch-enemy, Davis down his throat; they
shoved his brother, the Nebraska John the Baptist, after
Davis, and so made it impossible for him to yell.

This joke upon Bryan was worth all the long sessions, all
the lost sleep, all the hard usage of the *gluteus maximus*. I
shall be snickering over it for many long years. I shall recall
it upon the scaffold, and so shock the sheriff with a macabre
smirk.

BREATHING SPACE

August 4, 1924

This would seem to be a good time for the prudent voter to
keep his ears open and his mind in the same state. Of only one
of the four eminent men on the two major tickets is much
known, and even of that one, the Hon. Mr. Coolidge, there is
less known than there ought to be. It is established that he is

a stubborn little fellow with a tight, unimaginative mind, but it is certainly not established that he is a man of any genuine ability. He made a dreadful mess of the Daugherty business and of the Denby business, trying to hang on and to let go at the same time, and he made an even worse mess of the business of handling Congress. He seems to have very little capacity for dealing with men, and indeed, despite his bucolic stubbornness, very little resolution of any kind. The chances are that if he is elected in November his administration will be one of turmoil and difficulty, and that it will end in scandal and disaster.

Big Business, it appears, is in favor of him, and with it Little Business. The fact should be sufficient to make the judicious regard him somewhat suspiciously. For Big Business, in America, is almost wholly devoid of anything even poetically describable as public spirit. It is frankly on the make, day in and day out, and hence for the sort of politician who gives it the best chance. In order to get that chance it is willing to make any conceivable sacrifice of common sense and the common decencies. Big Business was in favor of Prohibition, believing that a sober workman would make a better slave than one with a few drinks in him. It was in favor of all the gross robberies and extortions that went on during the war, and profited by all of them. It was in favor of the crude throttling of free speech that was then undertaken in the name of patriotism, and is still in favor of it. It was hot against the proceedings which unveiled the swineries of Fall, Doheny, Daugherty, Burns and company, as Dr. Coolidge himself was. Now it is in favor of Dr. Coolidge. He may be, as they say, a virtuous and diligent man, but he is surely in very bad company.

What is to be said of Dr. Davis? His press-agents, it appears, lay stress on two things: that he is highly intellectual, a man who reads books, and that he is a very successful lawyer. The two merits, alas, do not often go together, nor is there any evidence that either is of much public value in a President. The last reader of books who sat in the White House got the United States into a ruinous war, increased the public debt by $25,000,000,000, destroyed the Bill of Rights, and filled the Government service with such strange fowl as Bryan, Lansing, Palmer, Burleson and Colonel House. This bookworm was also a lawyer, though a bad one.

Dr. Davis is said to be a good one. But is there any reason to believe that, among lawyers, the best are much better than the worst? I can find none. All the extravagance and incompetence of our present Government is due, in the main, to lawyers, and, in part at least, to good ones. They are responsible for nine-tenths of the useless and vicious laws that now clutter the statute-books, and for all the evils that go with the vain attempt to enforce them. Every Federal judge is a lawyer. So are most Congressmen. Every invasion of the plain rights of the citizen has a lawyer behind it. If all lawyers were hanged tomorrow, and their bones sold to a mah jong factory, we'd all be freer and safer, and our taxes would be reduced by almost a half.

Dr. Davis is a lawyer whose life has been devoted to protecting the great enterprises of Big Business. He used to work for J. Pierpont Morgan, and he has himself said that he is proud of the fact. Mr. Morgan is an international banker, engaged in squeezing nations that are hard up and in trouble. His operations are safeguarded for him by the man-power of the United States. He was one of the principal beneficiaries of the late war, and made millions out of it. The Government hospitals are now full of one-legged soldiers who gallantly protected his investments then, and the public schools are full of boys who will protect his investments tomorrow. Mr. Davis, it would seem, approves this benign business, and, as I say, is proud of his connection with it. I knew a man once who was proud of his skill at biting off little dogs' tails.

This brings us to the candidates for the Vice-Presidency. Of the Hon. Mr. Dawes it is sufficient to say that he is a shining light in both Big Business and the law. He is what they call well heeled and is frankly sympathetic with other men who are well heeled! When, after the war was over, certain Congressmen began asking what had become of some of the money appropriated for its conduct, Mr. Dawes appeared before them, gave them a good round cursing, and so scared them into silence. What became of the money was never found out. Then the learned gentleman turned his attention to schemes for policing labor. His masterpiece, it appears, involved the copious cracking of heads. All the Rotary Clubs and Chambers of Commerce are in favor of Mr. Dawes. He is the pet candidate of the country bankers. Most of them, in fact, are sorry that he doesn't head the ticket.

Of the Hon. Mr. Bryan I can tell you little, save that he wears a skullcap and is a brother to the eminent Jennings. Jennings was hot against Dr. Davis and threatened to bolt the ticket if he was nominated. So they put Brother Charley on it, and thus spiked him. Brother Charley has gone on in politics out in the cow States by promising, if elected, to reduce the price of coal and gasoline. His opponents, in the main, have promised to raise the price of corn and wheat. Confronted by such a choice, the husbandmen have commonly voted for Charley, as for the least of two swindlers. In brief, a politician rather above the average. Unlike Brother Jennings, he is said to be doubtful about the scientific accuracy of Genesis, but the eloquence of Jennings will suffice to hold the rustic Fundamentalists in line. In his early days Charley was sporty, and had something to do with horses. But now, with his skullcap, he looks like a country undertaker. The job he aspires to has been held in the past by John Adams, Thomas Jefferson, John C. Calhoun and Hannibal Hamlin. More recently it has been held by Garrett A. Hobart, Charles W. Fairbanks and the Hon. Mr. Coolidge.

The Hon. Mr. LaFollette remains. He has no hope, it would seem, of actually seizing the throne; all he dreams of accomplishing is to throw the election into the House of Representatives, where, holding the balance of power, he will be able to dictate the election. But what good will that do him? His right of dictation, practically considered, will be simply a right to choose between the Hon. Mr. Coolidge and the Hon. Mr. Davis. Dr. LaFollette himself will probably be the third man, but no one believes that either side will consent to his election —and the House will be restricted to the three high men; it cannot go outside for a candidate.

In brief, his power, assuming that he keeps both Dr. Coolidge and Dr. Davis from getting a majority in the Electoral College, will have only what the lawyers call a nuisance value. He will be able to scare everyone half to death, and yet he will be unable to get anything for himself. But won't it be possible for him, with both gangs at his mercy, to strike a bargain with either one or the other? Won't both be willing, in return for his support, to adopt his program, and so give him a great moral victory? Of course, of course! Both sides will be willing to promise anything, on a stack of Bibles a mile high. And whichever side promises most, and so fetches Dr. La Follette, will ditch him two hours after its candidate is inaugurated.

But another possibility remains. La Follette is surely no flapper in politics. It may be that he will refuse to believe either party. In that case there will be no election at all, and March 4 will come without a new President in waiting. What will happen then? Dr. Coolidge, I presume, will try to hold on —and ten thousand eager patriots will apply for injunctions and mandamuses against him. In other words, the whole comedy will be transferred to the Supreme Court of the United States. In yet other words, it will become infinitely low and buffoonish, infinitely amusing. Nine lawyers, including one good one, will elect the President. I give warning that I shall need the Stadium to laugh in.

But this is not yet. The time has not come for overt mirth. The perspicacious subject of the Republic, for a month or two, will listen much and say little. We'll know more about the candidates by September 1. And what we find out about them may make the show even more charming than it is today.

LABOR IN POLITICS

August 11, 1924

The Hon. Mr. LaFollette, I take it, is too old a bird to attach much importance to the American Federation of Labor's indorsement of his candidacy. Theoretically, this indorsement will bring him the 2,926,468 votes of the Federation's members, and the six or seven million votes of their wives, sons, daughters, brothers, sisters and other well-wishers. But actually, it will be worth vastly less to him. For labor, in America, seems quite unable to function politically, and at every election its vote is hopelessly divided. In November, I dare say, hundreds of thousands of union men will cast their votes for the Hon. Charles G. Dawes, perhaps the most bold and bloodthirsty enemy of unionism ever heard of in American politics.

It is hard to make out why this should be so. Perhaps one reason lies in the fact that labor leaders, in the Republic, are mainly mountebanks who are for themselves long before and after they are for labor. and that it is thus easy for the professional politicians to corrupt them. Both parties bid for their support by promising them jobs, and so they are divided, and their influence upon their followers, at least in political matters, is greatly weakened. The enthusiasm of a given labor leader for this or that ticket is usually too transparent to deceive even union men. Everyone knows that he has been promised something, and in most cases everyone also knows precisely what it is.

I do not know how many labor leaders now recline at their ease in public offices in the United States, but the number must be very large. In almost every State there are jobs that were created expressly for them, and have no other utility. And in Washington there are many other such jobs. Moreover, it is easy to fetch large numbers of them by appointing them to gaudy honorary commissions and sending them on junkets at the public expense. There is a type of labor leader, indeed, who would rather strut about in a plug hat than get a job. Some of these peacocks have gone very high in the movement, and are as hot against radicals as so many Wall Street bankers.

But perhaps the political impotence of labor is due more largely to the fact that the American workingman, like every other American, has ambitions, and is thus disinclined to think of himself as a workingman. In other words, he refuses to be class conscious. What he usually hopes is that on some near tomorrow, he will be able to escape from work and go into business for himself, and so begin oppressing his late colleagues. This dream makes him resist the regimentation that must inevitably go with every really effective labor movement. In particular, it makes him resist all efforts to control his vote. He values his freedom as a citizen more than he values his welfare as a workingman, for he will be a citizen all his life, whereas, as I have said, he has a secret but indomitable faith that he will some day cease to be a workingman.

Has anyone ever noticed that union men are radical in proportion as the trades they practice diminish this hope? At the extreme Left stand the railroad engineers and firemen, who were for LaFollette long before he was an actual candidate. After them come the steel workers and coal miners, and the copper miners and lumbermen of the West. It is easy to see why. A locomotive engineer, save he be insane, must know very well that he can never hope to own a railroad of his own. A steel worker is in the same boat: if he saved all his wages for a hundred years, he would still lack enough to buy a blast furnace. And so with the miners and the lumbermen.

But in the smaller trades there is still hope, and it shows itself in the politics of their practitioners. Consider, for example, old Sam Gompers. Sam, in those far-off days when he worked, was a cigarmaker. Well, a cigarmaker, at that time, could go into business for himself the moment he had saved $50. It is not so easy today, but Sam remembers only yesterday. He is almost wholly devoid of class consciousness. He thinks of himself, not as a workingman, but as a public man, and the familiar companion of Dr. Coolidge, President Willard and Judge Gary.

The needle trades may appear to offer evidence against this notion, but there is far more appearance than substance in it. The garment workers, in the happy days when any thrifty workman, after five or ten years at the machine, could start a sweatshop of his own, were anything but radical. They had nothing to do with the early adventures of such visionaries as Debs and Powderly, nor were they run amok by Herr Most. It was only after their old hope began to fade—after it had become a practical impossibility for any ordinary slave to escape from the sweatshop—that they turned to Socialism. Now they are resigned and class conscious—and very radical.

No doubt the other trades that still hold aloof will follow them as escape from servitude becomes more and more difficult.

It will be a long, long while, perhaps, before such workingmen as electricians, locksmiths and chimney-sweeps turn to the Left, for all that one of them needs to go into business for himself is a set of simple tools, but in other trades the thing is growing more nearly impossible as year chases year. Not many of the working bakers of today will ever own bakeries of their own, and not many of the plumbers will ever become boss plumbers, and not many of the carpenters will ever be contractors. The brew-workers went to the Left long ago, and the machinists are going even now. Soon or late the last door of escape will be closed, and a man who begins at the bench will die at the bench.

But hope, I believe, will linger long after the last reality has been squeezed from it, for men never abandon it without a hard struggle. When it is no longer supported by facts it will be supported by occasional miracles. Even today one sometimes hears of a railroad president who started as a fireman, or a coal operator who once mined coal. Moreover, the windows will remain open after the door is closed. Any plumber of to-day, when he loses hope of setting up a studio of his own, is free to become an osteopath, a bootlegger or a labor leader. It is hard for a man with that possibility always before him to become class conscious.

As I say, the Hon. Mr. LaFollette is no novice in politics, and so it is highly improbable that he sets much value upon the indorsement of the American Federation of Labor. He knows very well that all of its bosses are against his principal ideas, and that most of its members are with them. The statement of Gompers and company shows very plainly why it indorsed him. Both of the great parties, at their conventions, showed it the door, and so it was forced to go to LaFollette to save its face. But it is no more a radical organization than the Sulgrave Foundation or the Rotary International. On the contrary, it is stoutly and even violently conservative.

LaFollette's real strength among the workingmen lies in the regions outside the Federation pale, and even outside the pale of the railroad brotherhoods. He will get most of his labor votes, not from organized labor at all, but from unorganized labor. It is there that discontent is greatest, for the Federation and the brotherhoods are wholly selfish, and not only refuse to help the poor fellows without their ranks, but even give capital a hand in oppressing them. The migratory laborers of the West, if they had votes, would all vote for LaFollette. For both of the major parties are against them, as the Federation of Labor is against them, and their efforts to protect themselves from oppression have only converted oppression into persecution. They are in precisely the position that all workingmen would be in if Dr. Dawes could have his way.

But despite all this, Dawes will get a great many labor votes —perhaps as many as La Follette. The White House ante-rooms are already filled with labor leaders, all eager to kiss hands and pledge their fealty. LaFollette, as everyone knows, has only the remotest chance of getting into the White House; Dr. Coolidge is pretty sure to stay there. Once his safety is assured, he will not be ungrateful to those who saved him from the Reds. There will be jobs and jobs to give out, high-sounding dignities to distribute. Some of them will go to patriotic labor leaders, and a few weeks later these worthy men will be in Washington, elegantly done out in full-dress evening dress-suits, and dining amicably with Mr. Vice-President Dawes.

THE NEW WOODROW

August 18, 1924

A week having been devoted by the principal Democratic journals of the country to deluging the Hon. John W. Davis with cataracts of pomade, vaseline, goose-grease, cold cream and other unguents, perhaps it may be lawful now to observe that his historic speech of acceptance was, after all, no very great shakes—that any lawyer of the general intelligence of, say, a bank cashier or a Federal judge might have delivered one just as good, and that many lawyers, even without the aid of wind music and the huzzahs of bootleggers, would have probably done better.

Dr. Davis, of course, is no Harding. That is to say, he is no donkey. He employs the English language in a manner that shows he has a decent respect for it. He is adroit and ingratiating. His manner, even when he rants, is polished and refined. One cannot imagine his own rhetoric making him puff and sweat. Nevertheless, it remains mere rhetoric at bottom, and hence hollow. Only once in his speech, and that when he indulged himself in the banality of denouncing poor Fall, Denby and Daugherty, did he come down to plain propositions, clearly stated. The rest was mere sound and fury, signifying nothing. It was the immemorial blather of a candidate for office under democracy, addressing multitudes unfamiliar with ideas and incapable of thought. It was the sort of sonorous bilge that delights Kiwanis Clubs, attendants at Methodist revivals, and the editorial writers for party newspapers.

I point specifically to three salient passages—those dealing with the wholesale corruption at Washington, with Prohibition and with the so-called League of Nations. What did Dr. Davis have to say about these enormously important issues—perhaps the most important now before the country? He had nothing to say—that is, nothing that was precise, apposite and illuminating. He simply lathered each one with rhetoric and then passed on. Here, for example, is what he said of Prohibition:

> For no reason that is apparent to me the question has been asked, as, perhaps, it will continue to be asked until it has been definitely answered, what views I hold concerning the enforcement of the Eighteenth Amendment and the statutes passed to put it into effect. Why the question? Is it not the law? I would hold in contempt any public official who took with uplifted hand an oath to support the Constitution of the United States, making at the same time a mental reservation whereby a single word of that great document is excluded from his vow.

And so on, and so on. Who could imagine any more disingenuous begging of a question? You know and I know, and Dr. Davis well knew when he emptied this nonsense upon the Clarksburg moonshiners, that no one had ever solicited him to agree to disregard the Eighteenth Amendment—that for all its wholesale violation by millions of Americans, no proposal that the President of the United States formally repudiate and nullify it has ever been made by anyone. In other words, he knew quite well that the question he asked himself had never been asked of him by any other man. And he knew quite as well that another and very different question *had* been asked of him, to wit, Do you favor *changing* the Volstead act?

This real question he evaded, and it must be assumed that he evaded it deliberately, for he is surely not stupid enough to confuse it with the other. That is to say, it must be assumed that he deliberately dodged a highly important and pressing issue because it was dangerous—because answering it like an honest man might lose votes for him. Such is the shifty politician we are now asked to venerate! Such is the new candidate for the shoes of Washington and Jefferson!

Try to imagine Washington skulking up an alley in any such manner. If you can imagine it, then go out into the street and give three cheers for Dr. Davis.

His discussion of the colossal thieving that went on under Harding was even less frank. In brief, what was his contention? Simply that all this thieving was started in Washington by the Ohio gang—that nothing of the sort had ever been heard of there until poor Gamaliel took the oath. He rang the changes upon his thesis, and it took him to his highest peak of eloquence. The days of 1917 and 1918 were "heroic" and full of "moral grandeur"; no jobholder under the Martyr Woodrow showed the slightest "taint of dishonesty or corruption"; it is a "libelous suggestion" that the Harding reign of mirth had anything to do with any "demoralization attendant upon the great war."

What is to be thought of an educated man, even though he be a politician, who discharges such arrant nonsense upon the public air? Does anyone seriously believe that Dr. Davis has never heard of the airship scandals, with their loot of $900,000,000—9,000 times as much as Fall got? Or that he is unfamiliar with the operations of the Alien Property Custodian and the Chemical Foundation? Or that he has no knowledge of the stupendous stealings that went on in the shipyards, the munition plants and at the army camps during the war? The truth is, of course, that Dr. Davis knows about all these things quite as well as you and I know about them.

Yet he tries to make it appear, in a public statement of the first importance, that he doesn't. He deliberately evades the bald and inescapable facts. Are such childish evasions the marks of a candid man? And when a man is guilty of them is it a reason for making him President?

The learned gentleman's dealing with the League of Nations issue was almost equally disingenuous. On the one hand, he credited the League of Nations with a high virtue and utility which everyone knows it has not shown; and on the other hand he talked vaguely and without sense of the vast benefits to be derived from American participation in its chicaneries.

I know of very few persons who are against a League of Nations *per se.* Almost everyone believes that such an organization, if honestly administered, would tend to promote peace in the world, and so lift the present excessive burden of taxation. It could not, perhaps prevent wars altogether, but it might at least help to diminish their number. The objection to the present League of Nations is that it has no such object in fact, and no such effect. It is simply a convenient device for enabling the victors in the late war to hold on to their loot. In so far as it has worked, it is because they have agreed upon the division; in so far as it has failed, it is because they have quarreled.

How would it improve this gang of thieves by adding one more thief—and that one a very rich and bold one? The sole effect of the addition, it seems to me, would be to make quarrels more frequent. The United States, already safely within the English orbit, would simply aid England in her struggle against France, and so force France to look for help elsewhere. The United States, meanwhile, would not give her services for nothing—that is, her bankers and their political valets would not give their services for nothing. Are they doing so in London today? Did they do so in Paris a year ago? Go ask the European taxpayers who are about to pay a bonus of 7 per cent for American money, and then start paying interest on it at 7 per cent for 99 years!

If the United States joined the League, indeed, probably the only visible effect would be a vast intensification of the general distrust and dislike of Americans, already violent enough, God knows. We would be the capitalists of the firm, and the honest debtors and working men would naturally hate us. In the end the temptation to get their money back by combining against us would be almost irresistible. If we go in, then let us simultaneously order a Goose-Step Day for at least once a month.

I do not argue that there is any ready solution for the present international problem. I merely argue that Dr. Davis' solution is vague and nonsensical—that it is almost as bad as Dr. Harding's unintelligible scheme of a World Court. Its author attempted no plausible exposition of it. He did not bother to come down to details and specifications. In other words, he did not talk like a sensible man presenting an idea to other sensible men; he talked like a politician spouting empty words from the stump. His whole harangue had that character. To praise it as a clear statement of issues, and to argue that it dealt with them candidly and illuminatingly, is simply to utter nonsense.

MEDITATIONS ON THE CAMPAIGN

August 25, 1924

Having now devoted a solid month to examining the high and low words of the partisans of the Hon. John W. Davis, of Wall Street, West Virginia, I can only report that I have yet to encounter any sound reason for voting for him. The more these partisans argue that he is a true Progressive, and hot for all the sure cures now on tap, the more they prove that the Hon. Mr. LaFollette is even truer and even hotter. And the more they try to make it appear that he is, notwithstanding, a safe and sane man, and one to be trusted fully by every citizen with money in the bank, the more they make it plain that the Hon. Mr. Coolidge is even safer and saner, and still more to be trusted.

In a word, the Hon. gentleman falls between two stools. He is, in a very real sense, not in the fight at all; he is simply a sort of bystander—far from innocent, perhaps, but still not actively engaged. The actual combatants are the Hon. Mr. LaFollette and the Hon. Mr. Coolidge. Each of these great statesmen stands for something that is simple and obvious—something that anyone may understand. Dr. Coolidge is for the Haves and Dr. LaFollette is for the Have Nots. But whom is Dr. Davis for? I'm sure I don't know, and neither does anyone else. I have read all his state papers with dreadful diligence, and yet all I can gather from them is that he is for himself.

A sense of this fact seems to be going through the country. The Davis campaign is at a standstill. LaFollette is belaboring Coolidge, and the friends of Coolidge are belaboring LaFollette, but no one seems to think it worth while to belabor Davis. He is simply concealed in the crowd, like a bootlegger at a wedding. The sore men, in so far as they have any intelligence at all, seem to be unanimously in favor of LaFollette, and the Babbitts, with sound instinct, are all hot for Coolidge. But who is hot for Davis. Not even the political morons south of the Potomac. They will probably vote for him, as they would vote for the devil or even the Pope on a Democratic ticket, but they are no more hot for him than a Federal Judge is hot for the Constitution.

In all this there is a great deal more than mere accident. What ails the hon. gentleman, primarily, is simply the fact that he lacks all the qualities of leadership—that he is fundamentally not a leader at all, but only a follower. His career, as it is described by his friends, is quite devoid of anything plausibly describable as intellectual enterprise. There is no record that he has ever taken the lead in anything, either as statesman or as politician. He was so little original and rambunctious as a Congressman that the attention of the late Woodrow, who hated all men of forceful personality, was attracted to him, and he was made Solicitor-General. He was so careful and undistinguished as Solicitor-General that he was promoted to the Court of St. James. He was so easy a mark at the Court of St. James that the English gave three cheers when they heard that he had been nominated for the Presidency.

What share has the hon. gentleman had in the great political controversies of the past ten years—the most troubled era since the Civil War? Absolutely none. What has he had to say about Prohibition? Nothing save a few disingenuous platitudes. What about the League issue? Nothing but vague nonsense, by the Creel Press Bureau out of Crewe House. What about the Ku Klux? Not a word. What about the growth of paternalism in government, the idiotic multiplication of laws, the intolerable increase of jobholders? Several years ago, when he was president of the American Bar Association, he delivered a feeble harangue upon the subject—a harangue reading much like a warmed-over *Evening Sunpaper* editorial of six or eight months before. Since becoming a candidate he has evaded the matter. No one knows clearly what he thinks about it.

His presidency of the American Bar Association coincided exactly with a revolt against the wholesale invasions of the Bill of Rights that were begun under Wilson and continued under Harding. Lawyers in all parts of the country took part in this revolt—men as diverse as Senator Thomas J. Walsh and Dean Roscoe Pound of Harvard, Clarence Darrow and Feather Duster Hughes. But Dr. Davis took no part in it. To this day he has uttered no word about it. Is he in favor of shoving men into jail without jury trials, or is he against it? No one knows.

The learned gentleman's complete failure as a public man, indeed, has forced his partisans to fall back upon his eminence as a lawyer. But what is this eminence worth—that is, in a candidate for the presidency? It seems to me that it is worth precisely nothing. A man might be the most successful lawyer in the United States, and yet be quite unfit for the office of county sheriff, Congressman, or even Federal judge. There is nothing in the daily life of a trial lawyer that prepares a man to execute the laws; his experience only increases his competence to evade and make a mock of them. He is engaged professionally, day in and day out, in defending persons who have done so. Dr. Davis has been so engaged for years.

Now he says that he is proud of his career. Why not? His clients, in the main, have been very well heeled, and they have made him rich. I have nothing to say against his satisfaction. It seems to me that it is quite honorable to desire to be rich. It is also quite honorable, at all events in America, to want to be a successful lawyer, an adroit jail-robber. All I contend is that these aspirations are incompatible with the yearning to be President of the United States. The two things simply do not hang together. It is as if I, who have devoted my whole life to advocating Darwinism and other such heresies, should suddenly print a card announcing my candidacy for a bishopric, or, to make the analogy closer, for the stool of St. Peter. The majority of the faithful, I believe, would resent my candidacy, and with sound reason. In the same way a great many Americans resent the candidacy of the Hon. Mr. Davis.

Perhaps the fact explains, in part, the palpable flaccidity of his campaign. But there is a better explanation, I believe, in his lack of all the qualities of genuine leadership—his apparent incapacity to get ahead of ideas and pull them along with him. He is a highly respectable man, but he is nothing else.

Even Dr. Coolidge, for all his puerility, has this capacity. In his whole life he has probably never thought an original thought, but he has at least shown a talent for dramatizing the thoughts of others. In the present campaign he has very neatly seized the leadership of the Babbitts. Every idea that is honorable and of good report in Pullman smoke-rooms, on the verandas of golf clubs, among university presidents, at luncheons of the Kiwanis Club and where sweaters and usurers meet—all this rubbish he has welded into a system of politics, nay, of statecraft, of jurisprudence, of epistemology, almost of theology, and made himself the prophet of it. He has shoved himself an inch ahead of his lieges. He is one degree hotter for the existing order than they are themselves.

On the other rampart stands Dr. LaFollette, obviously a genuine leader, even to the eye of his bitterest enemies. No one has ever accused LaFollette of following anyone. He has always been in the forefront of the fray, alike when the going was good, as in Wisconsin when he mowed down the Babbitts, and in Washington during the war, when his foes tried to dispose of him, American fashion, by hitting him below the belt. LaFollette is so gaudily the leader that he is followed by thousands who are hot against him. The sheer force of his personality drags along the whole pack of visionaries. His own cellar contains relatively few jugs of peruna, but he is so thrilling that his guests willingly bring their own.

If all these guests could agree upon one brand LaFollette would carry twenty-five States, including Illinois and New York. But they simply can't. For Progressives are like Christians in this: that they hate one another far more than they hate the heathen. The devil doesn't have to fight the Catholics: he leaves the business to the Ku Klux, *i.e.*, to the Methodists and Baptists. Just so the Progressives devour one another, to the delight and edification of the Babbitts. Some of them, resisting even LaFollette's vast magnetism, have already turned upon him. Others have begun to row among themselves. I believe that by the Tuesday following the first Monday in November the whole pack will be in chaos, and dog will be eating dog. Cal, as I argued several weeks ago, will get the labor vote, old Sam Gompers to the contrary notwithstanding. And he will also get many another vote now credited to LaFollette. My guess is that he will be elected to the woolsack of Washington and Lincoln by an immense majority.

NOTES ON THE STRUGGLE

September 15, 1924

As the campaign wears on it becomes more and more depressing to contemplate the choice before the voters of this eminent and puissant Republic. The Hon. Mr. Davis, I begin to believe, is already out of the running. If he ever becomes formidable it must be by a sort of miracle. What remains? On the one hand the citizen may vote for Senator LaFollette, and so give his ballot to a scheme of reform that, viewed in the friendliest fashion, is full of highly dubious ideas. On the other hand, he may vote for Coolidge, and give his indorsement to a political philosophy that is ignorant, selfish, narrow and dishonest.

It is common to say that Wall Steet is unanimously in favor of Coolidge, and the fact is urged against him. It is not quite a fact. Wall Street, indeed, is seldom unanimously for anything. It divides as often as Main Street, and sometimes far more sharply. In the present case it shows some sturdy Davis sentiment and even a flicker or two of LaFollette sentiment. There are bankers who forget their safe-deposit boxes, just as there are clergymen who forget the collection plate. But if all that is worst in Wall Street be accepted as representative of the whole, then it may be said with complete truth that the Street sweats and prays for Cal. He is the favorite of all its jackals. They believe that they will be safe if he is elected, and they are right.

Why do they distrust the Hon. Mr. Davis? For the reason, I dare say, that he is too much a member of the lodge, too familiar with the secret aspirations of the grand kleagles and imperial wizards. Once he were in the White House, Wall Street could do nothing further for him, and he would be under a strong temptation to capitalize his immense knowledge of its ways. The money changers greatly prefer a ductile ignoramus, eager for flattery: he is vastly easier to work. The ideal is one who has been tried on the track. Dr. Coolidge has been tried. And found satisfactory.

One reads the speeches of the hon. gentleman and his running mate in a bruised sort of amazement. Is it actually possible that such drivel is admired, and makes votes? Turn, for example, to Dr. Coolidge's defense of the Supreme Court, made here in Baltimore a week or so ago. His fundamental contention, it must be plain, was sound enough. The Supreme Court may be bad, but a Congress free to make laws without any constitutional check would be a hundred times worse. But consider some of his arguments. Among other things, he argued that the Supreme Court was the chief existing safeguard of the right of trial by jury!

It would be hard to imagine anything more idiotic. The Supreme Court, as a matter of fact, has done more to destroy the right of trial by jury than any other agency. The whole system of Federal courts is now engaged, and has been engaged for years past, upon a deliberate and successful effort to blow it to pieces, first at the behest of Big Business and then at the behest of the Anti-Saloon League, and the Supreme Court has stood in the forefront of that conspiracy from the start. Upon the very fact, indeed, the partisans of Dr. LaFollette ground their demand that its powers be reduced and rigidly limited. Yet Dr. Coolidge stands up in public and argues solemnly that the Supreme Court is the guardian of the Bill of Rights, and that all persons who criticize it are enemies of the Constitution!

How is one to account for such dreadful nonsense? Is the eminent gentleman a numskull, or does he believe that all the rest of us are numskulls? Or can it be that he has borrowed a leaf from the book of his eminent associate, General Dawes? The scheme of General Dawes is simple: when his argument needs it, he lies. I point to his endless denunciations of Dr. La-Follette as the candidate of the communists. No one knows better than Dawes that LaFollette repudiated the communists long before his nomination, and that they are bitterly against him today. Nevertheless, he seldom makes a speech without trying to identify LaFollette with communism. In brief, Dawes is a fraud, and yet, if Dr. Coolidge is called to glory, he will be President of the United States!

Such are the two statesmen who seem destined at the moment, to triumph in November: a man whose chief arguments are nonsensical and a man whose chief arguments are mendacious. It is a curious fact, and charmingly illustrative of American character, that such assaults upon common sense and common decency do not lose votes, but rather make them. When Coolidge talks of the Supreme Court defending the Bill of Rights there is not laughter, but applause. And when Dawes libels LaFollette by depicting him as an agent of the Bolsheviks, the Rotarians do not hiss him; they cheer him.

Nevertheless, two extremely vulnerable men, and a properly planned attack, I believe, would do them great damage. So far, unluckily it has not been made. LaFollette, busy with his archaic visions of monopolies and his lamentable schemes to curse the country with more and more jobholders, has left the offensive to his running-mate, Wheeler, obviously a third-rate performer. Davis, instead of dissipating the fog with blasts of honesty and common sense, has devoted himself chiefly to academic pronunciamentos, many of them very evasive. His solitary statement of his position on the Prohibition question was disingenuous and discreditable—a plain dodging of the plain issue. It fooled neither the drys nor the wets and so got him nowhere.

What he appears to lack is simply courage—the only thing that can save his bacon, if it is to be saved at all. If he keeps on pussy-footing he will fade out of the picture completely, especially if McAdoo and Al Smith take to the stump for him. They will probably make very few votes for him; they will merely shoulder him out of the limelight, and cause the voters to forget him. His chance, slim at best, lies in a bold and vigorous attack.

The best opening for him, I believe, is offered by Prohibition. Despite all the effort to pump up other issues, the wet-or-dry issue remains the liveliest in all parts of the country. The Ku Klux issue is everywhere submerged in it, and beside it all the other issues now heard of grow pale. Not one American in a hundred is actively interested in the League of Nations; not one in a thousand is noticeably wrought up about the petty stealings of the friends of Dr. Daugherty; not one in ten thousand ever shows any excitement about States' rights. But Prohibition is talked of everywhere, endlessly and with passion, and especially is it talked of in the big cities.

Well, it is precisely in the big cities that Dr. Davis must win, if he is to win at all. Let him pledge himself to law enforcement all he pleases. If he also pledges himself to work for a modification of the Volstead act he will sweep New York, Chicago, St. Louis, Boston, Baltimore and a dozen other big cities, and some of these cities will carry States with them. Moreover, there will be some very populous States among them, with many votes in the Electoral College—more than enough to counterbalance the loss of half a dozen of the dry cow-states. The wet vote in most of the big cities now seems to be edging toward LaFollette. In two cases out of three its loss will be borne by Davis, not by Coolidge. In other words, the wet vote in the cities is largely Democratic.

But can Davis afford to shock the dry South? Why not? The South is helpless, as usual. It will have to vote for him, wet or dry, or see its whole political organization go to pot, with the accursed Moor triumphant. Moreover, what reason is there to believe that the South is actually dry? I know of none. The truth is that the Anti-Saloon League, like its secular arm, the Ku Klux Klan, is everywhere in difficulties in the South, and that a secret ballot tomorrow would probably show every State south of the Potomac, with the possible exception of North Carolina, to be wringing wet. The people down there, in truth, tire of government by Methodist dervishes, and nothing would please them more than a fair chance to prove it.

Here is Dr. Davis' chance. The prize offered to him consists of New York, Maryland, Missouri, and probably Rhode Island, Connecticut and Massachusetts—in all, 101 electoral votes, enough to give poor Cal, with LaFollette on his back in the cow-States, the fan-tods. Will he grab it? My prediction is that he will not. Instead, he will continue to make speeches about American idealism and the "moral grandeur" of the late Martyr Wilson.

THE COOLIDGE BUNCOMBE

October 6, 1924

One of the chief arguments made for Dr. Coolidge is that the majority of business men are for him. If this were true, then it would be fair to conclude, not only that business men put their private profits above the public good—which they probably do in fact, precisely like the rest of us—but also that they are singularly lacking in sense and prudence. For if anything is plain today, it must be that another Coolidge administration, if it is inflicted upon us, will end inevitably in scandal and disaster. The day good Cal is elected every thieving scoundrel in the Republican party will burst into hosannas, and the day he is inaugurated there will be song and praise services wherever injunctions are tight and profits run to 50 per cent. There will follow, for a year or two, a reign of mirth in Washington, wilder and merrier, even, than that of Harding's time. And then there will come an explosion.

How all this will benefit legitimate business I can't make out. The only business men who will gain anything by it will be the one who manages to steal enough while the going is good to last him all the rest of his life. All the others will get burnt in the explosion, as they always do when political dynamite is set off. Do they quake today before the menace of LaFollette? If so, let them consider how LaFollette came to be so formidable. Three years ago he was apparently as dead as Gog and Magog. The Farmer Labor party snored beside him in the political morgue; Socialism was already in the dissecting room. Then came, in quick succession, the oil scandal, the Veterans' Bureau scandal, and the intolerable stench of Daugherty. In six months LaFollettism was on its legs again, and now it is so strong that only a miracle can keep the election out of the House.

When so-called radicalism is denounced this sequence of cause and effect is only too often overlooked. It is assumed that men become radicals because they are naturally criminal, or because they have been bribed by Russian gold, or because they have not been properly Americanized. But the thing that actually moves them, nine times out of ten, is simply the conviction that the Government they suffer under is unbearably and incurably corrupt. The Doheny-Denby oil arrangement made thousands of them. The wholesale burglary of the Veterans' Bureau made thousands more. And the exposure of the Department of Justice under Daugherty and Burns lifted the number to millions. The notion that a radical is one who hates his country is naïve and usually idiotic. He is, more likely, one who loves his country more than the rest of us, and is thus more disturbed than the rest of us when he sees it debauched. He is not a bad citizen turning to crime; he is a good citizen driven to despair.

Where the government is honestly and competently administered radicalism is unheard of. Why is it that we have no radical party of any importance in Maryland? Because the State government is in the hands of reasonably decent men—

above all, because the State courts are honest and everyone knows it. And why is radicalism so strong in California? Because the State is run by a dreadful combination of crooked politicians and grasping Babbitts—because the fundamental rights of man are worth nothing there, and anyone who protests against the carnival of graft and oppression is railroaded to jail—above all, because the State courts are so servile, stupid and lawless that they almost equal the Federal courts under the Anti-Saloon League. No honest man in California is safe. There are laws especially designed to silence him, and they are enforced by kept judges with merciless severity. The result is that California is on fire with radicalism—that radicals pop up twice as fast as the Babbitts and their judicial valets can pursue and scotch them.

What I contend is that the Coolidge Administration, if it is inflicted on us is bound to be quite as bad as the Harding Administration, and that the chances are that it will be a great deal worse. In other words, I contend that it is bound to manufacture radicalism in a wholesale manner, and that this radicalism will be far more dangerous to legitimate business than the mild stuff that Dr. LaFollette now has on tap.

I believe that the Coolidge Administration will be worse than that of Harding for the plain reason that Coolidge himself is worse than Harding. Harding was an ignoramus, but there were unquestionably good impulses in him. He had a great desire to be liked and respected; he was susceptible to good as well as to bad suggestions; his very vanity, in the long run, might have saved him from the rogues who exploited him. Behind Harding the politician there was always Harding the business man—a man of successful and honorable career, jealous of his good name. Coolidge is simply a professional politician, and a very petty, sordid and dull one. He has lived by job-seeking and job-holding all his life; his every thought is that of his miserable trade. When it comes to a conflict between politicians and reputable folk, his instinctive sympathy always goes to the politicians.

He showed this sympathy plainly in the Denby and Daugherty cases. To say that he was not strongly in favor of both men is to utter nonsense. He not only kept them in office as long as he could, despite the massive proofs of their unfitness; he also worked for them behind the door, stealthily and ignominiously. To this day he has not said a single word against either of them; all his objurgations have been leveled at those who exposed them and drove them out. He kept the asinine Teddy Roosevelt, Jr., in office until a week or so ago, and then gave him a parting salute of twenty-one guns. He is even now trying to promote Captain Robison, the man who arranged the Doheny oil grab. Who has forgotten that he wanted to appoint Daugherty to "investigate" that colossal steal? Or that he was in close and constant communication with Ned McLean, Daugherty's and Fall's friend, during the whole of the inquiry?

No amount of campaign blather will suffice to wipe out this discreditable record. Coolidge pulled against the oil investigation from the start; he pulled against the Daugherty investigation from the start; he let Daugherty and Denby go at last only under pressure, and after trying to hit their opponents below the belt. His sympathy has been with such oppressed patriots all his life, and it is with them today. If he is elected for four years every professional politician in the Republican party will rejoice, and with sound reason. There will be good times for the boys—and Fall, Daugherty and company will be safe.

But will the country be safe? It is not so certain. Those business men who think only of easy profits tomorrow might do well to give a thought or two to the day after. They have seen a very formidable radical movement roll up under their noses. If they have any sense, they will not be deceived by the argument that it has been set in motion by "agitators." What agitators? Who and where are they? I can find no such persons. LaFollette

stumped the country for years and got nowhere. Only his own
State heeded him. But last winter he began to get a response,
and soon it was immense and vociferous. That response came
from men and women who had become convinced at last, and
with good logic, that government by professional politicians was
intolerably and hopelessly rotten—that the only remedy was to
turn them out, and then make laws to prevent them coming back.

Personally I doubt that such laws, if made, will work. In other
words, I am not a radical. I believe that all government is evil,
and that trying to improve it is largely a waste of time. But
that is certainly not the common American view; the majority
of Americans are far more hopeful. When they see an evil they
try to remedy it—by peaceful means if possible, and if not,
then by force. In the present case millions of them tire of the
degrading Coolidge farce, with its puerile evasion of issues, its
cloaking of Denby and Daugherty, its exaltation of such political jugglers as Slemp and Butler, its snide conspiracy to rob
LaFollette of honest votes in California. They tire of it and
want to end it. What now, if they are forced to stand four
years more of it? What if they must see it grow ever worse and
worse?

To timorous business men, in this year 1924, LaFollette may
look dangerous. But let them ask themselves what sort of radicalism will probably be afoot in 1928, after four more years of
Coolidge.

MR. DAVIS' CAMPAIGN

October 13, 1924

Every day, for at least a month past, I have heard the whisper that the Hon. John W. Davis was about to bust loose and shake the country with some hot stuff. And every day he has kept on prattling his amiable nothings.

Surely, by this time, even his most devoted partisans must begin to notice the plain fact that the hon. gentleman has blown up and is no more. As for me, I can recall no candidate for the Presidency, not even the Hon. Alton B. Parker, who ever carried on a more ineffective campaign. It is not that the Hon. Mr. Davis has made an amateur's blunders. It is not that he lacks eloquence. It is not that he has come under suspicion of grave crimes and misdemeanors. It is simply that he is too timorous a man to rise to the situation that confronts him—that he is ruining himself by playing safe.

All of his speeches that I have read, probably two dozen, might have been made just as well by a university president or by one of the wind-jamming Babbitts who address Kiwanis and Rotary. Here, perhaps, I libel the university presidents. As a class, they are platitudinous and nonsensical enough, God knows, but there is at least one among them, Dr. Butler, of Columbia, who actually says something when he speaks. Dr. Davis says precisely nothing. Even his girlish flings at the Ku Klux Klan are without substance. What he says is simply what everyone now says. If he is really against the Klan, why doesn't he give it a wallop where it is tender? That is to say, why doesn't he denounce its connection with the sinister enterprises of the Methodist and Baptist churches, and the Anti-Saloon League? If he is opposed to the entrance of religion into politics, here is his chance to say so plainly. Instead, he is content to poll-parrot academic objurgations that are five years old, and so thin that even the Southern newspapers now bawl them.

The learned gentleman is still worse when he gets upon the subject of what he calls personal liberty. His pleas for this great boon have all the heat and force of a flapper's demand that her beau stop kissing her. They almost recall the sermons on Ibsen and Maeterlinck that used to be delivered by intellectual suburban rectors twenty-five years ago. The orator, it appears, is hot for something, but it never becomes clear just what that something is. Does he favor personal liberty? Then precisely *what* personal liberty? Only one brand of it has been subverted of late in anything approaching a wholesale and public manner. This one brand he never mentions. About it he is elaborately and disingenuously silent.

The omission does not escape his auditors, even at meetings packed with ward heelers, and the fact was shown some time ago in Chicago. In the midst of the hon. gentleman's most affecting eloquence, at the exact moment when he began to hymn liberty in words that would have moved a lieutenant of cossacks or even a Federal judge, the gallery began to yell "Give us beer!" The eminent speaker, as I say, was eloquent, but that gallery was still more eloquent. It said more in three austere, pathetic words than he had been saying in a thousand. But he was unaffected. He took no notice of the interruption. Instead, he kept on arguing, lawyer-like, that liberty was ordained by law, and citing statute and precedent to prove it. I daresay, though I don't know, that he quoted various Federal judges. The man simply lacks humor.

If he had it, he couldn't make any campaign at all. His job is really too grotesque. A lawyer on leave from the ante-room of J. P. Morgan, with a brief waiting for him against the day he is beaten, he has to posture before the populace as a Liberal. A jobholder under the late Woodrow, and hence privy to the colossal stealing that went on in Washington in that idealistic era, he has to gabble about its "moral grandeur" and to pretend to be indignant over the puerile purse-snatching of Fall and the friends of Daugherty. A candidate dependent upon the votes of Southern Methodists and Northern Catholics, he has to be against the Ku Klux Klan without being against it, and to whoop for liberty without scaring the Anti-Saloon League.

I lack the honor of the gentleman's acquaintance, but all who know him say that he is, in private, a man of the highest and sweetest tone, a fellow marked by rectitude in all its more delicate varieties, one who would neither rob an orphan nor let a guest go dry—in short, a gentleman. My reply to that is that going into politics is as fatal to a gentleman as going into a bordello is fatal to a virgin. As he stands before us he is not in the locker-room at Piping Rock; he is rampant upon a stump, discharging certain ideas. My contention is that these ideas are full of evasion and hypocrisy, that uttering them is incompatible with intellectual integrity—to get to the heart of it at once, that gentlemen do not do such things.

Why, indeed, should they? Running for office is not obligatory; the man who does it does it voluntarily. Well, if it is impossible to do it without going upon the streets intellectually, then why do it at all? What is the prize in the present case? A public office that has been held, in the recent past, by such blobs as Harding and Coolidge. I can imagine, nevertheless, a man wanting it. He may put Harding and Coolidge out of his mind, and think of McKinley, Taft and Rutherford B. Hayes, or even, if he is vain enough, of Washington and Adams. But why should he be willing to sacrifice his freedom and his honor in order to get it? What is there in it that is worth the blush seen in the shaving-glass?

The concept of honor, of course, is foreign to the professional politician, as it is, indeed, to the average and normal American —foreign and also abhorrent, as becomes evident every time the Anti-Saloon League, the American Legion or any other such organization is heard from. But the man before us is not a professional politician, nor even an average American: he is put in the show-case as a gentleman. Why should a gentleman try to get votes by false pretenses? I can't imagine any situation justifying it; certainly, there is none before us now. Is Davis wet or is he dry? If he is wet, as I hear, then he is trying to hornswoggle Prohibitionists into voting for him. And if he is dry, then he is trying to bamboozle the wets.

The attempt, I believe, will not work. If, as appears plain, his campaign is making no progress, it is chiefly because he has shown no frankness and courage—because his transparent evasions and his deliberate misstatements of known fact have made all the more reflective varieties of men suspicious of him. He will carry the Southern States, where thinking is forbidden by law, and he will get the support of the jobholders and jobseekers of his party in the North. But he has obviously aroused no enthusiasm in other circles. Compared to him, even the dreadful Coolidge is a candid man. Coolidge says nothing, true enough, but that is simply because he has nothing to say. His complete lack of ideas is what delights the sort of men who favor him, for they have learned by bitter experience that ideas are dangerous.

Davis is blowing up for the same reason that Governor Ritchie blew up at the Democratic National Convention: because he is playing close to the board at a time when only boldness could help him. Dr. Ritchie had an excellent chance to make a stir in the convention by tackling the Anti-Saloon League, the Ku Klux Klan and all the other branches of the Methodist-Baptist political machine head-on, and I daresay that his private inclination was to do it, for he is a frank man. But the professional politicians among his advisers were all against it, for politics is incurably evasive, and so his candidacy came to nothing. When the deadlock was at its height, one blast upon his bugle horn might have started a stampede for him. Instead, he was given a sleeping draught and locked in a room.

Davis goes the same route and for the same reason. The politicians who manage his campaign are all plainly in favor of pussy-footing. It is their notion that, if he is careful and avoids scaring anyone, he may slip through—partly by the aid of the Hon. Al Smith in New York and partly by the aid of the Hon. Mr. LaFollette in the Bible Belt. This notion, I presume to opine, is full of holes. The Hon. Al Smith ran ahead of the Cox-Roosevelt ticket by a million votes; he'll probably run ahead of the Davis-Bryan ticket by even more, and so leave it on the beach in New York. And the Hon. Mr. LaFollette, when the time comes to count the ballots, will probably turn out to have captured almost as many of them from Davis as he has captured from Coolidge.

THE VOTER'S DILEMMA

November 3, 1924

Though he is praised in lush, voluptuous terms by the president of the Johns Hopkins University, the Imperial Wizard of the Ku Klux Klan, the *Wall Street Journal*, the Hon. Frank A. Munsey, the proprietor of the *Saturday Evening Post* and other such agents of a delicate and enlightened patriotism, and though his election, barring some act of God, seems to be as certain as tomorrow's dawn, it is difficult to see how any self-respecting man will be able to vote for the Hon. Mr. Coolidge without swallowing hard and making a face.

For if the campaign has developed anything at all, it has developed the fact that the hon. gentleman, for all the high encomiums lavished upon him, is at bottom simply a cheap and trashy fellow, deficient in sense and almost devoid of any notion of honor—in brief, a dreadful little cad. I doubt that any man of dignity, even among his most ardent supporters, has any respect for him as a man. His friends are all ninth-raters like himself. Even in the trade of politics, until the martyrdom of the illustrious Harding heaved him into the White House, he was regarded not as a leader, but as a docile camp-follower. He remains essentially a camp-follower today. He will be safe, but he will be ignoble.

Those who support him because of his safeness tend to forget, I fear, the rest of it. They inevitably wriggle themselves into the position of contending that nothing else matters. It is, I believe, a dangerous doctrine. The four years of Coolidge will be four years of puerile and putrid politics. The very worst elements in the Republican party, already corrupt beyond redemption, will be in the saddle, and full of intelligent self-interest. It will be a debauch of grab. And it will be followed by a revolt that will make the cautious radicalism of Dr. La-Follette appear almost like the gospel of Rotary. Let the friends of safety paste that in their hats. They are trying to put out a fire by squirting gasoline upon it.

Compared to Dr. Coolidge, the Hon. Mr. Davis is obviously a man of enormous superiorities—in fact, it is hard to discover a single element in which he is not superior, and clearly so. He knows more, he is of greater dignity, his pronunciamentoes have more apposite and force, his everyday associations are more decent, he has the mien and manner, not of a bookkeeper in a lime-and-cement warehouse in a small town, but of an educated man and a gentleman.

What ails him, as I have more than once argued, is simply his lack of boldness, and particularly of boldness in the purely political sense. I believe that he has been hobbled and his campaign ruined by the professionals who surround him—all of them so stupid that they could not even manage the convention which nominated him. As a result, his arguments have been feeble, and the country has noted the fact. A sturdy believer in the constitutional rights of the citizen, he has been forced to avoid mention of the rights so grossly violated by Prohibition.

An honest opponent of corruption in government, and out-spoken against the swineries that went on under Harding, he has had to be silent about the far worse swineries that went on under Wilson.

These evasions leave the hon. gentleman with one leg up and one leg down. They have led him, as evasions always do, into downright mendacities, blushful to contemplate in an honorary bencher of the Middle Temple. I allude here to his rumble-bumble to the general effect that no Democratic national admin-istration has ever seen a scandal. If he has forgotten the airship scandal, then surely the country has not forgotten it. Thus an air of equivocation and unreality has got into his discussion of the whole subject, and his campaign has grown progressively feebler. If it were not for the unintelligent support of the South —which is to say, of the Ku Klux that he has denounced—he would be out of it altogether. The East has heard him without attention, and the West has been too busy listening to La-Follette to pay much heed to him.

There remains, then, the Wisconsin Red, with his pockets stuffed with Soviet gold. I shall vote for him unhesitatingly, and for a plain reason: he is the best man in the running, *as a man*. There is no ring in his nose. Nobody owns him. Nobody bosses him. Nobody even advises him. Right or wrong, he has stood on his own bottom, firmly and resolutely, since the day he was first heard of in politics, battling for his ideas in good weather and bad, facing great odds gladly, going against his followers as well as with his followers, taking his own line always and sticking to it with superb courage and resolution.

Suppose all Americans were like LaFollette? What a coun-try it would be! No more depressing goose-stepping. No more gorillas in hysterical herds. No more trimming and trembling. Does it matter what his ideas are? Personally, I am against four-fifths of them, but what are the odds? They are, at worst, better than the ignominious platitudes of Coolidge. They are

better than the evasions of Davis. Roosevelt subscribed to most
of them, and yet the country survived. Whatever may be said
against them, there is at least no concealment about them. La-
Follette states them plainly. You may fancy them or you may
dislike them, but you can't get away from the fact that they are
whooped by a man who, as politicians go among us, is almost
miraculously frank, courageous, honest and first-rate.

The older I grow the less I esteem mere ideas. In politics,
particularly, they are transient and unimportant. To classify
men by examining them is to go back to the stupid days of conscientious Republicans and life-long Democrats. Let us leave
such imbecilities to Ku Kluxers, Fundamentalists and readers
of the New York *Tribune*. There are only men who have character and men who lack it. LaFollette has it. There is no shak-
ing or alarming him. He is devoid of caution, policy, timidity,
baseness—all the immemorial qualities of the politician. He is
tremendous when he is right, and he is even more tremendous
when he is wrong.

The argument against him seems to follow two lines: that he
is a red radical and in secret communion with the Russians, and
that he was against the late war and refused to support it. The
first allegation is chiefly voiced by the Hon. Mr. Dawes, a man
wholly devoid of honor. It is met by the plain fact that all the
American communists are opposed to La Follette and denounce
him with great bitterness. The second charge is well-grounded.
LaFollette not only voted as a Senator, against American
participation in the war; he also refused flatly to change his
views when he failed to prevent it.

What followed is well remembered. While the uproar lasted
he was practically barred from the Senate Chamber. His colleagues, eager to escape contamination, avoided him; he was
reviled from end to end of the country; all the popularity and
influence that he had built up by years of struggle vanished
almost completely. Try to imagine any other American poli-

tician in that situation. How long would it have taken him to grab a flag and begin howling with the pack? How much would his beliefs and principles have weighed against the complete collapse of his career? I attempt no answer. I simply point to the other Senators who had been, before the declaration of war, in the same boat.

But LaFollette stuck. The stink-bombs burst around him, but still he stuck. The work of his whole life went to pieces, but still he stuck. Weak friends deserted him and old enemies prepared to finish him, but still he stuck. There is no record that he hedged an inch. No accusation, however outrageous, daunted him. No threat of disaster, personal or political, wabbled him for an instant. From beginning to end of those brave and intelligent days he held fast to his convictions, simply, tenaciously, and like a man.

I repeat my question: Suppose all Americans were like him? In particular, suppose all politicians among us were like him? Suppose trimming went out of fashion, and there were an end of skulkers, dodgers and safe men? It is too much, perhaps, to hope for, even to dream of. LaFollette will be defeated tomorrow, as he deserves to be defeated in a land of goose-steppers and rubber-stamps. The robes of Washington and Lincoln will be draped about a man who plays the game according to the American rules.

AUTOPSY

November 10, 1924

The Hon. Mr. Coolidge was elected to the shoes of Lincoln by 10,000,000 plurality. The Hon. Tom Walsh, out in Montana, got through by the skin of his teeth. There is juicy material for the political pathologist in these facts, for the Hon.

Mr. Walsh is the man who uncovered Fall and forced out Denby, and the Hon. Mr. Coolidge is the man who did more than any other, by public bull and private wire, to bring that business to wreck. I say nothing of the Hon. Mr. Wheeler, the foe of Daugherty. The Hon. Mr. Wheeler was beaten so badly that little remains of him save a grease spot. Anon the friends of Mr. Daugherty, aided by the friends of Mr. Coolidge, will mop up the grease spot, put it on trial, and try to railroad it to jail.

What does all this mean? That the people of the United States are *not* against robbing the Government? I suspect as much. More, I have suspected it for years. Yet more, I have argued it for years. Who, indeed, can recall a time when the act was actually dangerous—as dangerous, say, as spitting on the sidewalk or carrying a bottle of wine to a sick friend? Certainly it is not dangerous in this, our prosperous and Christian age. None of the thieves who trimmed Uncle Sam at Hog Island during the war have ever gone to jail. The airship contractors are still at large, their billion of loot in their pockets. So are all the camp contractors. So is Doheny. So is Fall. And they will stay at large, happy, at peace, venerated by the general, until they are snatched up to bliss eternal.

Dawes deserves special mention. Dawes is the man who put down the investigation of the war frauds. He went gallantly to the rescue of all the prehensile dollar-a-year men, and saved them from jail. The scandal of their colossal thieving fell upon Democratic shoulders, and Dawes was a Republican—but *Brüderschaft* above partisan spite! Today he is heir-elect of the greatest moral republic ever heard of—the exemplar and despair of other nations. Let the Bolsheviki murder Cal, as they murdered the illustrious Harding, and Dawes will wear the sword of George Washington.

A thought somehow staggering. It is almost as if Dr. Billy Sunday should be made Pope. But let us not commit the error, so common among Progressives of all wings, of shuddering over it too piously, of seeing in it too much of the lamentable. Dawes, in Washington's day, would have been barred from the higher political preferment, as not a gentleman. But he is very typical of the America in which he lives, and in particular of the business America now triumphant. His ethical ideas are simple and devoid of cant. He believes that any man deserves whatever he can get. This is also the notion of at least 98 per cent of his countrymen.

The fact explains their indifference to what is called public corruption. They are not in favor of stealing *per se*, but stealing from the Government somehow seems to them less reprehensible than other kinds. Perhaps it is mainly because the Government is impersonal—that robbing it does not bring any concrete man to ruin. Perhaps it is also because the Government can instantly replace whatever it loses. Every individual knows, of course, that when he steals from the Government he steals some of his own money—that he will be forced, as a citizen, to make good some of the loss—but he also knows, or, at all events, hopes, that his share of the swag will be infinitely larger than his share of the damage.

This hope is usually well-grounded. If he gets anything at all, he gets more than he can possibly lose. The profiteers of the war days were themselves heavily mulcted; they had to pay enormous taxes. But they had enough skill at their business to get back much more than they paid—and that sort of skill, in a commercial society, is always admired. No wonder. It is the sort of skill that every man is trying to summon up; its exercise is the chief aim of human ambition. A few succeed gloriously; the rest fail. The latter, of course, envy the former, but not malignantly, not to the extent of wishing them in jail. The occasional effort to run them down and make them disgorge is enjoyed, as every other man-hunt is enjoyed, but it is regarded as bad sportsmanship to shoot the fox.

In all this there is a concept of the Government as something

remote and, as I have said, impersonal—something separate
from and antagonistic to the body of citizens. That concept is
certainly not unsound. The politicians who constitute the Government try to make it appear, to be sure, that they carry on
their business in an altruistic spirit—even Dr. Coolidge, for example, gives out that he is a slave to Service, as Dr. Fall and
Dr. Daugherty did before him—but that pretension deceives no
one. Every citizen of any intelligence whatever knows that the
aim of the Government, *i.e.*, of the politicians, is simply to
squeeze him all it can. It is not his servant, but his enemy. If it
could do so safely it would strip him to his hide.

Thus he sees nothing wrong in taking a hack at it in return
when the chance offers. When he steals from it, he is not stealing
from his neighbors, honest and hard-working men like himself,
but from a vast and shadowy organization of professional
thieves, all of them inimical to him. Life in a democracy tends
inevitably to become a mere combat between the two gangs—the
professionals on the one hand and the amateurs on the other.
The former is not made up exclusively, as Dr. LaFollette and
his friends seem to think, of bankers and other such magnates.
There is room in it also for more lowly men, if only they can
muster the courage to enter it. During the war all of the union
men of the country, by pooling their strength, managed to
horn in; they stole almost as much, in all probability, as the
dollar-a-year men. And ever since then the soldiers, deprived of
their fair share at the time, have been trying to get it belatedly.
The chief argument for the bonus is not that the veterans of
the war leaped to the defense of democracy, for at least four-
fifths of them, as everyone knows, tried to avoid service. The
chief argument is that, when they were forced into the army,
they were deprived of their equitable chance at the loot then on
tap.

The difference between the two gangs is that that of the professionals is supported by an unfair advantage—that it has the

law on its side. It controls not only the executive and legislative arms; it also controls the courts, and what that advantage is worth has been shown in the cases of Daugherty and Wheeler. The other gang is almost unarmored. The Government is always able, when so disposed, to single out a few of its ringleaders and clap them into jail. But the Government gang is well-nigh immune to punishment. Since the first days of the Republic less than a dozen of its members have been impeached, and only a few understrappers have ever been put into jail.

Thus the combat which constantly goes on parallels the one between the Anti-Saloon League and the bootleggers. The Anti-Saloon League is quite as criminal as the bootleggers; it devotes itself professionally to violating the Bill of Rights. But its control of the Government puts it above the law. It appoints the very judges who try its enemies. In consequence, its members and agents commit their crimes almost unmolested, and only one of them, in fact, has ever got into jail—and that by a sort of accident. But public opinion is mainly on the side of the bootleggers. They not only make an appeal to the good sportsmanship of the crowd, which sees clearly the unfairness of the combat; they are also closer to the crowd than the Anti-Saloon League, which is largely ecclesiastical in character, and hence a natural object of suspicion to plain men.

In the late election the Anti-Saloon League was everywhere on the side of corruption. It allied itself with the Ku Klux in the South and Middle West, it worked hand in hand with the Daugherty gang of political thieves in Ohio, and it supported Teddy Roosevelt II in New York—the same Roosevelt who helped Doheny and Sinclair to grab the navy's oil reserves. It is curious to reflect that this grossly corrupt and evil organization came very near getting control of the State of New York, and with it of the largest and most civilized American city. It was defeated only by the great popularity of the Hon. Al Smith. That is to say, it was defeated only by the votes of Jews and

Catholics, neither of whom, by the current dogma, ought to be allowed to vote at all.

TWILIGHT

October 17, 1927

Having pussy-footed all his life, it is highly probable that Dr. Coolidge will go on pussy-footing to the end of the chapter. There is nothing in the known facts about the man to indicate any change of heart. He was born with that pawky caution which is one of the solid qualities of the peasant, and he will hang on to it until the angels call him home. It has made life comfortable for him, as the same quality makes life comfortable to a bishop or a mud turtle, but what it will cost him in the long run! The verdict of history upon him is not hard to forecast. He will be ranked among the vacuums. In distant ages his career will be cited as proof of the astounding fact that it is possible to rise to the highest places in this world, and yet remain as obscure as a bookkeeper in a village coal-yard. The present age has produced other examples: King George of England, that King of Italy whose name I forget, and perhaps six of the nine judges of the Supreme Court of the United States.

Dr. Coolidge, if he had any enterprise and courage in him, would be the most enviable man in the world today. For he faces nearly a year and a half of almost imperial power—and no responsiblity whatever, save to his own conscience. If, as I believe, he is honest in his withdrawal from the race for his own shoes, then he is free to do anything he pleases, and nothing can happen to him. He could, if he would, force almost any conceivable legislation upon Congress. He could bring irresistible pressure to bear upon the Supreme Court. He could clear out the frauds and imbeciles who infest the high offices of government, and put in decent men. He could restore the Bill of Rights.

All these things he could do in his seventeen months, and without going outside his constitutional prerogatives. But there is not the slightest chance that he will do any of them, or that doing them will so much as occur to him. He has been plodding along in the goose-step too long for him to attempt any leaping and cavorting now. He will pass from the Presidency as he came into it—a dull and docile drudge, loving the more tedious forms of ease, without imagination, and not too honest.

When I speak of honesty, of course, I mean the higher forms of that virtue—the honesty of the mind and heart, not of the fingers. I suppose that, in the ordinary sense, Dr. Coolidge is one of the most honest men ever heard of in public life in America. True enough, he did his best to hush up the Daugherty scandal, and connoisseurs will recall that a great deal of lying had to be done to hush up his hushing up. But no one ever alleged that he was personally corrupt. The Ohio Gang never took him into its calculations. If he went to its rescue, it was not to protect thieves, but simply to prevent *scandalum magnatum*—a more dangerous thing, in an inflammable democracy, than a little quite stealing. His motives, one may say, even transcended the partisan; they were, in a certain sense, almost patriotic.

But of intellectual honesty the man apparently knows nothing. He has no taste for cold facts, and no talent for grappling with them. There is no principle in his armamentarium that is worth any sacrifice, even of sleep. Human existence, as he sees it, is something to be got through with the least possible labor and fretting. His ideal day is one on which nothing whatever happens—a day sliding into a lazy afternoon upon the *Mayflower*, full of innocent snores. There is no record that he has ever thought anything worth hearing about any of the public problems that have confronted him. His characteristic way of dealing with them is simply to evade them, as a sensible man evades an insurance solicitor or his wife's relatives. In his speeches, though he knows how to write clear English, there is nothing that might not have occurred to a Rotarian, or even to a university president.

All his great feats of derring-do have been bogus. He kept out of the Boston police strike until other men had disposed of it: then he echoed their triumphant whoops in a feeble falsetto. He vetoed the Farm Relief bill because he couldn't help it— because signing it would have made trouble for him. He opened fire upon poor Daugherty only after the man was dead and the smell of his carcass unbearable. He intrigued for a third term until it became obvious that he couldn't get it without a fight, and then he fled ignominiously, leaving his friends upon a burning deck.

There is something deeply mysterious about such a man. It seems incredible that one with such towering opportunities in this world should use them so ill. The rest of us sweat and struggle for our puny chances, and then wreck ourselves trying to turn them into achievements. But here is one who seems content to pass by even great ones: he appears, indeed, to be scarcely conscious of them when they confront him. During his years in the highest office among us the country has seen a huge slaughter of its ancient liberties, a concerted and successful effort to convert every citizen into a mere subject. He has done nothing to stop that, and he has said nothing against it. Instead, he has devoted himself to puerile bookkeeping. The man who had a million in 1923 now has, perhaps, a million and a quarter.

But who, in the long run, will give a damn? Of what use are such achievements to the progress of the human race? Who knows what the tax-rate was in 1847, or who benefited by it, or who was in favor of it or against it? History, it seems to me, deals with larger issues. Its theme, when it is not written by mere pedants, besotted by names and dates, is the upward struggle of man, out of darkness and into light. Its salient men are those who have had a hand in that struggle, on one side or the other. What will such history say of Coolidge? It will say even less, I believe, than it says of John Tyler, who at least had the courage to take himself off the scene in a blaze of treason.

Laws multiply in the land. They grow more and more idiotic and oppressive. Swarms of scoundrels are let loose to harass honest men. The liberties that the Fathers gave us are turned into mockeries. Of all this Dr. Coolidge seems to be almost un- aware, as he is apparently unaware of any art or science save party politics. He has to be sure, adverted to the subject in an occasional speech, but only in weasel words. What has he done about it? He has done absolutely nothing.

What he could do if he wanted to, even in the short time re- maining to him, is almost past calculation. He could stop the grotesque crimes and oppressions of the Prohibition blacklegs with a stroke of the pen. He could bring a reasonable sanity and order into the whole Prohibition question, and open the way for its candid reconsideration. He could clear out the Department of Justice, and return it to common decency. He could prepare and advocate an intelligent plan for the national defense, and put an end to the disingenuous and dangerous debate which now goes on. He could restore our dealings with foreign nations to frankness and honesty. He could improve the Federal bench by appointing better men. He could shame Congress into some regard for the honor of the nation.

All these things a man of diligent enterprise and laudable ambition could do—and if not all of them, then at least most of them. It might take some fighting, but he would win that fight- ing, for all men of any decency would be with him. He could turn the flow of national events back to the sound principles upon which the Republic was founded, and get rid of the follies and dishonesties that have displaced those principles. He could con- found rogues and hearten honest men. He could leave behind him, win or lose, the memory of an honorable and useful life. He could make it something, once more, to be an American.

But he will do nothing of the sort. The year and a half ahead of him, like the years behind him, will be years of ignoble emptiness. He will keep on playing the politics of the village grocery. The best men of his time will continue to lie beyond his ken, and he will continue to recreate himself with the conversation of cheap-jacks and ignoramuses. There will be the familiar reports of his brave intentions, and the familiar disappointments. He will eat so many more meals, make so many more trips on the *Mayflower* with rogues and bounders, hear so many more reports from herders of votes, and make so many more hollow speeches. The stove will be spit on regularly. The clock will be wound up every night. And so, at last, he will pass from the scene, no doubt well rewarded by those who admire him with intelligent self-interest—an empty and tragic little man, thrown by fate into opportunities beyond his poor talents, and even beyond his imagination.

CAL AS LITERATUS

December 24, 1928

Those bustling connoisseurs of folkart who are forever breaking into raptures over Charlie Chaplin, Edgar A. Guest, Ed Wynn, Will Rogers and Groucho Marx have let a masterpiece slip by them undetected. I allude to Dr. Coolidge's letter to the Hon. Joseph Pulitzer II, editor of the St. Louis *Post-Dispatch*, written at Superior, Wis., on August 10, and published in the *Post-Dispatch's* fiftieth anniversary issue, on December 9. It was, in form, simply a note felicitating that great journal on its birthday. But in substance it was a treatise on the sorrows of the Presidency, and in manner it was incomparably naïve, earnest, eloquent and charming. For the first time since August 2, 1923, the real Calvin Coolidge got into print. For the first time in five years he set forth his honest sentiments in his own homely words.

A grammatical schoolma'm, to be sure, might easily find grave flaws in his letter. There are so many, indeed, that I detect a few myself. In the very first sentence there is the clumsy rustic phrase, "planning *on* celebrating," and in the first paragraph there are a dozen banal rubber-stamps of speech, including "thriving town," "respectable age," "great metropolis," "leading figure," "force of character" and "worthily carrying on." In another place "restrictive" is misused in place of "restricted," and further on the tautological "thoughtful minded" does duty for "thoughtful." In half a dozen places "towards" is used where "toward" would have been better.

But all that is beside the point. Shakespeare mauled the language far worse, yet even schoolma'ms now endure him, and even respect him. The main thing is that Dr. Coolidge wrote simply, innocently, artlessly—that he forgot all literary affectations, and set down his ideas exactly as they came into his head. The result was a bald but strangely appealing piece of writing —a composition of almost Lincolnian austerity and beauty. The true Vermonter was in every line of it. At one place there was even a dour Vermont jocosity: "I have often remarked that at least I had one distinction. I have been the healthiest President that the country has ever had."

You will find nothing a fourth so good in any of Dr. Coolidge's state papers. With their high-falutin solemnity, their turgid thinking and their heavy, Johnsonian clomp of phrase, they seem to belong to a wholly different man. The reason is not far to seek: they *do* belong to a wholly different man. He is the anonymous expert who is employed at the White House, at the cost of the groaning taxpayer, to concoct them. What his name is at the moment I don't know, but a few years back he was Judson C. Welliver, now the editor of the Washington *Herald*. Welliver went into office with Harding, and remained under Coolidge until November 1, 1925.

He is a journalist of the highest skill and knows how to write simply and charmingly, but he is also a fellow with a sense of humor, and during his service under Harding it pleased him to make his boss talk and think like an earnest but somewhat stewed Congressman. Harding himself never detected the joke; he was far too stupid—in fact, he was almost illiterate, as his inaugural address, which he wrote himself, demonstrated painfully. So he went on spouting Welliver's gaudy bombast until an assassin's bichloride tablets finished him, in the full belief that he was making a vast impression on the learned. That he was being laughed at behind the door never occurred to him, for his pastor, bootlegger, golf caddy and other confidantes were at pains to keep the fact from him.

Under Coolidge, Welliver revised the Presidential style, and for the better. It became measurably simpler and clearer. But it continued to be in essence, a device for flabbergasting newspaper editorial writers without actually saying anything—it continued to roar like a hurricane without letting loose any compromising ideas. Dr. Coolidge liked it, for it served him well. Out of it arose his reputation as a profound thinker, a man of subtle sagacities. It whirled by like a brass band, leaving the same vacuum behind it. When Welliver withdrew, his successor was instructed to get more of the same stuff out of the same barrel. He has been doing it ever since, to the satisfaction of his employer and all right-thinking Americans.

His last masterwork was a speech on the history of aërial navigation, delivered before a congress of aviators a week or two ago. It sounded so much like the multiplication table that Senator Fess of Ohio, a former schoolmaster, hastened to have it printed in full in the *Congressional Record*. The aviators heard it with their mouths open, wondering what it was about. They scattered to their homes convinced that Dr. Coolidge was a deep one—perhaps almost as deep as Arthur Brisbane, Otto Kahn or Andy Mellon.

But such virtuoso pieces by staff literati plainly do not represent the real Coolidge. Far more literate than his martyred predecessor, whose only studies of English syntax were made at the night school of the Elks in Marion, Ohio, he is still intrinsically a rural Vermonter, and hence devoid of academic artifices. The professors at Amherst, you may be sure, did not fool him. He heard their lectures on style with all due respect, but he knew very well that he could beat them at any really difficult and useful exercise, from lassoing an hysterical heifer to spitting at a mark, and so he clung to certain mental reservations. When they told him that "planning to celebrate" was right and "planning on celebrating" wrong, he wrote down "planning to" in his notebook, but continued to make it "planning on" elsewhere.

Such a man, when he lets himself go, almost always writes very well. His thoughts may not be profound, but their sincerity makes up for that lack, and they conquer by their freedom from the customary whoopla. It is hard for a simple man, so writing, to write really bad English. The language, indeed, seems to have been made for such men. It is extraordinarily rich in homely and pungent phrases, made to shock grammarians and delight the rest of us. All of its so-called rules may be broken without any damage to clarity or eloquence. The more they are broken, the more effective the style, as readers of Mark Twain and Carlyle well know. The chief aim of every conscious stylist, in English, should be to write like a simple man, unspoiled by pedagogues. The best English ever written is in the King James Bible. The worst is to be found in the thunderous blather of Dr. Johnson and among the sugar-teats of Walter Pater.

The real Coolidge, long concealed behind the false whiskers

of a professor, emerged in the letter to Dr. Pulitzer. There were no ideas in that letter of any originality or importance, and the English, as I have said, was loose and indecorous, but all the same it was capital stuff, and deserves to be remembered. Let us hope that when the time comes for him to write his autobiography the august author will do it with his own pen and in the same style, and not hire a professional rhetorician to pump the thing full of wind, and so make nonsense of it.

It is conceivable that, in speaking of Dr. Coolidge's singularly strutting and hollow state papers, I have been unjust to Dr. Welliver, and to the unknown Welliver II who now warms his old stool. It may be that both of them composed chaste and sound scripts, and that their eminent patron himself turned them into the fustian that has grieved us voluptuaries, thus seeking to knock the eye out of Brisbane, J. Ham. Lewis, Paul Elmer More and Andy Mellon. There are high precedents for it. Abraham Lincoln, in his early days, wrote like a schoolmaster inflated with helium. He was fifty before he achieved the simplicity that made him immortal.

Whatever the facts in the case of Dr. Coolidge, I can only reiterate the hope that, now that he has tried being his authentic self, he will stick to that line for the rest of his days. He has a natural talent for the incomparable English language, hitherto concealed by timidity, conscience or some vague sense of duty to Amherst and its professors. Let him write the chronicles of his reign in the stark, salty, unaffected, damn-the-grammarians phrases of his letter to Dr. Pulitzer, and he will go down into history, not only as the least colicky of Presidents, but also as the only artist, save one, among them all. But let him do it in the manner of his customary speeches and state papers, and he will descend forever into the nothingness of those who are admired by schoolma'ms.

THE COOLIDGE MYSTERY

January 30, 1933

The brethren who had the job of writing eulogies of the late Dr. Coolidge made very heavy weather of it, and no wonder, for such papers are difficult to do at best, and they become almost maddening when they must be done under pressure. The right hon. gentleman, who had always been more or less baffling to journalists, and hence a source of serious professional concern to them, threw them the hardest of all his hard bones in the end by dying so unexpectedly. I dare say that a poll of the editorial offices of the country would have given him at least thirty years more of life. He seemed, in fact, to be precisely the sort of man who would live to a vast and preposterous age, gradually mummifying in a sort of autogenous vacuum. But he fooled all the amateur actuaries by dying suddenly and melodramatically, and in what for a Vermont highlander was only the beginning of his prime.

I have accumulated a large number of obituaries of him, and examined them with some care. Their general burden seems to be that he was "a typical American." But was he? Alas, the evidence brought forward to support the thesis runs against it instead. For it appears that a typical American, in the view of the journalistic *Todsäufer*, as in that of the authors schoolbooks, is one who wins his way to high place by heroic endeavors and against desperate odds—and that was certainly not the history of Dr. Coolidge. On the contrary, his path in life was greased for him like that of a royal prince, and there is no evidence that he ever met a single serious obstacle from birth to death, or had to pause even once to get his breath and bind up his wounds.

He came into the world under one of the luckiest stars that ever shined down on mortal man. There was nothing distinguished about his family, but it was at least very respectable, and his father was a man of local importance, and rich for his place and time. If young Cal was ever on short commons no record of the fact survives. He was well fed, he was well schooled, and when the time came for him to launch into life he got a quick and easy start. Going direct from college into a prosperous law office—apparently by the influence of his father—he got into politics almost immediately, and by the time he was 27 he was already on the public pay roll. There he remained continuously for precisely thirty years, advancing step by step, always helped by fortune and never encountering anything properly describable as opposition, until he landed finally in the gaudiest job of them all, and retired from it at 57 with hundreds of thousands in gilt-edged securities.

The typical American, whether in politics or out, is a far different fellow. Whatever his eventual success, his life is normally one of struggle, and he goes through it flogged by a dæmon. If it has its perihelions of triumph and glory, it also has its nadirs of defeat and despair. But no defeat ever stopped Coolidge, and no dæmon gnawed at his liver. His life, for all its blinding lights, was as placid as that of a nun in a convent. The heavenly hierarchy seemed to be in a conspiracy to protect him, and help him along. Asking for nothing, he got everything. In all history there is no minute of a more implacable destiny, or of an easier one.

I recall well the day that he was nominated for the Vice-Presidency in Chicago—a blistering July Saturday in 1920. There had been, as everyone knows, a bitter battle for the Presidential nomination, and it went to the late Dr. Harding by a despairing sort of compromise, and only because he was too obscure to have any serious enemies. The battle over, half the delegates rushed out of the steaming hall and started for home. The nomination of a Vice-President was almost forgotten, and when some one recalled it the only candidates who turned up were fifth-raters. Hiram Johnson, defeated for the Presidential nomination, refused it scornfully, as beneath his dignity. So Henry Cabot Lodge, who was presiding, suggested Coolidge, who came from his own State and was one of his satellites, and Coolidge it was. The balloting took perhaps ten minutes. Then the remaining delegates also rushed out, for the hall was an inferno.

Immediately afterward I retired to the catacombs under the auditorium to soak my head and get a drink. In one of the passages I encountered a colleague from one of the Boston papers, surrounded by a group of politicians, policemen and reporters. He was making a kind of speech, and I paused idly to listen. To my astonishment I found that he was offering to bet all comers that Harding, if elected, would be assassinated before he had served half his term. Some one in the crowd remonstrated gently, saying that any talk of assassination was unwise and might be misunderstood, for the Armistice was less than two years old and the Mitchell Palmer Red hunt was still in full blast. But the Bostonian refused to shut down.

"I don't give a damn," he bawled, "what you say. I am simply telling you what I know. I know Cal Coolidge inside and out. He is the luckiest ———— ———— in the whole world!"

This Bostonian knew a lot, but not all. He was right about the early translation of Harding to bliss eternal, but wrong in assuming that it would have to be effected by human agency. He had not yet learned that Coolidge was under the direct patronage and protection of the Archangels Michael, Raphael and Gabriel, who are to ordinary angels as an archbishop is to an ordinary man, and to archbishops as an archbishop is to a streptococcus. It is quite impossible to account for his career on any other theory. There were massive evidences of celestial intervention at every step of it, and he went through life clothed in immunities that defied and made a mock of all the accepted laws of nature. No man ever came to market with less seductive goods, and no man ever got a better price for what he had to offer.

The achievements of the deceased, in fact, almost always turn out on inspection to have been no achievements at all. Did he actually break up the celebrated Boston police strike? He did not. It was broken up by other men, most of whom were not even in his confidence; all he did was to stand on the side lines until the tumult was over. Did he tackle and settle any of the grave problems that confronted the country during his years in the White House? He tackled few of them and settled none of them. Not a word came out of him on the subject of Prohibition. Not once did he challenge the speculative lunacy that finally brought the nation to bankruptcy. And all he could be induced to do about the foreign debts was to hand the nuisance on to poor Hoover.

His record as President, in fact, is almost a blank. No one remembers anything that he did or anything that he said. His chief feat during five years and seven months in office was to sleep more than any other President—to sleep more and to say less. Wrapped in a magnificent silence, his feet upon his desk, he drowsed away the lazy days. He was no fiddler like Nero; he simply yawned and stretched. And while he yawned and stretched the United States went slam-bang down the hill—and he lived just long enough to see it fetch up with a horrible bump at the bottom.

It was this snoozing, I suspect, that was at the bottom of such moderate popularity as he enjoyed. The American people, though they probably do not know it, really agree with Jefferson: they believe that the least government is the best. Coolidge, whatever his faults otherwise, was at all events the complete antithesis of the bombastic pedagogue, Wilson. The itch to run things did not afflict him; he was content to let them run themselves. Nor did he yearn to teach, for he was plainly convinced that there was nothing worth teaching. So the normalcy that everyone longed for began to come back in his time, and if he deserved no credit for bringing it in, he at least deserved credit for not upsetting it.

That this normalcy was itself full of dangers did not occur to anyone. The people generally believed that simple peace was all that was needed to cure the bruises and blisters of war time, and simple peace was what Dr. Coolidge gave them. He never made inflammatory speeches. He engaged in no public combats with other statesmen. He had no ideas for the overhauling of the government. He read neither the *Nation* nor the *New Republic*, and even in the New York *Times* he apparently read only the weather report. Wall Street got no lecturing from him. No bughouse professors, sweating fourth-dimensional economics, were received at the White House. The President's chosen associates were prosperous storekeepers, professional politicians, and the proprietors of fifth-rate newspapers. When his mind slid downhill toward the fine arts, he sent for a couple of movie actors.

Is anything to be said for this *Weltanschauung?* Perhaps a lot. The worst fodder for a President is not poppy and mandragora, but strychnine and adrenalin. We suffer most when the White House busts with ideas. With a World Saver preceding him (I count out Harding as a mere hallucination) and a Wonder Boy following him, he begins to seem, in retrospect, an extremely comfortable and even praiseworthy citizen. His failings are forgotten; the country remembers only the grateful fact that he let it alone. Well, there are worse epitaphs for a statesman. If the day ever comes when Jefferson's warnings are heeded at last, and we reduce government to its simplest terms, it may very well happen that Cal's bones now resting inconspicuously in the Vermont granite will come to be revered as those of a man who really did the nation some service.

3

Onward,
Christian Soldiers:
Hoover & Al

N O CAMPAIGN AND PROBABLY NO SET OF CANDIDATES GAVE
Mencken greater opportunity to roll out gay copy from his
typewriter than the 1928 presidential canvass. And in many
ways the pieces he turned out in the years immediately before
and during this episodic clash of personalities and religious and
temperance prejudices may well have represented Mencken at
his finest hour. For the times were ripe for him. The nation
was still living well and had not yet fallen upon the hard days
that followed the bleak Tuesday in late October when the average prices of fifty leading stocks, as compiled by the *New York
Times*, dropped nearly forty points between 10 A.M. and the
3 P.M. stock exchange closing hour. And even though the campaign of 1928 surfaced some short tempers and ugly rumors,
the country at large, in a prosperous and expansive mood, could
dismiss for the moment partisan differences on election day.
They joined in applause as young Charles Lindbergh cast his
first vote for Hoover, while another national hero—the immortal Babe Ruth—voted for "Al."

As the two front runners for the major parties were inching
ahead toward certain nomination quite a spell before the 1928

conventions, Mencken warmed to his reportorial tasks with obvious relish. On personality, he found Hoover and Al "as far apart as Pilsner and Coca Cola," and his sympathies for the "Happy Warrior"—as Franklin Roosevelt would immortalize Smith in placing his name before the Democratic convention of 1928—are lustily proclaimed.

Unlike the campaign of 1920, the canvass of 1928 placed two figures before the voters who had long been familiar public faces. The fact that the Democratic platform came out for repeal this time, while the Republican party still declared in favor of prohibition (despite Senator Wadsworth's admonition to the gentlemen of the Resolutions Committee to vote as they drank)—this gave Mencken something to make his copy crackle, but his discussion here, of course, covers familiar ground.

His treatment of the religious issue that pounded beneath the surface of the 1928 campaign, however, opens a new bigotry bin for us and serves as an awful reminder of the fantastic untruths that circulate in the passing political parade. As usual, Mencken's handling of these absurdities is devastating.

Mention of the name Marshall in the first piece of this section calls for a brief word of comment. Charles C. Marshall was a New York attorney closely associated with the Anglican Church and an authority on canon law. It was Marshall who, in an open letter to Governor Smith published in the *Atlantic Monthly*, called upon Smith to say what he would do as president if a conflict arose between the Constitution and laws of the United States and the doctrines of the Roman Catholic Church. In reply Smith said that he had been "a devoted Catholic since childhood. . . . and I recognize no power in the institution of my Church to interfere with the operations of the Constitution of the United States or the enforcement of the law of the land."

Elsewhere, Mencken's aside about Hoover—"a Republican only as an afterthought"—refers to the fact that in 1920 Hoover's name had been entered in the Michigan presidential preference primary as a Democrat. And even as the 1928 Republican preconvention campaign got under way many old-timers shook their heads questioningly as they raised doubts about Hoover's true Republicanism.

The reference to Coolidge's friends still hoping for a draft should be weighed in the light of the laconic eight-word statement released by the President at Rapid City, South Dakota, on August 2, 1927, the fifth anniversary of the day he had been sworn in as the nation's chief executive at Plymouth Notch, Vermont: "I do not choose to run for President in 1928." What Mencken emphasizes about the draft-Coolidge movement, of course, is that the friends of the President persisted in believing right down to the balloting for presidential nominees, in June of 1928, that Cal would sweep the convention in a ninth-inning rally and be triumphantly recommissioned by his party for another go at the presidency. The chance never came!

Mencken's observations about the outcome of the election and the unity of the Democratic party in 1928 suggest that prediction was not his strong suit. He was wrong in seeing Al's chances of election as "very good," and even more so in saying that Smith would have the solid South behind him. (He failed to carry Virginia, Florida, North Carolina, Tennessee, and Texas, though he did win more popular votes throughout the nation than had any previous Democratic presidential candidate.) However, Mencken himself later calls attention to the fact that Hoover, "if he had not been counted out," might have carried even more states in the South (Hoover lost Alabama by just 7,000 votes in a race where several times that number of ballots were declared invalid because of improper marking).

The close of this particular section of Mencken's pieces—"The Men Who Rule Us"—takes us to May 19, 1930. Mr. Hoover had been in office a year and a half. It is only in disbelief, of course, that we can read Mencken's statement that Hoover's chief problem of the moment concerns his relation "to the ac-

complished and unconscionable politicians—clerical and lay,
who run the Anti-Saloon League." Hardly a funny statement
for these unfunny times as the depression deepens and unem-
ployment climbs!   M. M.

AL SMITH AND HIS CHANCES

July 5, 1927

The chief danger confronting the Al Smith boom lies in the fact that it started too soon. A whole year must elapse before the Democratic National Convention actually nominates its candidate, and most of the possibilities of that year run against good Al. He may say something grossly offensive to the Ku Kluxers who now cast sheeps' eyes toward him, and so send them fleeing to their klaverns. Or he may say nothing, and so lend support to the growing suspicion that, after all, he has nothing to say. Or worst of all, the great ecclesiastical organization of which he is an humble satellite may say or do something so inept and preposterous that his chances, and those of every other Catholic, will go down to zero for another generation.

This last possibility is not to be dismissed as remote. The Catholic hierarchy in America, at the present moment, is surely not overburdened with men of wisdom and discretion. It can show no leader comparable to Archbishop Ireland, and none even remotely comparable to Cardinal Gibbons. It has good administrators in plenty, but few statesmen, and the few do not seem to be in high places. Can you imagine Cardinal Gibbons calling in the police to rough a meeting of birth-control fanatics, as was done by certain eminent ecclesiastical dignitaries in New York a couple of years ago—to the scandal of the church and the mirth of the town? Can you imagine him succumbing to the blandishments of the Comstock Society and supporting a new Comstock Act frankly designed to make it impossible for a man accused under it to offer any defense? Can you imagine him letting one of his parish priests set off such an orgy of wowser-

ism as now disgraces Boston? If so, you can imagine more than
I can.

It seems to me that such blunders show bad ecclesiastical
management. Will it improve? Perhaps. But not soon enough,
I suspect, to relieve Al of his hazard. Whether for good or for
ill he is thought of by the country as the Catholic candidate,
and his fortunes are thus bound up with the acts and attitudes
of the church. As one who would be delighted to see him in the
White House, if only as a merited rebuke to the Methodist-
Baptist tyranny which now oppresses the Republic, I confess
frankly that my hopes are cooled every time I contemplate William Cardinal O'Connell and Patrick Cardinal Hayes.

As for Al himself, he seems to be marking time. The other
candidates, great and small, discuss the problems that lie before
the country with more or less courage and sagacity: from him
comes precisely nothing. No one knows what he thinks about
the foreign policy, romantically so called, of the Hon. Mr. Kellogg. No one knows what he thinks about the clamor of the
Middle Western yokels to be fed out of the public crib. No one
knows what he thinks about the Philippines, or about the various
plans to reduce the income tax, or about the control of the Mississippi, or about Muscle Shoals or Teapot Dome. No one
knows, even, what he thinks about prohibition.

In brief, no one knows his views upon any of the major questions that will confront him if, when and as he reaches the White
House. Why is he silent? Only two answers are possible. One is
that he is holding his tongue because he is afraid to set up controversies and lose delegates—in other words, because he esteems
delegates more than he esteems principles, and is willing to get
them by false pretenses. The other is that he really has nothing
to say. Both answers show a considerable plausibility, and especially the second. The plain fact is that Al, as a good New
Yorker, is as provincial as a Kansas farmer. He is not only not
interested in the great problems that heave and lather the coun-

try: he has never heard of them. His world begins at Coney Island and ends at Buffalo.

This attitude of mind, in a man of his upbringing and worldly experience, is surely not unnatural. For years New York City has been gradually sliding away from the rest of the country, and today it is almost as much foreign soil as Paris or Warsaw. In ideas as in manners it is the complete antithesis of the Middle West, the West and the South. What Kansas or Tennessee or Utah venerates, New York laughs at. What New York esteems is diabolical to Kansas, Tennessee and Utah. This split, it seems to me, has been productive of much good. It has made New York a refuge for civilized Americans, and so saved them to the country. But it has made the typical New Yorker the narrowest of provincials—and Al, in more than one way, is the most typical New Yorker ever heard of.

His silence about Prohibition is not so easily explained: its roots are to be sought, I believe, in policy rather than in indifference. Unless all report goes for naught his private views are those of any other New Yorker of his class: he is against the dry millennium without qualification, and would be glad to see the Volstead Act repealed and the Eighteenth Amendment expunged from the Constitution. But he has never said so in plain words. On the contrary, his extremely rare references to this grand subject of subjects have been excessively discreet, and no one can prove today, by his deliberate and recorded words, whether he is for the Eighteenth Amendment or against it. It is even hard to determine clearly whether he is for or against the Volstead Act.

This uncertainty is being turned to use by the eminent New York politicians who now promote his candidacy. They employ it against their brethren of the South, in the hope of hauling the latter into camp. If Al came out flatly against the Anti-Saloon League his apple-cart would be upset in the South, and in the Middle West the outraged yokels would make a bonfire of it. But so long as he keeps quiet on the subject, it remains possible for his backers to do business with the local politicians of those wilds, whose one yearning is for jobs, and who are thus quite willing to trade with any candidate likely to lead them to the trough.

It is surely no secret that such negotiations are under way. There is ground for believing, indeed, that overtures have been made to many dry leaders, including the Hon. Dan Moody of Texas. Dan is as dry as the Rev. John Roach Straton, but he pants for higher office, and even the Vice-Presidency would soothe him. So there is talk both in Fourteenth street and in Holy Austin of putting him on the ticket with Al, and of posturing both of them upon a platform declaring that, whatever the difference of opinion about this or that law, the Democratic party must be, is, and ever shall be for Law enforcement.

Considered from the austere standpoint of moral science, this would be a dishonorable and disgraceful arrangement, for its plain purpose would be to get Al into the White House by hornswoggling both the wets and the drys. But I need not argue, I hope, that honor has no place in politics: the one aim is to get the job. A candidate of much loftier pretensions than Al—the Hon. John William Davis, LL. D.—was quite willing to go into action upon a precisely similar platform three years ago, and Al himself, as everyone knows, was willing too, and made every effort to get the chance.

But Prohibition seems likely, during the coming year, to develop into a far more lively and exigent issue than it was in 1924, and so a straddle upon it may turn out to be impossible. Some new Marshall may rise from the wilderness, to press Al for an answer upon it, as the original Marshall pressed him for an answer in the matter of his relations to the Catholic Church. If that happens, he will face a far more difficult situation than he faced then. For if he declares for anything short of a rigid enforcement of the Volstead Act, the fires of the Ku Klux, the

Anti-Saloon League and the Methodist Board of Temperance, Prohibition and Public Morals will flame from every hill south of the Potomac and west of the Ohio, and if he permits himself that declaration he will hand the whole of the wet and wicked Northeast, and maybe a substantial part of the Northern Middle West, over to Ritchie or Reed or some other such agent of the devil.

Thus the next year promises to give the worthy Alfred something to think about. His boom, at the moment, seems to be prospering mightily. Job-hungry Democrats from all over the Bible Belt are in treaty with his managers. The eminent *Nation* reports that even the villagers in the remotest deserts of Texas are beginning to think of him kindly. But the worst is to come. It is in the nature of enthusiasm to cool. It is the essence of politics that the hero of today, is pursued by wolves tomorrow.

THE STRUGGLE AHEAD

December 5, 1927

That Dr. Coolidge and his attendant pediculæ still cherish the hope that he will be drafted next year must be manifest to anyone who gives eye to their maneuvers. Observe how carefully, despite all his show of withdrawing, they avoid indicating a favorite among the other candidates. It would be natural, if they believed in his protestations, for them to turn to some one else, and any man they favored would leap to the front of the pack instantly, for the whole rabble of Federal jobholders would be for him. But they keep out of it with great care, and so all the candidates lag painfully, and none of them seems likely to muster enough votes to win. Thus, when the fatal day comes, Cal will have to be dragged from behind the egg-stove to take the nomination. Such, at all events, is the palpable theory of the bucolic Machiavellis who advise him and whose conversation he delights in.

The other aspirants, it seems to me, are all pretty weak, both as candidates and as men. The ablest of them, plainly enough, is the Feather Duster, Mr. Hughes, but he is the sort of able man who lacks conscience: he has wasted his brains upon trashy enterprises. Moreover, he once disgraced the Supreme Court of the United States by intriguing for office while he was a member of it. True enough, this intriguing was not unlawful, nor was it forbidden by the hogpen *mores* that prevail in American politics: nevertheless, the historian will find it hard to square the business with any plausible concept of the dignity and integrity of the judiciary.

Dr. Hoover, despite the touching confidence of my learned colleague, Dr. Kent, is even worse. He may be gifted intellectually, but he certainly manages to conceal it when he says anything, either *viva voce* or in writing. His grand achievements all diminish rather than increase on analysis. What he did in Belgium and in the Mississippi flood area might have been done quite as well by any other reasonably competent engineer. Finally, is he an American or an Englishman? The answer was by no means certain in 1914, and a vigorous opponent in the campaign might very well revive its uncertainty.

Of the rest, Dr. Lowden presents the most engaging personality, but he is a city lawyer running as a tribune of the farmers —something not unlike an Elk running as a dry. It is hard to believe in his program for their relief. Whether it is sound or not, it will make only enemies for him in the cities—and whoever wins next year will have to do it with city votes. It must be plain that Dr. Lowden is making no progress. To the vast majority of voters he remains only a name, and what little they hear about that name is disquieting.

As for Dr. Dawes, he is considerably more formidable, and

the whisper goes 'round that Wall Street is in favor of him, and secretly grooming him to grab the nomination. But I believe that Dawes would be an extremely vulnerable candidate, and that any Democrat of noticeable campaigning talents could bring him down, Wall Street or no Wall Street. He made such an ass of himself on the stump when he was running with Dr. Coolidge that he had to be hauled off and silenced. There are court decisions that handle him harshly, and they could be used against him with devastating effect.

The rest of the Republican candidates are mainly jokes. Senator Curtis, the Senate leader, is simply a dull party hack, with no claim to consideration save his regularity. Senator Norris is an honest Liberal, and could no more get the nomination than Oswald Garrison Villard. James J. Davis, the preposterous Secretary of Labor, is a professional joiner and back-slapper. Senator Borah, after having long been a professional Liberal, is now a professional Prohibitionist. The others slope down hill to nothingness. There must be a dozen more, but all of them put together could scarcely carry even Vermont against Al Smith.

Al, indeed, has been leaping ahead so fast of late that it now seems impossible to stop him. Counting in certain delegations whose attachments to favorite sons will be of the loosest, he will have a majority in the convention, and if he is discreetly handled —as he was certainly not at the New York convention—it should be possible to convert that majority into two-thirds without any serious difficulty. The Ku Kluxers, to be sure, will still be on hand, and some of them will be very violent, but they will be fewer than they were the last time, and they will lack the leader that they had in Dr. McAdoo, now taken to the woods.

Al's greatest handicap the last time—that is, after the appalling imprudence of his Catholic friends, and especially of his clerical friends—lay in his apparently incurable forthrightness. An adherent of the Latin rite, he let the fact be known upon all possible occasions, and flaunted it in the faces of the trembling Methodists and Baptists. A convinced and practicing wet, he damned Prohibition in loud tones, and publicly consorted with scofflaws. But since that time he has learned prudence and is to-day a fair match for Dr. Coolidge in that department. His speech of last week before the lady politicians of New York is a typical example of his present willingness to talk pianissimo. His words were sweet, but they meant exactly nothing.

His last previous formal broadside was well-aimed and im-mensely effective. It was, in essence, a defiance of the Pope—or, at all events, it was so interpreted in the South. Al appeared to serve notice upon Rome that, in all matters of civil government, he was prepared to wrap the flag about him and defy the whole College of Cardinals. This curious document, as everyone knows, was mainly written by a priest; nevertheless, it took the wind out of the sub-Potomac Ku Kluxers, and scores of the leading statesmen of that region began jumping aboard the Smith band-wagon. Since then Al has let well enough alone. With McAdoo down and out, and no other white, Protestant, Nordic hero of any force or effect in sight, he seems likely to fetch whole bat-talions of Southern delegates on the floor of the convention, and to sweep the South itself at the election ensuing.

This propitious development of his campaign, I confess, pains me somewhat, for I am in the pay of both Senator Reed and Governor Ritchie, and naturally want to see either or both of them win. But if Al is nominated, and Dawes, Hoover or a drafted Cal stands opposed to him, there will be some compensa-tion, at least, in the gaudiest contest seen in years. For Al is a rabblerouser of high gifts, with a special talent for abuse, and any man that the Republicans are likely to nominate will be easy meat for him. His arguments, I suspect, will often be thin, but he will give a good show—and a good show is about the best we can ask from politicians in these pussy-footing later years.

The only actual issue is Prohibition, and Prohibition, it is very probable, will be carefully concealed by both parties before the campaign begins. My guess is that both will declare for Law Enforcement in their platforms, and in words almost identical. The Republicans will mean 10 per cent Law Enforcement and the Democrats will mean 8 per cent: that will be the only difference between them. But if Al is the Democratic candidate he will get practically all of the wet votes, for the wets will know that the Democratic 8 per cent will represent a compromise between the 16 per cent of the Southern drys and his own 0 per cent.

There are no other issues. Al is in favor of economy, and so are Cal and the rest of the Republican candidates. Governor Ritchie's issue of State's rights, it seems to me, is likely to make a great deal of progress in the years to come, but the time for it is not yet. The people of the United States are gluttons for punishment. They will stand a great many more doses of Federal usurpation before they revolt at last. Today they complain only of Prohibition: they will have a lot more to complain of before the tale is told.

At the moment the campaign for State's rights is thus mainly legalistic. It has yet to produce any throbbing of hearts. But I believe that Governor Ritchie will be well advised if he sticks to it. He has it by the collar—and he will still be of the political child-bearing age in 1932 and 1936. There is no telling when some super-gorgeous obscenity in the Federal courts may set the plain people to yowling.

AL
—

April 23, 1928

Has the art and mystery of politics no apparent utility? Does it appear to be unqualifiedly ratty, raffish, sordid, obscene and low down, and its salient virtuosi a gang of unmitigated scoundrels? Then let us not forget its high capacity to soothe and tickle the midriff, its incomparable services as a maker of entertainment.

I point to the spectacle now unfolding before the judicious in Moronia Felix, the late Confederate States. Six months ago all the principal statesmen down there were warning the Northern Democrats, in hushed, dissecting-room tones, that any effort to make Al Smith the party nominee this year would bust the Solid South wide open, and revive all the miseries of the Civil War. But now, suddenly confronted by the practical certainty of his nomination, whole regiments of them are leaping upon the bandwagon with shrill, eager hosannahs, and before the ides of June those who yet linger will be leaping too!

Perhaps I ought to except a few hardboiled and consecrated men, pledged against the Pope until Hell freezes over—for example, the Hon. J. Thomas Heflin, of Alabama. Their pastors still encourage them to stand firm; there is a great deal of earnest praying in their behalf. But I have grown so cynical with senility that I begin to doubt even these. Good Tom, it must be apparent, faces a very trying situation. If he carries his struggle against the Vatican to the floor of the Houston convention, and is there put to rout, he will be in difficulties indeed. For he must then either swallow Al and so desert the Bible, or lead a bolt and so commit mayhem upon the Democratic party. In either case, he'll be sure to get a dreadful beating for it later on.

The other Confederate publicists are more prudent. They believe it to be highly probable that Al will be nominated, and they know very well that if he is the Solid South will support him, Rome or no Rome. So they make the aforesaid leaps for the bandwagon. Closeted in their praying-rooms, they have been told by the angels that intolerance is a wicked thing, and, what is more, unprofitable to men aspiring to offices of public trust. As I hint, these first converts were only the shock troops. The main army will begin to march anon.

It seems to me that all gabble about splitting the Solid South is nonsense. Wherever its solidity is actual, it will remain solid, and perhaps for another generation to come. It is simply impossible, in most Southern States, for a self-respecting man to be a Republican. His neighbors of that party are either black rascals who live by preying upon their own people, or white rascals who live by flattering and vicitimizing the black ones. The jobholders foisted upon him when the Republicans are in power at Washington are almost unanimously rogues. He regards them, high and low, as the rest of us regard Prohibition agents.

This man naturally desires to see a Democratic President in the White House, if only because the phenomenon relieves him of the oppression of such vermin, and puts what he regards as measurably decenter men in their places. If in addition, he is one who aspires to public office himself, his yearnings in that direction take on the quality of holy zeal. So long as a Republican is in the White House he must content himself with State offices. All the Federal jobs are monopolized by go-getters who, in his view, are but little above the menacing hordes of blacks.

Most politicians, as everyone knows, are of low intellectual visibility, but not many of them are so stupid that they can't tell a hawk from a handsaw. In the South they are all acutely aware that the votes of the region are necessary to the Democratic party—that it can't win without them. And when it loses, they get no Federal jobs, and the reign of Republican blacklegs continues. Thus they always support the national ticket and roar for the national platform, no matter how violently both outrage their private pruderies. They supported Bryan and they supported Alton B. Parker. They whooped it up for Cox and they whooped it up for Davis. If the Devil were nominated, they would swallow him. And when the time comes they will swallow Al.

I am inclined to suspect that his chances of being elected are very good. He will not only have the Solid South behind him— a bit scared and reluctant, perhaps, but still essentially solid— he will also have all the big cities of the North, which means that he will carry easily five or six of the most populous States. Nor will he lack support in the Southwest or even in the Northwest. Best of all, he will probably have Hoover in front of him, and that means that he will have one of the most transparent and vulnerable frauds in American history. The man is a Republican only by a prudent afterthought, just as he is an American only by a prudent afterthought. He looks hollow, and he is hollow. The Democrats should be able to blow him up in six weeks of campaigning.

I have heard it argued that Al, if he wins at the polls, will be elected by false pretenses—that he really can't do anything for the wets who will be his chief supporters. But that is not altogether true. Those who point out that, as President, he will confront dry majorities in both houses of Congress, and that in consequence he will be unable to get rid of the Eighteenth Amendment or even to materially modify the Volstead Act— these pessimists forget that despite all such burdens, a President still has plenty of power. There is, for example, his power to appoint Federal judges. It is sufficient alone to get him almost anything he wants in the way of law.

At present, as everyone knows, the Anti-Saloon League claims a sort of right of veto over Federal judges, and over Federal district attorneys and other law officers with them. In most cases, I suppose, it doesn't actually name Dr. Coolidge's appointees—though certainly it has done so in a few cases—but it seems pretty clear that he seldom if ever appoints a judge to whom it actively objects. With Al in the White House, the Anti-Saloon League will lose that right of veto, along with its other vast and extra-legal powers, and so will the notorious Methodist Board of Temperance, Prohibition and Public Morals. Al's view of these indecent organizations is that of any other rational man. He regards them as vile, and he will certainly not adorn the bench with their nominees and partisans.

Instead he will appoint judges whose general ideas are in accord with his own—men free from wowserian influences, and with a proper respect for the Bill of Rights. There are plenty of such men on the bench of his own state: that bench, indeed, is noted for its enlightened Liberalism, as the bench of the Maryland Free State is, and it can show some jurists of very high learning—for example, Cardozo, J. The next President will have to replace a majority of the justices of the Supreme Court and perhaps a majority of the inferior Federal judges. They are, in the main, elderly men, and suffer in health, like the rest of us, from the current scarcity of potable light wines and beers.

If Al names lawyers of genuine learning and independence, instead of the fourth-raters whom, in the main, Dr. Coolidge has appointed, the Senate will confirm them despite the Anti-Saloon League. It has seldom, in history, rejected a nominee of notably sound qualifications; even the desperate fight made against Mr. Justice Brandeis failed in the end. Five Liberal justices on the bench of the Supreme Court would be sufficient to pull the teeth of Prohibition. For it is the bench, not Congress, that has made the Volstead Act the dreadful *reductio ad absurdum* of sound law and decent government that it is today. In their complaisant eagerness to give its outrageous oppressions force and effect, the judges have fallen perforce into an almost complete sacrifice of the Bill of Rights. But a few decisions would be enough to restore that battered charter. And restored, it would reduce the Methodist frenzy to flog and harass the rest of us to impotence.

Perhaps the soundest of all reasons for voting for Al in November lies in the probability that he will thus rehabilitate the bench, which has been badly damaged by Prohibition, both in legal dignity and in public respect. But that is not why the Southern Ku Kluxers will vote for him. They will vote for him because they (or their leaders) are hungry for jobs—because they will conclude, after due prayer, that is better to risk being sold down the river to the Pope and the Jesuits than to go on gaping at the swill-trough from afar, and mourning sadly like a calf taken away from its mamma.

THE IMPENDING COMBAT

May 28, 1928

All the political seers and sorcerers seem to be agreed that the coming Presidential campaign will be full of bitterness, and that most of it will be caused by religion. I count Prohibition as a part of religion, for it has surely become so in the United States. The Prohibitionists, seeing all their other arguments destroyed by the logic of events, have fallen back upon the mystical doctrine that God is somehow on their side, and that opposing them thus takes on the character of blasphemy. At Charleston, W. Va., not long ago, some of them were gravely discussing whether or not Jesus should be reprimanded *post mortem* for the miracle at Cana. And others have frequently maintained that violators of the Volsteadian rumble-bumble

should be publicly executed, as heretics were executed in mediæval Europe.

These earnest men, led by their appointed pastors, will make
a violent fight against the nomination of the Hon. Al Smith,
LL.D., at Houston, and if they fail to head him off, as seems
likely, they will continue that fight before the country. Henry
M. Hyde, who was lately in attendance upon the great Baptist
convention at Chattanooga, Tenn., the Jerusalem of the Fundamentalist Holy Land, tells me that all the Baptist evangelists
are preparing to take the stump against Al and the Harlot of
the Seven Hills, and that they are already in a lather of spiritual zeal. More, they will be joined by hundreds of pastors who
now serve cures: these cures will be abandoned for the duration
of the campaign.

There is even a great deal of wild talk in the South about
bolting the ticket, and the experts in political pathology at-
tached to the Washington bureau of the *Sunpaper* seem inclined
to take it more or less seriously. Myself, I view it lightly, for I
believe that the Democrats of the South are far dumber than
anyone has ever suspected, even in Boston or Harlem. They
would vote for the Pope himself if he were nominated at
Houston. But though they will fall into line in November, they
will undoubtedly do a great deal of hard sweating before its
first Tuesday dawns, and the evangelists who plan to operate
upon them will find it easy to fever and alarm them, and inci-
dentally to gather in their mazuma.

If Al is undone, either at Houston or at the polls, it will not
be because he is a Tammany man, nor even because he is wet,
but simply and solely because he is a Catholic. The issue grows
clearer every day. His defeat will be a smashing affront to all
Catholics, who will be notified thereby that the majority of their
fellow-citizens do not regard them as sound Americans. And
if he is nominated and elected it will be a no less smashing
affront to those millions of Protestants who believe in all sin-

cerity that Catholicism is inimical to free government, and that the election of a Catholic President will sound the death-knell of the Republic.

In either event, the result is bound to leave much bitterness. The campaign itself, as I have said, will be extraordinarily bitter. There will be absolutely no way to compromise the leading issue. The Catholics and their allies will stand pat, and the anti-Catholics and their allies will stand pat. Each side will have at the other with all the ferocity of so many Liberty Loan orators, vice crusaders or D.A.R. beldames. For religion is the greatest inspirer of hatred the world has ever seen, and it shows no sign of losing that character in its old age. Every effort to make the warring sects lie down together has failed. They quarrel incessantly, and they will keep on quarreling to the end of the chapter.

Why this should be so I don't know, but so it seems to be. The enmities set up by nationalism are as nothing compared to those set up by religion. A few hours after the formal conclusion of a bloody war the soldiers of the opposing armies are friends, and only those who stayed at home keep up the bawling. But when religion gets into a difference it is fought out to the death, and there is never any treaty of peace. Consider again, Prohibition. It used to be discussed good-humoredly, and the two sides kept up a certain show of politeness to each other. Even such violent partisans as Carrie Nation were viewed tolerantly. But the moment the Baptist and Methodist pastors began taking jobs with the Anti-Saloon League the contest became a bloody riot, and now it has come to such a pass that murder is a daily incident of it. Naturally, it is wets (and innocents) who are being murdered, for the pastors are on the side of the drys.

I recite these lamentable facts, not to deplore them, but to say that I do *not* deplore them. Life in America interests me, not as a moral phenomenon, but simply as a gaudy spectacle. I enjoy it most when it is most uproarious, preposterous, in-

ordinate and melodramatic. I am perfectly willing to give a
Roosevelt, a Wilson, a Fall, an Elder Hays, an Andy Mellon or
a Tom Heflin such small part of my revenues as he can gouge
out of me in return for the show that he offers. Such gorgeous
mountebanks take my mind off my gallstones, my war wounds,
my public duties and my unfortunate love affairs, and so make
existence agreeable. I'd rather read the *Congressional Record*—
or, failing that, any good tabloid—than go to see a bishop
hanged.

This show is good at all times, but it is best when some great
combat is in progress, and I can think of no combat more likely
to be violent and hence thrilling than one in which religious
zealots are engaged. However trivial its actual issues, it is
bound to show all the savagery of a dog fight. In the present
case that savagery will be there, but the issues will not be trivial.
The question to be decided, indeed, will be of capital importance
—that is, to the extent that any political question can be important. By their votes the massed morons of America will be
called upon to determine whether the unwritten law of a century
and a half, that no Catholic shall sit in the White House, shall
be abandoned forever, or whether it shall be reaffirmed and
given a new force and authority.

This is the first time that the question has come squarely before the so-called people, and no one can say how they will
answer. But the very fact that there is a doubt will give the
struggle an added fury. Thus I look for entertainment of the
first calibre, exactly to my taste in all its details, and as a sworn
neutral in theology I shall view it with the advantage of not
caring a hoot which side wins. If Al wins there will be a four
years' circus. And if he loses there will be a circus too.

Personally, I hope to vote for him. It will be the duty of every
lifelong Democrat. More, it will be a pleasure. For he is, I believe, an honest and worthy man, and it will be interesting to
observe how he deals with the great problems sure to confront

the next President—for example, the question of Prohibition. No matter what he does or says there will be roars of rage. If he tries to restore the Bill of Rights by appointing Federal judges unacceptable to the Anti-Saloon League, the Baptist parsons will yell that the Pope is upon us. And if he lets fall the slightest hint that the Eighteenth Amendment is also in the Constitution, the wets will bawl that he has betrayed them, that he is an ingrate, a traitor and a *Schuft*.

I do not envy Al, but neither do I envy any of the other gentlemen who make of Our America the greatest show since Rome caved in. There is such a thing as sitting in the audience without getting stage-struck, as going to bull fights without wanting to be either the matador or the bull. After all, it is the spectator who has the fun, not the clown. The clown has to daub himself with unpleasant paint, get into an absurd costume, and then expose his stern to the blows of the slapstick. Not infrequently, I daresay, they hurt. When the show is over he has to wash up, hunt for his collar-buttons, and paint his bruises with arnica. The spectator, by that time, is snoring in bed, or sitting comfortably in some quiet beer house, deploring the decay of art.

But the art of political buffoonery is surely not decaying, at least in the Federal Union. On the contrary, it seems to be improving year by year. When I was a boy, in the last century, Presidential campaigns were still corrupted by serious purpose. The candidates were such grave and learned men as Cleveland and Harrison, and the issues were of such character that they engaged political economists and statisticians. But now all that is happily past. The combat ensuing will keep to the level of a debate on Darwinism between a hedge pastor and the village atheist, with music by the United Brethren choir. It will break up in a fist fight, with ears torn off and teeth knocked out. It will be a good show.

REAL ISSUES AT LAST

July 23, 1928

The Democrats, as the party of opposition, have been making and forcing the issues in all the campaigns since the Civil War. They did it with the tariff, they did it with free silver, they did it with imperialism, and they did it with trust-busting. Now they do it again with Prohibition, and on some near tomorrow, I herewith predict formally, they will do it with the ever growing issue between the cities and the farms. Already, indeed, they have edged this last issue into national politics, for the Prohibition issue, in the last analysis, is no more than a part of it. The essential struggle in America, during the next fifty years, will be between city men and yokels. The yokels have ruled the Republic since its first days—often, it must be added, very wisely. But now they decay and are challenged, and in the long run they are bound to be overcome.

It is amusing to observe how issues rise and fall. In the first campaign that I remember, between Cleveland and Harrison, the tariff was everything, and the Democrats roared against protection as the Prohibitionists now roar against booze. But today there are no more free traders, save perhaps in laboratory jars, and the Democratic convention at Houston declared for protection without a single protest. Free silver is not only dead, but completely forgotten; even William Jennings Bryan, who got his inspiration direct from God, abandoned it before he was called above. As for trust-busting, both of the great parties are now against it. As for imperialism, both are in favor of it.

Senator Reed tried to make corruption an issue at Houston, and Dr. Bowers, the key-noter, gave him gaudy aid. But the delegates simply refused to get excited about it, and so did the country. The plain fact is that the American people are not against corruption. They do not loathe the successful thief, but admire him. It is precisely the most corrupt political machines that are the most secure. In Baltimore, where the Democrats steal very little, they are frequently unhorsed by the Republicans. But in Philadelphia, where the Republicans do their stealing with steam-shovels, it would take an earthquake to upset them. The plain people always prefer grafters to honest men, hoping to get their share.

Thus the issue of Prohibition emerges as the only one that the voters of the Republic are really interested in, and under it lies the issue of city or country hegemony. The yokels, it seems to me, are in for a drubbing, if not in November, then in some November not far ahead. The trouble with them is that they have lost all their old-time leaders to the towns, and are now led by a rabble of frauds and fanatics. The typical American statesman of the better sort, in the early days of the Republic, was a country gentleman. But now he is a city man—born on a farm, perhaps, but raised on hard paving-stones, and with urban prejudices in his blood.

The yokels hang on because old apportionments give them unfair advantages. The vote of a malarious peasant on the lower Eastern Shore counts as much as the votes of twelve Baltimoreans. But that can't last. It is not only unjust and undemocratic; it is absurd. For the lowest city proletarian, even though he may be farm-bred, is at least superior to the yokel. He has had enterprise enough to escape from the cow and the plow, and he has enjoyed contact with relatively enlightened men. He knows a great deal more than the rustic, and his tastes are more civilized. In the long run he is bound to revolt against being governed from the dung-hill.

His refusal to accept Prohibition is the first sign of that revolt. Prohibition is essentially a yokel idea. It mirrors alike the farmer's fear of himself and his envy of city men. Unable to drink at all without making a hog of himself, he naturally hates those who can. When a city man goes on a grand drunk, the police take charge of him humanely and he is restrained from doing any great damage. The worst that happens to him is that his wife beats him and he loses his job. But when a farmer succumbs to the jug his unmilked cows burst, his hogs and chickens starve, his pastor denounces him as an atheist (or even an Episcopalian), and he is ruined. Thus he favors Prohibition, especially if he is given to heavy drinking—first because he hopes it will protect him against himself, and secondly because it harasses his superior and enemy, the city man.

There are, of course, Prohibitionists in the cities also, but they are not numerous, and most of them will be found, on inspection, to be defectively assimilated yokels. The more intelligent countrymen, escaping to the cities, become urbanized very rapidly, and some of them take on a high polish. But there are others so dumb that it is impossible to civilize them, and they continue to be yokels. Baltimore houses a great many such poor nitwits. They support the Hell-fire ecclesiastics who survive among us, and are run amuck by Klan whisperings in every campaign. The time will come when the emancipated cities will send such morons back to the country.

I have never encountered a genuine city man, not obviously balmy, who was in favor of Prohibition. There seems to be something in the urban mentality that rebels against such imbecilities. Perhaps the fact is to be ascribed to familiarity with the police. The yokel, seeing policemen very seldom, retains a considerable fear of them, and a high respect for the laws behind them. But the city man takes the cops lightly, and the laws with them. He has no respect for laws as such; he respects them only when they are useful and plausible. Such grotesque concoctions as the Volstead Act he knows to be neither.

The yokel's answer to this sniffishness is that the city man is a scoundrel, and ought to be kept under restraint. His opposition to Prohibition, so the hedge pastors argue, is due to a consuming love of rum. But that argument quickly runs aground on the fact that the city man, despite the Eighteenth Amendment, still has all the rum he can consume. For he is not only contumacious; he is also ingenious, and knows how to beat laws that he dislikes. So the yokels and their spiritual advisers have to fall back on the doctrine that Prohibition is ordained of God, and is hence binding upon every good citizen, regardless of his private convictions. But the city man simply laughs at that. He observes that the chief agents of revelation are Methodist bishops, and he has heard too much balderdash from them to have any confidence in them.

If the Confederates stay in their Democratic cage, as seems likely, the coming campaign will be fought out between the big cities of the North and West and the farms. The chances seem to be very good that Al will carry every city in the nation, barring Philadelphia and a few other such Republican strongholds. The question is whether the yokels will be able to roll up majorities sufficient to beat him. The situation in Maryland will be paralleled in twenty other States. On the one hand the city wets will be for Al, and on the other hand the country drys and Ku Kluxers will be for Lord Hoover.

No other issue will play any part in the campaign. Even the religious issue will be no more than a phase of the larger issue of the country against the cities. The city man has few religious prejudices; he has, indeed, very little religion. When he is found to be disturbed about the Pope, it almost always turns out that he is a defectively assimilated yokel, with the hay still in his hair. I know of no genuine city man who worries about the ambitions of the Jesuits. What moves him is the fact that he is tired of being governed by his inferiors, and has begun to harbor an active desire to throw them off.

No matter what the result of the coming election, the issue is thus joined. It may be that, in the first battle, the yokels will win. They have many obvious advantages. A good many men of money are inclined to go with them this time, and there are more morons in America, as everyone knows, than intelligent men and women. But in the long run; it seems to me, they are bound to lose, for the city men are far sharper than they are, and will be able to break down their advantages one by one. I believe that the battle will go down in history as one of the first importance. Once the cities have liberated themselves from yokel rule, civilization will be free to develop in the United States. Today it is woefully hobbled by the ideas of peasants. We have many huge and grandiose villages, but, with the possible exception of New York and San Francisco, we have no cities. When an American, acquiring money, feels a yearning for civilized living, he has to go abroad. That is surely not a sound state of affairs. No one wants to civilize the peasant against his will, but it is plainly against reason to let him go on riding his betters.

CIVIL WAR IN THE CONFEDERACY

July 30, 1928

From the Potomac to the Pecos the South is in a lather. The campaign down there will be the most violent since Reconstruction days. On the one side are the Ku Klux klergy, desperately determined to put down Al and the Pope, even at the cost of taking the colored brother to their bosoms. On the other are the awakening *intelligentsia*, eager to meet the pastors in open battle and hopeful of beating them and ruining them. I omit the professional politicians: in the South, as elsewhere, they seek only jobs and are willing to take either side to get them. And I omit the great masses of saved and baptized morons, for the choice they will make will simply be between the Catholic bugaboo and the nigger bugaboo.

The real fight is between the Methodist and Baptist preachers, who struggle to hold the hegemony they have enjoyed so long, and the young Southerners, men and women, who tire of their incessant imbecilities, and are determined to get rid of them. It is not without reason that, in North Carolina, the sweating pastors direct their chief barbs at Chapel Hill, for at Chapel Hill is the State university, and it has done more to civilize the State than any other agency, or than all other agencies taken together. Quite naturally the clergy hate it. The Baptists never hold a convention or the Methodists a conference without hearing and applauding extravagant denunciations of it. But the more it is denounced, the more it seems to prosper.

So in all the other Confederate States. Even in such appalling back-waters as Mississippi the educated youngsters begin to be ashamed of the traditional Southern *Kultur*. They tire of the tyranny of the hedge parsons, and they tire of the swinishness of Prohibition. Everywhere they are organizing and taking to the warpath. Throwing off that romantic sensitiveness which formerly made them flare up at every word of criticism, however apposite and sound, they now admit frankly that the South needs an overhauling, and are determined to clean it up.

Even more than the rest of the country, the South is sorely misrepresented by its statesmen. Thinking of Alabama, one thinks of the Hon. J. Thomas Heflin. But the fact is that Heflin's days are numbered down there, and that his awareness of it is mainly responsible for his frantic clowning. All the decent newspapers of the State are against him, led by the excellent Montgomery *Advertiser*, and he has no following whatever among Alabamans pretending to be civilized. To accuse a student at the State university of taking him seriously would be as indecorous as accusing a student at the Johns Hopkins of accepting the theology of Dr. Howard A. Kelly. His strength lies among the Ku Kluxers of the villages and mean streets. But the Klan is passing, and he will pass with it.

The chief spokesman for North Carolina at Houston was the Hon. Josephus Daniels. It was as if one of the Goldsboroughs—Phil, T. Alan or the late Aristides Sophocles—had spoken for the Maryland Free State. The new North Carolina is almost everything that Josephus is not. It is, in many respects, the most advanced of all the Southern States, and he is one of the hollowest and dumbest of Southern politicians. Even his make-up is grotesque: he still clings to the black string-tie and long-tailed coat of the professional Southerner of the last generation. It is highly improbable that he could be elected to any office of dignity in North Carolina today. But he was in Wilson's Cabinet, and so he was sent to Houston, and there he disgraced the State with his maudlin bellowing about Prohibition.

So elsewhere. Carter Glass spoke for Virginia, with the witch-burner, Bishop James Cannon, Jr., at his side. Tennessee was made ridiculous by a boozing dry. The chief representative of Texas in the convention news was Gov. Dan Moody. Moody is still young, but he belongs to a decaying order. The superstitions of his remote Baptist village hang about him. The Texans of his generation—that is, those of any education—are against him by odds of at least ten to one. They are tired of government by crossroads theologians. They are tired of the Anti-Saloon League and its intolerable corruptions. They hope to convert Moody, who is almost unique among Southern drys in that he is actually a teetotaler. If they fail, they will retire him to private life.

The thing that is changing the South is prosperity. So long as the overwhelming majority of its people were poor, as they were until a decade or so ago, they had to stay in their wallows, and no glimmer of enlightenment ever reached them. Their schools, in the main, were fifth-rate, and they had few intelligent newspapers. Thus they succumbed easily to the clergy of the hell-fire sects, who penetrated to the most remote villages and met with no challenge. What the poor whites heard from the

outside world they heard from the lips of these pious ignoramuses.

Where the pastors plowed the politicians reaped. The gentry
were driven out of public life, and all the offices began to go to
go-getting trash. There ensued a carnival of corruption. Not
Tammany in its worse days was ever so debauched as some of
the State machines. The Anti-Saloon League and the Klan
came along to help this process, and the war fury, artfully
stirred up from Washington, gave them massive aid. It became
dangerous in the South to be intelligent. The whole region
seemed to be plunged in imbecility, and without hope of getting
out. Every Baptist pastor became a neighborhood Pope. The
Anti-Saloon League was supreme in politics. The Klan elected
Governors and Senators. Thousands of young Southerners, in
despair, moved North.

But with the end of the war came a swift reaction, and on its
heels prosperity. Boys and girls began to flock to college. With
money in their treasuries, the States overhauled their school
systems. Newspapers began to make money, and with money
came boldness. Soon leaders made their appearance—Harris in
Georgia, Hall in Alabama, Wright in South Carolina. The
Klan, drunk with power, committed suicide. The Anti-Saloon
League, going from excess to excess, aroused its opponents to
action. In a few years there was a complete change. The Young
South began to be heard from, demanding an end of abomina-
tions, social, religious and political. The war for liberation,
plainly enough, would be a long one, with the issue in doubt, but
at all events there was going to be a war.

Today, it seems to me, there is every reason for the Young
South to be confident. It has already, as in North Carolina,
won substantial victories, and everywhere it is gaining strength.
More and more young Southerners are going to college, traveling, reading good books, coming into contact with ideas. The
colleges they go to are still, in many cases, bad, but the young-

ster who goes to even the worst college is less likely than he was before to view gravely such statesmen as Tom Heflin and such theologians as the Rev. Dr. Two-Gun Norris. It is no longer sufficient, below the Potomac, for a Methodist bishop to speak in awful tones. He is beginning to be judged critically, and the more he is judged the less his voice is mistaken for the voice of God.

It will take, of course, a long battle to throw off the political parsons altogether. In the backwaters, no doubt, it will be forever impossible, as it has been in the North. The yokels in Michigan and upper New York are quite as idiotic as the yokels in Arkansas. But in the South, as elsewhere, there is an active movement to break the grip of these peasants and their shamans upon the government. In Texas, for example, the revolt against Prohibition and the Anti-Saloon League is clearly a revolt of the cities against the country. Houston, Galveston, El Paso, Dallas, San Antonio and Fort Worth sweat under the rustic tyranny as Baltimore sweats in Maryland. And the same thing is manifest in Georgia, Louisiana, South Carolina and Alabama.

As I say, the war will be a long one, but I believe that there will be plenty of recruits for it, and that in the end peasant-rule will be broken. It is plainly incompatible with civilized progress. Drained of all their best blood by the cities, the country districts subside into a futile malignancy. They are run by numskull windjammers, of the pulpit and the stump. They serve as recruiting depôts for such villainous organizations as the Klan and the Anti-Saloon League. They are against every variety of enlightenment, and every common decency. The old naïve belief in their virtue and wisdom must be abandoned, and they must be stripped of their power to harass and impede civilization, as they have been stripped of it in all the countries of Europe. In this necessary and sanitary business, I believe, the emerging South will take a leading part.

AL AND THE PASTORS

August 6, 1928

With the nomination of Al in the hot, hell-bent city of Houston, I resumed an old vice: the reading of denominational papers. Whether Catholic or Protestant, they are always full of amusing stuff, but especially when they are Protestant and evangelical. As of July 10 I subscribed to all the Baptist and Methodist organs south of the Potomac, and have been refreshing my soul with them ever since. They pour in at the rate of three or four a day, nearly every one with its furious, first-page blast against poor Al. From them I learn a great deal that is confidential and surprising about the plot of the Pope to seize the United States, but even more about the troubles of his rivals of the Baptist and Methodist rites.

These brethren, I gather, are far from easy in mind. Convinced by their searchings of the Scriptures that the election of Al would cause the downfall of the Republic, they yet show a painful fear that the Solid South will nevertheless support him. What alarms them most is the attitude of the daily newspapers of the region, all of which have kissed the Tammany blarney stone. Thus they have to turn aside frequently from their slaughter of the Pope to rebuke these traitors, and the result is a division and dispersal of their fire.

Of all the sheets that come in for denunciation the most hotly denounced seem to be the Richmond *News-Leader*, the Jackson (Miss.) *News*, the Atlanta *Constitution* and the Raleigh *News and Observer*. All four are edited by consecrated, Christian men —the *News-Leader* by the gifted Dr. Douglas S. Freeman, the *News* by the Hon. Frederick Sullen, the *Constitution* by the Hon. Clark Howell, and the *News and Observer* by the eminent Josephus Daniels. Dr. Freeman is the leading Baptist layman of Richmond, Dr. Daniels is the leading Methodist of North

Carolina, and the Hon. Mr. Sullen was converted by Dr. Billy
Sunday and is to the front in all pious works. Nevertheless, all
have dedicated their papers to Al, and so they are bitterly reviled by their colleagues of the evangelical press. The Richmond
Christian Advocate even goes to the length of hinting darkly,
though without saying it out loud, that Dr. Freeman is "now
owned and controlled by Catholic and Jewish interests."

Worse, there is a certain amount of treason within the fold
of the pastors themselves. The case of Monsignor Warren A.
Candler, the Methodist ordinary of Atlanta, has already got
into the newspapers. He is a brother to Asa G. Candler, the
coca-cola magnate, and hence has access to a great deal of
money, and must be listened to when he speaks. Bishop Candler
refuses to come out against Al; more, he warns the clergy of his
diocese against taking the church into politics. Two of his colleagues on the bench of bishops join him. It is all very disturbing.

Nor is there any lack of dissent lower down the scale. I pick
up the *Christian Index* of Atlanta, "the organ and property
of the Baptists of Georgia," and find its whole first page given
over to a solemn remonstrance by the Rev. John D. Mell. He
addresses himself "to the Baptist preachers in Georgia," and
says:

> The members of your churches are divided. Reason, judgment
> and prudence are going to be dethroned as the campaign pro-
> gresses. If you take the high office to which you have been called
> down into the strife, and become a partisan in your community,
> you will lose the affection of nearly all of those you oppose, of
> many of those whose candidate you espouse, and you may, in
> some cases, even lose your pulpits. I have known, in my time,
> several strong preachers to lose their pulpits that way, and they
> were just as sincere as you are, and, perhaps, just as wise.

Editor Louie D. Newton, of the *Index*, gives his best space
to this warning, but he makes no reference to it in his editorials.

Instead, he gives over three pages to articles taking the opposite line—one a report of the dry conference at Asheville, N. C., on July 18 and 19, another a long treatise by the Rev. A. T. Robertson, professor of New Testament interpretation in the Southern Baptist Theological Seminary, arguing that John the Baptist, if he were alive today, would be against Al, and a third by the Rev. T. F. Calloway, pastor of the First Baptist Church of Thomasville, Ga., full of hot stuff against the Pope. Dr. Robertson is one of the great whales of the Southern Baptist connection. He has many learned degrees, is the author of a textbook of New Testament Greek, and belongs to the American Philological Association. I offer the following specimen of his logic:

> It is better to have a head like that of John the Baptist and lose it for the sake of righteousness than not to have such a head and keep it.

So far as I can make out, but one evangelical journal of the South has refused to join the hue-and-cry against Al. That is the *Southern Christian Advocate* of Columbia, S. C., the home of the celebrated Senator Cole L. Blease and (according to Dr. Blease himself) of some of the most accomplished booticians in the entire South. The editor of the *Southern Christian Advocate* went to the Asheville conference and told the brethren there that "in South Carolina circumstances were such that all problems since 1876 had been worked out within the Democratic party, and that however many there might be who would never vote for Smith, few could be expected to vote for Hoover, and that the State would remain in the Democratic column."

The editor himself says that he will not vote for Al, and he gives plenty of space in his paper to those who advocate voting for Lord Hoover, but he refuses to go so far himself. Apparently, one of the considerations that keeps him in line is the fact that his Democratic State executive committee has decided that persons who confess that they will vote for Hoover cannot take any part in the Democratic primaries. He protests against this scheme to hog-tie dry Democrats, and says that it is "contrary to all fairness and the Constitution of a country of freemen." In other Southern States the same rule has been put into effect, and it has brought forth the same remonstrances. But the politicians stand pat, and so the pastors can only rage and roar.

Most of them do it with hearty goodwill. I can find but one, indeed, who pleads for Christian charity. He is the Rev. Livingston Johnson, editor of the *Biblical Record* of Raleigh, N. C., a Baptist organ. He says:

> Nothing can be gained, but much may be lost, by intemperate language or unkind conduct toward others. We should do our duty fearlessly, uninfluenced by what others may say or think, if our consciences are leading us to pursue courses different from theirs; but we should pray for grace to prevent us from saying anything that would alienate our friends, or create wounds that this life may be too short to heal.

Dr. Johnson adds to this plea the strange doctrine that "we preachers should remember that our chief work in the world is to offer the Bread of Life to hungry souls."

During the two weeks following Al's nomination there was but little mention of his religion. He was denounced simply as a wet, or as a member of Tammany. But now practically all of the denominational papers have at him as a Catholic, and devote a large part of their space to assaults upon the Pope. The principal charge leveled against His Holiness is that he is in politics, and eager to get political control of the United States. This ambition is opposed on the ground that church and state ought to be kept separate, but it is common for an embattled editor to argue in the very next column that it is not only permissible for the Baptist and Methodist churches to go into politics, but even a moral duty.

Many of the reverend editors have been led by their researches to raise the old question, for long hotly debated by Southern theologians, whether a Catholic is a Christian at all. The Rev. A. M. Pierce, of the *Wesleyan Christian Advocate* of Atlanta, apparently thinks not: he is "strongly persuaded," he says, that Catholicism is only "a degenerate type of Christianity" and ought to be displaced by "a purer type." To that end, he says, "various Protestant churches are working on different mission fields." But other editors are not so sure. In the Richmond *Christian Advocate*, for example, space is given to a Norfolk contributor who appeals to Catholics as fellow-Christians, and says "I have not yet, and I pray God I never will, knock any church that stands for Jesus Christ." Not many, however, go that far.

Meanwhile, it is curious to note that certain Romish practices have begun to get lodgment in the Bible Belt. For example, the *Biblical Record,* of Raleigh, gives over a column and a half on its first page to an account of a *retreat* at Ridgecrest, N. C., in June! More than sixty Baptists took part in it.

THE HOOVER MANIFESTO

August 13, 1928

Dr. Hoover's speech of acceptance shows how much he profited by his years of training in the British service: it suggests in almost every line the speeches that English politicians make on great and solemn occasions. That is to say, it is couched in correct and stately English, it sounds all the current shibboleths with a hearty smacking of the lips, it breathes a spirit of highly self-conscious righteousness, and it is almost, if not quite, devoid of clear and cogent ideas. Such speeches resound from end to end of the Motherland whenever a Prime Minister in difficulties goes to the country. They shake the rafters of St. Stephen's whenever a Bolshevik member pushes home an embarrassing question. They are better, it must be granted, than our crude colonial stuff. The illiterate imbecilities of a Harding are not in them, nor the completely meaningless phrases of a Coolidge. Nevertheless, they are mainly wind.

It seems to me that the canto on Prohibition offers a fair measure of the Hooverian mind and genius. The learned candidate does not dodge the question. Though he shoves it into the second half of his speech, he appears to realize that it will be the main issue in the campaign, and he is willing to discuss it. But what has he to say about it? What is his proposal for putting an end to the obscene saturnalia which now disgraces the country, with Prohibition agents and bootlegger-gunmen running a race in crime? His proposal, as I gather it, is simply that Law Enforcement be piled upon Law Enforcement! His remedy for Prohibition agents is more Prohibition agents!

His "organized searching investigation of fact and causes" sounds promising, but he immediately erects a high fence around it. He is unalterably opposed to repealing the Eighteenth Amendment, and argues that modifying the Volstead Act would be nullification, and hence immoral. What remains? Nothing, it would seem, save to go on hiring criminals to make more criminals, to go on loading the Federal courts with judges and district attorneys satisfactory to the Anti-Saloon League, to go on sacrificing peace, order and the Bill of Rights to the pious frenzy of the Methodist Board of Temperance, Prohibition and Public Morals. Such is the best thought of the Republican Pericles upon the question that has brought more turmoil and bitterness into American life than any other since the Civil War.

The rest of the eminent aspirant's address keeps to the same depressed and depressing level. It is correct, it is respectable, it states the orthodox Republican doctrine in sonorous words, but there is not the slightest sign in it of fresh and vigorous thought, nor of even the most elementary courage. The whole thing reads like an article in a third-rate magazine, written by a laborious newspaper reporter and signed by some official nonentity. It states the obvious in banal terms, and then proceeds to elaborate it without imagination. There are touches of Dr. Frank Crane in it, and more of the preposterous Brisbane. God made Dr. Hoover virtuous, but He also made him dull.

The evasions in the speech are far more interesting than the forthright asseverations. Consider, for example, the brief paragraph upon religious intolerance, now launched upon us by Prohibition. As a Quaker, the hon. gentleman is opposed to it. In fact, he is hot against it. But at once it appears that he is not hot enough to denounce the only kind of intolerance actually on tap. What he opposes is denying "the right of every man to worship God according to the dictates of his own conscience"— which no one, so far as I know, has ever proposed to do. On the matter of blacklisting a public man on account of his faith he is completely silent. In other words, he is completely silent about the real issue, the while he loses flabby platitudes about a purely academic one.

So again when he deals with the corruption that has gone on in Washington under his very nose and without a word of challenge from him. First he tries disingenuously to make it appear that "both political parties" had their hands in this mess, and then he proceeds to the idiotic *non sequitur* that "there must be no place for cynicism in the creed of America." In other words, the odorous doings of Fall, Daugherty and company must yet leave us optimists! All is well, even when a President of the United States tries to shield a Daugherty. All is well, even when the courts fail to bring a Sinclair to book. And all is well, too,

I suppose, when a moral candidate for the Presidency gets the nomination with the aid, cheerfully sought and granted, of the Vare gang, the remains of the Ohio gang, the Anti-Saloon League, and the rabble of boughten Negro delegates from the South.

But perhaps it is unfair to Lord Hoover to examine his harangue too critically. It was addressed, not to rational men, but to the far-flung and innumerable simians of the radio. We have come to such a pass in the United States that it is no longer safe for a candidate for high office to be too candid or to show too much intelligence. Al and his friends, like Senator Bruce here at home, seem to believe differently, but before the campaign has gone very far they will probably discover their error. In any combat before the mob the victory goes to the hollower of the two combatants. Let one of them really say something, and at once he is suspect. Let him say something that has not been said before, and he is as good as ruined.

Thus the salient object of a candidate for the Presidency, in these days of complete ochlocracy, is not to discuss the issues before him frankly and realistically, but to get rid of them by swathing them in disarming and meaningless words. He is surrounded by professional politicians, which is to say, by men whose lives are made up of fears. The world that they confront is a world of bold and bellicose minorities, each very touchy. Their aim is to offend no one unnecessarily. They see victory, not as a conquest of ideas, but as a series of adroit escapes from them. The ideal politician is Dr. Coolidge. His opinions are harmless because they are mainly unknown.

Dr. Hoover belongs to the same school. In his campaign he will profess every form of respectability ever heard of, but he will leave dangerous topics to more reckless men. If there is any fighting in the grand manner, Al will have to do it. He will make a gaudy show, but I don't believe he will gather in any votes by it. The American people prefer safer men. That is to say, they prefer vacuums. Coolidge, of course, is perfect and unapproachable, but the air pump has worked wonders with Hoover.

His progress, since 1920, in the art and mystery of practical politics has been really marvelous. He advanced upon the Chicago convention a plain and forthright man, with a great deal of inconvenient candor behind him. His débâcle there taught him a lesson, and he has been learning ever since. Barred from Cleveland by the Coolidge flames, he devoted himself to preparing for 1928. When his cohorts reached Kansas City they included almost every scoundrel in his party, from Vare at the top to the Confederate blackamoors at the bottom. He was nominated by the most ghastly combination of job-brokers and corruptionists ever gathered into one hall.

These men are now upon his back, but his respectability is sufficient for the burden. He is the highest type of Christian public man—virtuous and yet humanely tolerant of sin, correct in all his so-called ideas, innocent of speculative heresies, patriotic so long as it pays, full of reassuring words, pious, undramatic, safe. If he is elected, he will make a careful and cautious President. There will be no roars from the White House. The sounds issuing from it will be all coos. To answer every demand of fact there will be a soothing generalization. The stream already gushes. "New and gigantic forces have come into our national life. . . . Science has given us new tools. . . . Peace has been made. . . . Grave abuses have occurred. . . . All should have equality before the law. . . . There must be no place for cynicism in the creed of America."

He will begin to run for reëlection at 12 o'clock noon of March 4, 1929. Nothing will issue from him to imperil his fortunes in 1932. There will be plenty of pap for the customers of the *Saturday Evening Post*, but there will be plenty, too, for the practical and indomitable boys now bearing the burden in the heat of the day. Daugherty will vote for Hoover. So will Sinclair. So will the booters and the Prohibition agents.

ONWARD, CHRISTIAN SOLDIERS!

August 24, 1928

The holy war against Al in the late Confederate States seems to be breaking into two halves. On the one hand, some of the Methodist and Baptist papers begin to be extremely polite to him, and warn their customers that it is unChristian (and, what is worse, unwise) to have at opponents too hotly. On the other hand, there are journals which pile indignation upon indignation, and devote practically all of their space to philippics against Al, Raskob, Tammany, the Beer Trust and the Pope.

A good specimen of the former class is the *Southern Christian Advocate*, of Columbia, S. C.—like all the multitudinous *Christian Advocates*, a Methodist organ. In the current issue I can find but two references to Al, and both of them are quite inoffensive. Nor does Pastor E. O. Watson, the editor, print anything against the Pope. So with the *Biblical Record* (Baptist), of Raleigh, edited by Pastor Livingston Johnson. Dr. Johnson, indeed, is so moderate that he feels moved to explain his lack of ferocity. Some of his subscribers have protested against it. Says he:

> Because we have not used more vitriolic language some have thought that the editor was weakening in his position. The writer has simply endeavored to keep a cool head, as he has two or three times advised others to do.

Dr. Johnson prints several articles defending political activity by the evangelical clergy, but he publishes no assaults upon Al, nor does he denounce the Catholic Church. The *Baptist Banner*, of Parkersburg, W. Va., swings even further to the Right. It prints long articles on "State Missions," "The Book of Romans" and "Are We Going to Let Country Churches Die?", but not a word about the great Christian uprising against Rome. The *Baptist Messenger*, of Oklahoma City, goes the same way. There is no denunciation of the Pope, and Al is barely mentioned. The editor, Pastor E. C. Routh, believes that "when great moral issues arise that affect the eternal destinies of a multitude" every consecrated Christian, lay or clerical, should speak out, but he apparently believes that this speaking out should be very circumspect.

The *Baptist Record*, of Jackson, Miss., one of the holy towns of the Chigger Belt, publishes a number of arguments against Al, but they are devoid of vituperation. One of its contributors warns the Mississippi Baptists that Rome "believes in ruling the world with an iron heel," and another sends in some quotations from a Catholic "Manual of Discipline," published in Philadelphia in 1926, showing that the Pope has "a right to annul those laws or acts of government that would injure the salvation of souls or attack the natural rights of citizens," and that Rome holds that "the state should aid, protect and defend the church." But there is nothing about the villainies of the Jesuits or the plots of the Knights of Columbus.

The *Southwestern Christian Advocate*, of Cincinnati, which has a considerable circulation in the South, defends the political parsons, but does not mention the Pope. The *North Carolina Christian Advocate*, Greensboro, reprints an editorial from the Hon. Josephus Daniels' paper, the Raleigh *News and Observer*, denouncing those Tarheel Democrats who have threatened to cut off the revenues of pastors advocating Hoover, but it is silent about the crimes of Rome, and its principal articles bear such titles as "The Place of the Beautiful" and "A Good Man Gone." The *Alabama Baptist*, of Birmingham, prints a few digs at Al and Raskob, but there is no violence in them, and the Catholic Church is not mentioned.

The Richmond *Christian Advocate* prints Bishop E. D. Mouzon's denunciation of the Pope and his janizaries, but not much of its own. It apologizes for discussing politics at all, on the ground that the newspapers show "a biased attitude," and promises not to be "inflammatory or bitter." The *Baptist Standard*, of Dallas, Texas, after saying that it "has not chosen to jump into partisan politics," complains that it is "being misunderstood," and that two other Baptist papers have "concluded that it is indifferent to the present crisis in our nation's life." The editor says that this is not so, but he indulges in no invective against Al. The *American Baptist*, of Lexington, Ky., takes much the same line. The editor is against Al, but he has nothing to say about the Pope and he is "opposed to mentioning the names of parties and candidates in resolutions passed by religious bodies." The Primitive Baptist organs are too busy hunting down heresy to bother with politics. In the *Primitive Baptist*, of Thornton, Ark., the campaign is not so much as mentioned.

The *Baptist Courier*, of Greenville, S. C., belongs to the other wing. It announces Raskob as "a private chaplain (*sic*) of the papal household," and says that "without doubt he has been on his knees before the Pope." Further, it prints an article entitled "The Romish Peril," by the learned Dr. A. T. Robertson, of the Southern Baptist Theological Seminary, in which he sounds a warning that "the Pope undoubtedly longs for the wealth and power of the United States to be in his hands." He goes on:

> He will never give up that hope. He will leave no stone unturned to gain that end. . . . Rome means to get control of the United States sooner or later. Protestants may well understand that purpose.

Dr. Robertson does not mention Al, but his meaning is plain enough. Dr. C. M. Bishop, writing in the *Texas Christian Advocate*, of Dallas, Texas, goes further. He identifies Tammany and the Pope with the horrendous beasts mentioned in the Book of Revelation, and heads his article "Unclean Spirits Like Frogs." In the same journal Dr. Bob Shuler, the chief rival of Dr. Amiée Semple McPherson in Los Angeles, pursues the melancholy subject in his well-known trenchant style.

In the *Baptist Advance*, of Little Rock, Ark., there are many waspish items about Al, Raskob, Tammany, the Pope and the Hon. Joe Robinson. One of them says that the Catholics in Hungary have protested officially against the erection of statues there to Luther and Calvin, and cites the fact as a foretaste of what will happen in the United States if Al is elected. Dr. Robinson's speeches against intolerance are denounced as "the ravings of a demagogue and the vaporings of an ignoramus." But the editor then grows a bit cautious, and says that "we have no desire or intention to lambast anyone who cannot adopt our views with reference to the present campaign."

The *Baptist Message*, of Shreveport, La., and the *Baptist and Commoner*, of Benton, Ark., are full of hot stuff against the Pope. The latter gives three and a half pages to a diatribe under the heading of "Is the Catholic Church a Christian Church." The answer is no. The Pope, it appears, is an impostor, for "Christ said He would send the Holy Ghost into the world to direct His work." So are all priests, for Christ "called His ministers preachers and shepherds, never priests." The papal title of pontiff is pagan. The Catholic Church is "a brutal, hell-born power," and its clergy are scoundrels.

They are always to be found at the bedside of the dying to extort money for the pretense of making prayers, and on hand to extort from the widow every penny possible for the same pretense. To meet them in the street or in the church, they seem to be devout: but when you come to know them you find that they are hypocrites and filled with iniquity.

All of them, it appears, are actively in politics. "Practically all the public offices in our large cities are held by Catholics. . . . The higher the percentage of Catholics, the higher the crime rate." The *Baptist Message* pursues the subject. "Every Catholic legislator, officeholder and jobholder," it says, "is expected always to remember that he is to hold office or job in the light of the fact that he is a Catholic." As for Al:

> During the Catholic Ecumenical Council, held in Chicago some time ago, while the Pope's official representative, Cardinal Bonzano, was passing through New York city, it is said that the Mayor of New York, who is also a Roman Catholic, and Governor Smith met this foreign churchman at the ship landing, and conducted him, with brass bands and military escort, to the New York City Hall, and there, placing him upon a *throne* erected for him IN THE CITY HALL—he, Governor Alfred Emanuel Smith, Governor of the Sovereign State of New York, in the United States of America, DID PROSTRATE HIMSELF BEFORE and BOWED THE KNEE to this foreign representative of a foreign potentate, and DID KISS THE RING on the hand of this foreigner, in token of his ABJECT SUBMISSION TO THE AUTHORITY OF THE POPE OF ROME.

The *Baptist Trumpet*, of Killeen, Texas, warns its readers that if Al is elected "the Romish system will institute persecutions again, and put the cruel, blood-stained heel upon all who refuse her authority," and points for proof to Revelation 11, 21, wherein "Rome is called by the name of Jezebel, because Jezebel was a heathenish woman, married to an Israelitish king." The *Christian Index*, of Atlanta, prints a long attack upon the Knights of Columbus by Pastor T. F. Calloway, of Thomasville, Ga., wherein he quotes "Priest D. S. Phelan, editor of the *Western Watchman*, as saying on June 27, 1912, that "if the Government of the United States were at war with the church, we would say tomorrow, *'To hell with the Government of the United States!'* "

The *Baptist Progress,* of Dallas, Texas, speaks of Al politely, but is hot against the Knights of Columbus. It says that "they claim that America justly belongs to the Catholic Church because a wise Jew, Columbus, who joined Catholics, discovered America in 1492." It argues that "the devil is behind both Romanism and the liquor traffic." In the *Baptist and Commoner,* previously quoted, Pastor J. A. Scarboro says the same thing, and points to texts in Daniel and Revelation to support him. He goes on furiously:

> The devil's crowd—Catholics, political demagogues, brewers, bootleggers, prostitutes—the whole motley bellygang are for Smith!

In the same paper Elder W. C. Benson rehearses his reasons for voting for Lord Hoover. I quote a few of them:

> To vote for Al Smith would be granting the Pope the right to dictate to this Government what it should do.

> A vote for Al Smith would be the sacrificing of our public schools. Rome says to hell with our public schools.

> To vote for Al Smith would be to say that all Protestants are now living in adultery because they were not married by a priest.

> To vote for Al Smith is to say our offspring are bastards. Are you ready to accept this?

And so on, and so on. I quote only a few specimens. Acres of such stuff are being printed. In some of the papers the Pope gets so much attention that he almost crowds out Prohibition. But most of them still have space to bawl out the wets. The *Wesleyan Christian Advocate,* of Atlanta, for example, denounces Governor Ritchie as one "who is not only wet, but blasphemously so." This may seem exaggerated—until one remembers that Prohibition is now an integral part of the neo-Confederate theology. To be wet down there is to be an infidel, and doomed to hell. Nothing that a wet says is honest, and nothing that a dry does is evil. The *Richmond Christian Advocate*, replying to a charge that Prohibition agents have committed more murders in the South than in the North, says complacently:

> It is a credit to these Southern States that the records show that they are trying to enforce the law, *even at the cost of human life.*

In other words, murder is a lesser crime than bootlegging! I doubt that many Southern pastors would dissent from that.

THE CAMPAIGN OPENS

August 27, 1928

Bilge goes with politics. Even Al must drench us with his bucket of it. I point to his pious allegation, in his speech of acceptance, that "standards of unblemished integrity characterized every act of the administration of Woodrow Wilson." Are the operations in alien property so soon forgotten? Or the business of the airship contracts? Or the transactions at Hog Island? Or the colossal cantonment steals? I surely hope not. More money was stolen under Wilson than under all other Presidents put together. From Good Friday, 1917, to the end of his second administration Jesse Smiths swarmed in Washington like autumn leaves in Vallambrosa.

I incline to suspect, indeed, that the historians of the future will say that what went on under Harding was no more than a hangover from what had gone on under Woodrow. Fall, after all, was a cheap skate. His loot, altogether, ran to less than $250,000. The boys, in the House with the Green Shutters took even less. Their main business was petty graft—a thousand dollars here and two thousand there. Perhaps the most valuable thing they got was the pick of the booze seized by prohibition agents. But under Wilson, with the war raging, the thing was done on a wholesale scale. The airship thieves, according to the most reliable statisticians, got nearly a billion. And the alien property operators probably got almost as much.

Thus Al blew a silly tin whistle when he talked of Wilsonian "integrity." Woodrow himself, true enough, was not corrupt, but neither was Harding. The members of the Wilson Cabinet kept out of jail, but Cabinet Ministers are not the only bene-ficiaries of graft. Washington, at the end of 1917, was a thieves' Utopia. There were 25,000 bogus majors loose in the town, and half of them were making it pay, and well. Was all this without the connivance of the administration? Perhaps. But the admin-istration was quick to put down anyone who protested against it. The Espionage act protected the patriots. When, later on, Harding tried to bring them to book they leaped from the shelter of the Espionage act to that of the Statute of Limita-tions.

But no doubt I push Al unduly. He is, among other things, a politician, and now and then he must function as one. More bilge, I daresay, will come out of him before the campaign is over. But not as much, you may be sure, as will issue from the moral recesses of Lord Hoover. Already, with their speeches of acceptance behind them, the difference between the two candi-dates is plain and shining. Hoover, by nature, is a trimmer and a platitudinarian. He first finds out what his customers want him to say, and then he says it, cautiously and without convic-tion. Al, on the contrary, is bold and forthright. He speaks clearly, and says something. He is his own man.

The odds in the campaign are against him, and he must know

it. No doubt his political instincts warn him to go carefully, to try to disarm opposition, to placate the whole swarm of raucous minorities. But there is more in him than the mere politician. Somewhere on the sidewalks of New York, without benefit of the moral training on tap in Kansas and Mississippi, he picked up the doctrine that it is better, after all, to be honest than to lie. It is not a popular doctrine in America. It is dangerous baggage in politics. It gets a man suspected and hated. But it has a merit nevertheless: it makes a man comfortable inside. Al has experienced that comfort, and he apparently likes it.

He seems to me to be the most refreshing and stimulating phenomenon that America has witnessed since the death of Grover Cleveland. He is, for all his political aptitude, the complete antithesis of the normal American politician. The usual writhing and crawling is simply not in him. Cocky, vulgar, even maybe low, he is never cheap. It would be impossible to imagine him intriguing for the Presidency as Hoover has intrigued for it, with the Anti-Saloon League, the Ohio gang, the Vare gang, the auction-block blackamoors from the South, and all the other degraded pimps and harlots of politics across the table. Al came into the campaign with clean hands. And win or lose, he seems determined to go out of it with clean hands.

His brush with William Allen White was a small thing, but it well displayed the qualities of the man. White's attack was characteristically disingenuous: the notions of honor prevailing among Kansas Methodists were visible in every line of it. In unctuous phrases he protested that he had no doubt of Al's rectitude, that he vastly admired and respected the man, but in the same breath he tried to make him out a defender of the worst sort of saloons, an advocate of race-track gambling, and a covert friend of prostitution. Another Kansas worthy, the preposterous Henry J. Allen, took a hand in the assault. His disingenuousness was even worse than White's.

Al met the onslaught with complete frankness. There was no

dodging of the issue in his reply, nor any attempt to swath the facts in weasel, Hooverian words. He admitted without reservation his votes against many "moral" measures, he announced his conviction that he had voted properly, and he closed by disposing of the whole "moral" flubdubbery in a few devastating sentences. His objection to it is that of any other rational man. It is the cardinal objection to Prohibition: that foolish and dishonest attempts at repression only make vice worse. Every man not a fanatic knows this to be true; he knows, too, that most of the professional proponents of "moral" legislation are plain rogues preying on fools. But not one American politician in a thousand ever summons up the courage to say so.

Al's bold saying so, it seems to me, marks a milestone in American politics. At last we contemplate a candidate who is frank and honest, sensible and unafraid. If the Methodist and Baptist witch-burners are against him, then let them be against him. He is not going to woo them with hypocritical commendations of their balderdash. The slimy side-stepping of Hoover is simply impossible to him. He says what he thinks in plain English. Those who vote for him will know precisely who and what they are voting for. And those who dislike his ideas and his frankness are free to vote against him and be damned.

I can imagine no candidate more likely to appeal to first voters. There is something charmingly young about him, despite his long years in politics. His essential point of view is not that of an old political hack, but that of an ardent and somewhat romantic youth, full of belief in the virtues of truth and eager for heavy odds and high adventure. Compared to him, Lord Hoover is no more than a pious old woman, a fat Coolidge. The two men differ as a soldier differs from a bookkeeper. They are as far apart as Pilsner and coca-cola.

It remains to be seen how much the professional politicians of his party will corrupt and denaturize Al before the campaign closes. My belief is that they will find him a hard egg. His

closest advisers are not politicians at all, but amateurs such as
Dr. Raskob, Mrs. Moskowitz and Judge Proskauer—all of them
violently opposed to the usual political flubdub. So far, they have
supported him against the professionals with great skill and
resolution. They seem determined, as he is, to carry the thing
through frankly and honestly. They prefer defeat with faces to
the front to victory on the belly, in the Coolidge-Hoover manner.

Nevertheless, Al will know what pressure is before he finishes.
Some of the most dreadful frauds in American political life have
a right of access to him. He must listen to Pat Harrison, the
Mississippi wet dry. He must listen to his running mate, old
Joe Robinson, almost a fit match for Curtis. He must listen to
many another mountebank, long schooled in politics as it is
practiced in the Bible Belt, with one eye on the Baptist pastor
and the other on the local wiskinski of the Anti-Saloon League.
He will hear every day how necessary it is to throw a bone to
Tennessee, to step softly over the susceptibilities of Oklahoma,
to remember the prejudices of the Decatur (Ark.) Methodists,
the Hagerstown (Md.) United Brethren, the Abilene (Texas)
Ku Kluxers. He will need all his strength to resist these whisperings.

But I believe it will not fail him.

THE SHOW BEGINS

September 3, 1928

Nothing could be plainer than the fact that, in the preliminary jousting of the campaign, Al has put it all over Lord
Hoover. So much, indeed, is admitted by all Hoover men of a
rational and realistic kidney. They pin their hopes, not upon
anything that their hero will do or say as the battle progresses,

but upon the bald fact that the natural chances run with him; that there are normally more Republicans than Democrats in the country; that the Republicans are always able to raise more money, and that their practical politicians are the more competent.

This last is made manifest at every national convention. The Republican professionals sometimes fight, but they seldom do it in deadly earnest. Thus the old ass, Charlie Curtis, found it quite easy to be against Hoover one day, and his running mate the next. But the Democrats claw and belabor one another with such violence that it is often impossible for them to pull together afterward. The sufferings of such drys as the Hon. Carter Glass and the Hon. Josephus Daniels are now visible to every eye. There are other Democratic drys who are in even worse condition. They want Al to win, for they itch powerfully for jobs, but they simply can't put their hearts into the business of electing him.

This earnestness commonly extends to the Democratic candidates, though not always. The Republicans put up Hardings, Coolidges and Hoovers, who are willing to do or say anything to be elected; the Democrats tend to burden themselves with Bryans, Wilsons and Smiths, who know precisely what they are in favor of, and talk about it all the time. Being in favor of things is obviously a dangerous habit in a Presidential candidate. It may get him a lot of votes, but on the other hand it may lose him a lot. So far, Al has apparently run, as they say, in the black, but at any moment he may say something that will alarm vast multitudes of morons, and so begin to run in the red. It is fear that piles up majorities—for the other fellow. Even Big Business in America is full of fears, despite its impregnable security. It is always seeing Bolsheviks under the bed. Al, I suspect, makes it a bit uneasy: he is too honest to be quite safe for prehensile men. But it trusts Hoover as completely as it trusts Vare, Chief Justice Taft or Elder Hays.

As I long ago argued, Hoover is one of the most adept politicians ever heard of in America. He has a natural instinct for the low, disingenuous, fraudulent manipulations that constitute the art and mystery of politics under democracy. He knows precisely how to posture as a Good Man without doing anything to justify the name. He has a strong nose, and can stand stenches without blenching. He is immensely liberal with other people's money. His so-called ideas are the safe, sonorous, meaningless platitudes of an editorial writer on a bad newspaper. He would have made a good bishop. No wonder he is admired by the sort of men who believe that the late Judge Elbert H. Gary was a great man!

But in all this virtue there is no corruption of innocence. His pre-convention campaign was a model of realism. The while he kept his show going with empty, highfalutin balderdash about Mississippi flood relief and other such moral and harmless subjects, he was gradually gathering into his corral all the worst political rogues in America. If any escaped him, no news of it has got out. The tattered veterans of the Ohio Gang came in to a man. The sturdy bravos of the Vare Gang followed, hayfoot, straw-foot. On their heels were the political parsons and shady lawyers of the Anti-Saloon League, and the fat black boys from the South, their hands out, disgracing their race. And all the miscellaneous rabble of Ku Kluxers, rum-runners, vote-buyers and jury-fixers. He welcomed them all, and they are all on his pay roll today.

His *garde du corps* presents an appalling spectacle. Even Harding, I half suspect, would have gagged at it. In Philadelphia it is even now all over the front pages, with tales of gross and unparalleled corruption. In Chicago the *Tribune*, which is supporting him, revolts against it as abominable and intolerable. In the South scores of its members are headed for jail—and hopeful of getting out after March 4. Some old and intimate associates perfume it. I name a few: Fall, Sinclair, Elder Hays,

Denby, Daugherty. They are all Hoover men. The Hon. William H. Anderson has not been heard from. But you may be sure that he is against Al.

It is amusing to reflect that some of the most vociferously self-righteous groups in America are on the side of this camorra, and doing all they can to turn it loose in Washington, as the Ohio Gang was turned loose by Harding. The whole Hoover campaign, indeed, shows a highly moral tone; every professional wowser in the United States seems to be taking a hand in it. Fat Herbert has all the Methodist bishops with him, as he has the Vare boys. He has the Anti-Saloon League, as he has the Ku Klux. He has the Baptist and United Brethren dervishes, as he has the boughten blackamoors and the survivors of the Ohio Gang. It is a pretty spectacle.

But not unprecedented. For a long while past, indeed, the whole "moral" movement in the United States has been in partnership with political corruption. It was the Anti-Saloon League, I believe, that made the capital discovery that crooked politicians were safer than honest ones—that it was easier to get them in line, and easier to keep them there. Since then all the other apostles of the uplift have learned that cynical lesson. The Klan, in its heyday, rubbed it in. Today, when one hears that the political parsons and their pediculæ are for this or that job-seeker, one concludes almost automatically that he is a scoundrel.

If there were any doubt of Al's bona fides otherwise, it would be proved by his refusal to have anything to do with these sorry soul-savers. He not only refuses to trade with them; he goes out of his way to denounce and defy them. Thus his campaign becomes, in some sense, a war upon them. If he is beaten every slimy Anti-Saloon League snooper in the land will rejoice, and every Baptist Ku Kluxer, and every filthy vice crusader, and every other rogue who has made piety pay. If he wins it will spell disaster to the whole wretched pack. For his victory will teach many a politician who now trembles before it that he may defy it safely, and thousands will proceed bravely to that defiance.

The Southern politicians do not need Al to show them the way. The "moral" attack is forcing them to experiment for themselves. If, as seems likely, the solid South remains solid, they will come out of the campaign with the discovery that the Methodist bishops, after all, do not own and operate the South —that it is possible to disobey their mandates and still win. The bishops themselves, I suspect, are not blind to that danger. It explains, on the one hand, the extreme cautiousness of the more intelligent of them and the unbridled ferocity of the more fanatical.

Win or lose, the time-worn political system of the late Confederate States seems booked for an overhauling. There is a widespread and growing revolt against the hegemony of the self-elected saints. The younger Southerners, male and female, rebel against their tyranny, and resent the derision that they bring down upon the South. They become too extravagant to be endured much longer. They try at the moment to enforce their mandates with all the dreadful devices of the medieval theologian. If they lose there will be a day of reckoning. And if they win it will only come the sooner.

The South cannot go on being an intellectual poor-farm, with ignorant and ignoble ecclesiastics as its overseers. It is growing too rich to submit to them. Their rule seems natural enough to peasants, but it irks persons who have been to school. Thousands of young Southerners are now in college, and many thousands more are on their way. The colleges that they go to are often bad ones, but even the worst has better things on tap than the village church. The very denominational seminaries that were set up to combat learning and propagate ignorance are under suspicion now; the denominational papers are full of complaints against them. They spread the poisons of the enlightenment. Not many of their graduates believe that Jonah swallowed the whale.

Or that man was created in the year 4004 B.C. Or that one who uses wine as Christ used it will go to Hell.

It is Al's good fortune that he has been chosen to lead this movement of deliverance, not only in the South, but everywhere in the land. Win or lose, he is a lucky man, for he will be remembered.

DER WILLE ZUR MACHT

September 10, 1928

When the news of Al's sinister triumph issued from Houston and the political parsons of the Confederate States began their furious assault upon him, it was predicted generally that they would quickly wear themselves out, as puppies wear themselves out chasing their tails. I can only report that I find no sign of it so far. Here and there, perhaps, a prudent pastor, his eye upon his poundings and the susceptibilities of his deacons, may have shut off his wind-machine, but enough others remain in action to keep the Bible Belt in an uproar. I read all the Methodist and Baptist papers printed below the Potomac: the letter-carrier brings them in by the armful. Two-thirds of them devote half their space to bawling that anyone who is against Prohibition is against God, and the other half to damning the Pope.

In each case their position is logically dubious. They excuse their violence in the matter of Prohibition on the ground that it is a moral question, and that they are bound by their oaths to horn into all moral questions, but they do not explain why they remained so silent while the Klan was flogging and barn-burning all over the South. They justify their assaults upon the Pope on the ground that the Catholic Church is a political machine with pretensions to secular power, but they overlook the fact that secular power is what they are trying to get themselves.

Here are inconsistencies, and the opponents of the embattled parsons push them home. In reply, they deny somewhat lamely, in the face of the plain facts, that they supported the Klan in its heyday, and then argue even more lamely that it was really a virtuous organization. A typical answer is that of the Rev. M. E. Lazenby, of the *Alabama Christian Advocate*, to a committee of laymen who want to know why he was "by indirection giving aid to the Klan at the time courageous newspapers were trying to rid the State of floggings by hooded bands." Pastor Lazenby answers that all the pother about the floggings was set up by a wet press in order that "Alabama could be won for the Al Smith column." In other words, they were imaginary—despite the very palpable stripes and welts that the victims exposed in court!

It is hard to argue with such frantic fanatics. Their definition of the truth, in the mundane field as in the ghostly, differs from that of other men, and they patronize a brand of logic that is almost as idiotic as that of university philosophers. But, if it is hard to argue with them, it seems to me that it is quite easy to understand them. Put it down that what moves them, fundamentally, is simply a yearning to run things, a lust for power, and all their multitudinous imbecilities take on a certain coherence, and even a sort of sweet reasonableness.

They got their first taste of power by adverse possession. The South, for years after the Civil War, was an intellectual poor farm, and in its remoter parts it reverted to the condition of the colonies at the close of the Seventeenth Century. Decent schools were few and far between, and only children of the relatively rich went to them. There were no newspapers of wide circulation, and in large areas there were no educated men. The best blood of the region had been wasted in the war, and what remained tended to be drained out. To this day Mississippi remains at the bottom of the whole list of American States on all cultural counts.

In the villages civilization was reduced to its elementals. The people had no intellectual interests, and no educated leaders. The only learning on tap was that of the one-room schoolhouse, and its teacher was commonly a peasant youth, but little raised above the common level. The only communal activity superior to the bald struggle for survival centered in the churches. They offered a hope of deliverance, if not in this world, then at least *post mortem*. The village pastor was the natural leader of the community. He alone could pretend to any knowledge above the simplest. He was ignorant, but he was still less ignorant than the rest. He became the neighborhood oracle.

The South, during the past twenty years, has made rapid progress materially, and *per corollary* culturally. It is going ahead quite as fast as any other part of the country. But though it is thus relatively progressive, it is still behind the North absolutely. In part, it has grown, but in part it has simply swollen. The ideas of the village—worse, of the remote and forlorn village—still pervade it. It has a countrified point of view. It still clings, for example, to the village attitude toward the parson. He remains an oracle, not only in the hills and swamps, but even in such towns as Atlanta and Birmingham. He continues to be a mighty man, listened to with respect and followed when he demands obedience.

But revolt against him is growing as the enlightenment spreads, and it naturally alarms him. He sees his power slipping from him, or threatening to slip from him, and he makes every effort to hang on to it. A man, commonly, of the lower orders, and unable to move ahead with the more intelligent of his people, he flings himself frantically upon every evidence of genuine advancement. He is against teaching the sciences in the schools; he is against the fine arts; he is against every infiltration of culture from without. He wants to keep his power, and he knows instinctively that he can keep it only by holding the populace at his own level.

Is it any wonder that this man gave a hearty welcome to the Klan—that he was, in fact, its chief supporter? It stood against everything that he feared, and its hooded mumbo-jumbo enormously reinforced and augmented his power. All over the South the Baptist preachers took to the nightshirt and tar pot with whoops, and thousands of Methodist parsons followed them. The Klan gave their pretensions a sort of secular authority; they felt the might of an army behind them. In the cities a few bold and iconoclastic holy men protested, but not many. Once the asphalt was left behind the evangelical clergy were almost unanimously Klansmen, and some of them were leaders in the floggings, burnings and other outrages which they now try to explain away.

Prohibition gave another powerful fillip to their sense of power. They were in favor of it, I daresay, quite honestly, and for reasons that were locally sound enough. The low-down Southerner, white or black, cannot drink decently; he can only get drunk and play the hog. But the battle for Prohibition was more than a struggle for a moral reform; it was also a clear-cut combat between the cities and the country, between the civilized centers and the areas of cornbread and revivals. Its sudden and unexpected success under cover of the war hysteria was a godsend to the parsons. They now had another army behind them, sworn to force their will upon their enemies, and the colossal authority and might of the national Government supported it.

Now they see that authority challenged and their own power in danger. No wonder they fight to retain it with savage fury! If it slips from them, as the support of the Klan is slipping from them, they will be reduced to impotence. The whole fabric of their hegemony is menaced. They are no longer fighting for Prohibition; they are fighting for their own high rights and prerogatives. The more frank—or the more indiscreet—of them admit it frankly. Even if Prohibition is a failure, they argue, it must be saved. The important thing is not to make men better, but to make them do what they are ordered to do. Soul-saving retires to the rear. The issue now is Law Enforcement.

The rancor against the Pope has similar springs. In their inflammatory warnings to their customers the parsons describe a Catholic Church which, in theory and practice, is precisely like their own churches. It pretends to the same right to the obedience of its communicants, the same right to dictate to public officers, the same infallible authority in all matters of morals. It is in politics, as they describe it, exactly as they themselves are in politics. If it triumphs, then it will seize and exercise the power that is now theirs. They prefer mightly to keep that power themselves. They are against the Pope until the last galoot's ashore. They hate him as a Mussolini hates a Communist, and for the same reason.

PROPHETICAL MUSINGS

September 17, 1928

Whatever the issue of the current combat between the political parsons and the Pope, it seems highly probable that the honest Prohibitionists are in for a sad time. There are plenty of them left in the Bible Belt, despite the lessons of the past eight and a half years, and many of them are in holy orders. These consecrated men have added the Volstead Act to the Ten Commandments, and give it far more faith and credit than they accord to any of the original ten. They believe quite seriously that the most heinous of all crimes is to use alcohol in the way it was used at Cana, and they look to Lord Hoover to stamp out the abhorrent practice completely.

If he loses to Dr. Schmidt the news will knock them out; it

will be the worst heard in the total immersion country since April 9, 1865. And if he wins their defeat and dismay will only be postponed, for he will be no more able to enforce Prohibition than Dr. Coolidge has been able to enforce it. The same old booticians will remain in business, the same old deacons will continue at the jug, and the front pages will be adorned with the same old thumping scandals. Hoover is no worker of miracles. He must achieve his prodigies by purely human means. So long as the chief of those human means are Prohibition agents and the agents continue to have hands, there will be booze enough for all.

Moreover, there is not the slightest reason to believe that fat Herbert will make any serious effort to put on the lid. He is far too wise to believe that it can be done, and there is too much enlightened self-interest in him to let him make the attempt. He knows very well what the result would be if he did. He would become the most unpopular President ever heard of, and his administration would be rocked by such scandals that those of Harding's day would pale beside them. There is nothing in the man to indicate that he will ever take such chances. He is a very careful fellow.

His pious declarations in favor of the Eighteenth Amendment and the Volstead Act are no more than what his eminent opponent calls boloney. Certainly no one who knows him believes that he is actually a Prohibitionist. He is simply a candidate for office, willing and eager to do or say anything that will get him votes, and the fortunes of war have made it more prudent for him to cultivate the drys than to cultivate the wets. If the thing ran the other way he would probably be quite as wet as Al is. His whole life has been spent among men to whom Prohibition is as loathsome as cannibalism. He came from London, the wettest town in the world, to sit in the Harding Cabinet, the wettest since the days of Noah. No one ever heard him utter a whisper against the guzzling that surrounded him. He was as silent about it as he was about the stealing.

The honest drys are forever embracing such frauds, and forever coming to grief. Is it so soon forgotten that Harding himself was elected as an ardent Prohibitionist, pledged to enforce the Volstead Act up to the hilt? His first act, once he was in office, was to appoint old Andy Mellon, a heavy holder of distillery stock, to the portfolio of the Treasury, with supreme command of Law Enforcement. His second was to arrange with the enforcement boys in Washington to supply him with tit-bits from their seizures. His boozing became so notorious that the late Wayne B. Wheeler remonstrated with him, and even threatened him. (The facts are all set forth in the recent biography of Wheeler, approved by the Anti-Saloon League.) Alarmed, he went on the wagon, and was dead in six weeks.

I am not arguing, of course, that Lord Hoover will carry on in Washington in the manner of Harding. He is a far more sedate and judicious man. He is not an Elk, but a Quaker, and Quakers are not lushers. But I remain unconvinced that he is really a Prohibitionist, save in the strictest candidatorial or Pickwickian sense. If proofs are brought forward that he is, I shall believe it. But simultaneously I shall begin believing, for good measure, that he was a Republican in 1916 and an American in 1914.

Thus the political parsons seem doomed to suffer, whether they unhorse the Pope or not. If Al is elevated to the ermine of Cal, then they will be *persona non grata* in Washington for four years, and maybe for eight, and their nerves will be lacerated by endless assaults. Congress will be bombarded with messages against the Volstead Act; the Federal judges nominated by the Anti-Saloon League, as they succumb to senility and bad booze, will be replaced by wets; Law Enforcement will be in the hands of its enemies. And if Lord Hoover wins they will be quite as badly off, for he is only a rice-convert, and he'll certainly not risk a second term by attempting the impossible.

But the clerical statesmen and witchburners are in for even

worse woes. By flinging themselves headlong into politics in the
South they have accomplished something that the slow progress
of civilization down there could not have accomplished in thirty
years: they have broken down the taboos that have hitherto
surrounded them. In sheer self-defense the Confederate politicians have had to resist them, and that resistance has taken the
form of denouncing them. Nine-tenths of the Southern newspapers join in. For the first time the deficiencies and demerits of
the parsons are openly discussed; for the first time they get a
dose of their own bitter medicine.

It seems to me that this is an innovation of the first importance, and that it is bound to have massive and permanent
effects. For years past the hedge pastors have operated in the
South almost without challenge. It has been regarded as an
indecorum to oppose them with any vigor, and an indecency to
question their *bona fides*. But now all that is suddenly changed,
and by their own act. Their very deacons, revolting against
their tyranny, call them names; the Southern newspapers denounce them openly and violently; they find themselves under
fire from all sides. The Southern intellectuals, a small body but
eager for battle, howl with delight. They look forward to rich
hunting. Henceforth they will be free to crack a clerical head
whenever they espy it—and they prepare for the sport with all
the enthusiasm of village Ku Kluxers flushing a fancy woman.

I look for punitive operations in the grand manner, once the
heir of Coolidge is chosen. If Al is slaughtered all the Southern
politicians will blame it on the parsons and roar for revenge.
And if Al wins they will seek with equal ardor to punish every
treason to him. Thus the parsons face a future full of strange
perils. Their old immunity is gone. Hereafter they must carry
on their gloomy campaigns in the open, without any taboos to
protect them. That highly salubrious change has been a long
time a-coming, but it has come at last.

Its effects are bound to be excellent. For years the South has labored under clerical domination at its worst. In every village some trashy divine has been cock of the walk, and even in the big cities the most preposterous Billy Sundays and John Roach Stratons have been treated with grave deference. No Southern newspaper ever called them to book in any forthright and effective manner, even when they filled the air with rantings against the veriest elements of sound knowledge and common sense. They were protected by what was regarded as their sacred character. Every pastor was a chartered libertine, free to bawl nonsense without challenge.

But now, by their own imprudence, the rev. brethren have exposed their hides. The free speech which currently prevails against them will continue after the present occasion for it has passed. All over the South newspaper editors learn that it is possible to tackle the clergy head on, and still survive. The more frantic they become, the more they lay themselves open to attack, and the more they are attacked the more the habit of attacking them will flourish. I look for good results, growing better as year chases year. The Southern intellectuals emerge from their storm-cellars and prepare for battle. The next time there is a Scopes trial it will have a different issue. The South seems to be delivered at last.

AL IN THE FREE STATE

October 29, 1928

It is difficult to make out how any native Marylander, brought up in the tradition of this ancient Commonwealth, can fail to have a friendly feeling for Al Smith in the present campaign. He represents as a man almost everything that Maryland represents as a State. There is something singularly and refreshingly free, spacious, amiable, hearty and decent about him. Brought up in poverty, and educated, in so far as he got any education at all, in the harsh school of the city streets, he has yet managed somehow to acquire what is essentially an aristocratic point of view, the habit and color of a gentleman. He is enlightened, he is high-minded, he is upright and trustworthy. What Frederick the Great said of his officers might well be said of him: he will not lie, and he cannot be bought. Not much more could be said of any man.

The contrast he makes with his opponent is really appalling. Hoover stands at the opposite pole. He is a man of sharp intelligence, well schooled and familiar with the ways of the world, and more than once, in difficult situations, he has shown a shrewd competence, but where his character ought to be there is almost a blank. He is the perfect self-seeker, pushing and unconscionable; it is hard to imagine him balking at anything to get on. His principles are so vague that even his intimates seem unable to put them into words. He is an American who came within an inch of being an Englishman, a Republican who came within an inch of being a Democrat, a dry who came within an inch of being a wet. He is what he is today because it has paid him well so far, and promises to pay still better hereafter.

It is a commonplace of the campaign that no one is passionately for him: all his most ardent support comes from those who are passionately against Al. In that support there is a grimly eloquent summing up of the two men. Al naturally arouses the distrust and dislike of all the anti-social elements, of all the mountebanks who prey upon vulgar ignorance and credulity, of all the racketeers, high and low. The goblins of the Klan are against him, and so are the waterpower exploiters. He is dreaded by the spies and boob-squeezers of the Anti-Saloon League, and hated by the witch-chasing Methodist bishops. The friends of Fall and Daugherty detest him, and the dupes of Heflin and Straton tremble at his name. All these sweet babies are for Hoover.

The issues of the campaign, as usual, have become tangled and obscured. There have been pointless, murky debates about the tariff, farm relief, government ownership, and other such inanimate and meaningless things. The true realities lie in the characters of the two candidates. Which is the more enlightened and courageous, the more likely to formulate rational and effective policies, the least likely to yield to privilege and power, the more trustworthy? The question almost answers itself. Al is for the free man because he is a free man himself. If his head failed him, his heart would carry him irresistibly that way. But Hoover will hedge. He will find excuses to hesitate. He knows who his masters are, and he will serve them.

On the one hand, he denounces every effort to hobble the water-power hogs as socialistic and tyrannical; on the other hand, he swallows calmly the intolerable contempt for private right that is Prohibition. On which side does he actually stand? What would he say if he were man enough to say what he really thinks? I believe that he is honest when he defends private right in the name of the water-power hogs, and dissembling when he denounces it in the name of the Anti-Saloon League. But he needs the votes of the dry fanatics, and so he is dry. He admits the failure of the Volstead act, but he is for it. He is against too much government, but he calls for more.

Certainly it would be hard to imagine a more devious fellow. He has all the limber knavishness of the low-down American politician without any of the compensatory picturesqueness. He is like a lady of joy who lacks the saving grace of being beautiful. He is a Zihlman, but not so transparent; a Goldsborough, but not so dumb. Hoover is not dumb. He has a good head on him, and knows what he wants. Almost by instinct, he turns to scoundrels. They swarm around him like flies around a molasses barrel. They, too, know what they want.

Compared to this sorry zany, with his fluid principles and tricky evasions, Al stands forth as every inch a man. It has been urged against him that his knowledge of some of the things he discusses is defective—that his equipment in certain fields of statecraft is less than it might be and ought to be. But that is mainly empty talk. He knows enough, and he can learn more. The basic sort of knowledge is his beyond a doubt: he can tell a rogue from an honest man through eight feet of oak. And the basic sort of integrity no one denies him: he is for the honest man at once, and until the last galoot's ashore.

In all his speeches there has been that simple note. It has been the *leit motif* of his whole career. Does he discuss the tariff? Then it is to discover why its benefits are so unequal, and to make them more equitable. Does he plunge into the Bad Lands of farm relief? Then it is because only charlatans have been there before him, and he wants to find out what fairness and candor can do. Does he play with the buzz-saw of government ownership? Then it is because bitter experience has taught him, as it has taught the rest of us, that the water-power hogs are incurably dishonest and disreputable—that a truce with them would be as hopeless as a truce with Adam-Zad the Bear.

His politics are thus simple, and to those debauched by the customary obscurantism they must inevitably seem somewhat naïve. But they have sufficed him in New York, and they would suffice him at Washington. There is, after all, no mystery in government, no arcanum closed to all save Vermont lawyers, mine-stock promoters, Pittsburg note-shavers, and other such adepts. The main and perhaps the only thing is to make being governed bearable, to hold down the rascals who live by the toil of the rest of us, to keep the brutal hoofing and looting of the plain man within bounds, to get a reasonable honesty and decency into the business. To this aim Al has addressed himself since his first days of power. He found New York one of the worst-governed States in the Union; he will leave it one of the best-governed.

So much for his virtues; there remains his charm. It seems to me that it is not enough that a President of the United States should be full of learning and rectitude; it is also important that he have good humor in him, and be likeable as a man. His business is not merely discharging words of wisdom; he must also manage men. If he is too vain and haughty to do it, as Wilson was, then the result is bound to be turmoil and disaster. If he is too idiotic, as Harding was, then it is riot and scandal. If he is too boorish, as Coolidge is, then it is sour and witless burlesque.

We have surely had enough such inept and preposterous fellows in the White House. Do all the major problems confronting the country, from farm relief and foreign policy, remain unsolved? Then it is mainly because the ship of state has lacked a competent pilot, able to win and command the crew. I don't think Hoover could do it. No one likes him in Washington, save the porch climbers who hope to work him. He is too cautious, suspicious, secretive, sensitive, evasive, disingenuous. He is another Coolidge, only worse. There is nothing in him, no human juices. He is like a balloon tire inside, as he is without. His administration, if he is elected, will be one of whispers, as his campaign has been.

Al is at the other end of the human race. Frank, amiable, tolerant, modest and expansive, he has the faculty of taking men into camp. They trust him at sight, and the better they know him the more they trust him. No man in American politics has ever had firmer friends among his enemies. His career, indeed, has been made by their aid, and it is Republicans who are his most devoted partisans today. He would bring to the White House the equipment of a genuine leader. He would face Congress with assurance and break it to his will. And he would give us the liveliest, gaudiest, most stimulating show ever seen in Washington since the days of Roosevelt.

I can imagine ageing men and women voting for Hoover as the safer of the two. They fear Al because he is so much alive. But what of the young? What of the first voters? Show me one who is not instinctively for Al, and I will show you one whose soul yearns for the robes of a Y.M.C.A. secretary or the white-satin badge that goes with consecrated B.Y.P.U. work.

THE EVE OF ARMAGEDDON

November 5, 1928

It has been, by God's will, a very bitter campaign, which is to say, an unusually honest one. Every effort to conceal the real issues—and both sides moved in that direction at the start—has gone to pot. If Al wins tomorrow, it will be because the American people have decided at last to vote as they drink, and because a majority of them believe that the Methodist bishops are worse than the Pope. If he loses, it will be because those who fear the Pope outnumber those who are tired of the Anti-Saloon League.

No other issue has got anywhere, nor will any other swing any appreciable number of votes. Al and Lord Hoover seem to be at one on the tariff, both say they are for economy, and both promise relief to the farmer though neither says how he is going to achieve it. When Hoover denounced Al as a Socialist it fell flat, for everyone knows that he is not, and when Al tried to hook up Hoover with Fall and Doheny it fell flat, for Americans are not opposed to corruption. Both sides have appealed alike to Negroes and Negro-baiters, and neither knows which way either group is going to jump. Labor, foreign policy, water power—all these questions are off the board.

There remain only Prohibition and religion, or more accurately, only religion, for Prohibition, in the dry areas, has long ceased to be a question of government or even of ethics, and has become purely theological. The more extreme drys, real and fake, simply refuse to discuss it. Throughout the Bible country belief in it has become a cardinal article of faith, like belief in the literal accuracy of Genesis. Men are denounced as traitors for so much as arguing that it ought to be discussed. Practically every one in those wilds guzzles more or less, as explorers quickly discover, but to suggest that Prohibition has failed and that something better is imaginable is as grave an indecorum as it would be to suggest to a Catholic theologian that the question whether the wine is really turned into blood at mass be submitted to a committee of chemists. In such fields *Homo sapiens* scorns and abominates human evidences. Challenged, he merely howls.

I daresay the extent of the bigotry prevailing in America, as it has been revealed by the campaign, has astounded a great many Americans, and perhaps even made them doubt the testimony of their own eyes and ears. This surprise is not in itself surprising, for Americans of one class seldom know anything about Americans of other classes. What the average native yokel believes about the average city man is probably ninetenths untrue, and what the average city man believes about the average yokel is almost as inaccurate.

A good part of this ignorance is probably due to the powerful effect of shibboleths. Every American is taught in school that all Americans are free, and so he goes on believing it his whole life—overlooking the plain fact that no Negro is really free in the South, and no miner in Pennsylvania, and no radical in any of a dozen great States. He hears of equality before the law, and he accepts it as a reality, though it exists nowhere, and there are Federal laws which formally repudiate it. In the same way he is taught that religious toleration prevails among us, and uncritically swallows the lie. No such thing really exists. No such thing has ever existed.

This campaign has amply demonstrated the fact. It has brought bigotry out into the open, and revealed its true proportions. It has shown that millions of Americans, far from being free and tolerant men, are the slaves of an ignorant, impudent and unconscionable clergy. It has dredged up theological ideas so preposterous that they would make an intelligent Zulu laugh, and has brought the proof that they are cherished by nearly half the whole population, and by at least four-fifths outside the cities. It has made it plain that this theology is not merely a harmless aberration of the misinformed, like spiritualism, chiropractic or Christian Science, but the foundation of a peculiar way of life, bellicose, domineering, brutal and malignant—in brief, the complete antithesis of any recognizable form of Christianity. And it has shown, finally, that this compound of superstition and hatred has enough steam behind it to make one of the candidates for the Presidency knuckle to it and turn it upon his opponent—basely to be sure, but probably wisely.

Certainly something is accomplished when such facts are exposed to every eye, and with overwhelming reiteration. It may be uncomfortable to confront them, but it is surely better to confront them than to be ignorant of them. They explain many phenomena that have been obscure and puzzling—the rise to power of the Anti-Saloon League, the influence of such clowns as Bishop Cannon, the Rev. John Roach Straton and Billy Sunday, and, above all, the curious and otherwise inexplicable apparition of the Klan, with its appalling trail of crime and corruption.

All these things go back to one source, and that source is now known. The problem before the civilized minority of Americans is that of shutting off its flow of bilge-water. Can that be done?

I am not so sure. The majority of rural Americans, with the best blood all drained to the cities, are probably hopelessly uneducable. Sound ideas make no more appeal to them than decent drinks. They prefer nonsense to sense as they prefer white mule to Burgundy. Abandoned for years to the tutelage of their pastors, they have now gone so far into the darkness that every light terrifies them and runs them amuck.

But though the job of enlightening them may be difficult, it should be worth trying. And if, in the end, there is only failure, then the way will be open for other and more radical remedies. For in the long run the cities of the United States will have to throw off the hegemony of these morons. They have run the country long enough, and made it sufficiently ridiculous. Once we get rid of campmeeting rule we'll get rid simultaneously of the Klan, the Anti-Saloon League and the Methodist Board of Temperance, Prohibition and Public Morals. We'll get rid of the Cannons and Heflins, the Willebrandts and Wayne Wheelers. And we'll get rid, too, of those sorry betrayers of intelligence who, like Hoover and Borah, flatter and fawn over the hookworm carriers in order to further their own fortunes.

It seems to me that Dr. Hoover has been exposed in this campaign as no candidate for the Presidency ever was before, not even the ignoramus Harding or the trimmer Davis. He went into it as a master-mind, a fellow of immense and singular sagacities; he comes out of it a shrewd politician, but nothing more. His speeches have been, on the one hand, so disingenuous, and, on the other hand, so hollow, that even his most ardent followers now take refuge behind the doctrine that he will, at all events, be safe—that he will not invite the Pope to Washington, or monkey with such divine revelations as the tariff and Prohibition, or do anything to alarm stock speculators, or make any unseemly pother about stealing.

Hoover, since the day he abandoned mine-stock promoting for Service, has always had the help of a good press. He knows how to work the newspapers. The Washington correspondents, in large majority, dislike him, but still they fall for him, for he is adept at the art of taking the center of the stage and posturing there profoundly. In the past his futilities were only too often overlooked, in the blinding light of his publicity. He went to the Mississippi in all the gaudy state of a movie queen, but came back with no plan to stop the floods there. He issued tons of reports of dull subjects, but said nothing. But always he got lavish press notices.

In the campaign, however, his old devices failed. His original plan, obviously, was to look wise and say nothing. His speech of acceptance was a mass of windy platitudes, almost worthy of Coolidge. But gradually Al forced him into a corner and he had to talk. What has he said? I defy anyone to put it into reasonable propositions. No one, to this moment, knows what he really proposes to do about the tariff, or about Prohibition, or about foreign affairs, or about water power, and in the matter of farm relief he has simply passed the buck. Theoretically an abyss of wisdom, he has chattered like a high-school boy. Once he muttered three sentences against religious intolerance. But the bigots kept on supporting him, and they will support him tomorrow, and he knows it and is counting on it.

AUTOPSY

November 12, 1928

Al Smith's body lies a-mouldering in the grave, but his soul goes marching on. He fought a good fight, and he was right. So far as I have been able to make out, not a man or woman who voted for him regrets it today. The phenomenon is almost unique in American politics. Usually, after a disastrous failure, the standard-bearer is heaved into Coventry and has to bear a lot of the blame. It was so with the pussyfooting Davis. It was so with the preposterous Cox. It was even so with Roosevelt: his last days, as everyone knows, were lonely and bitter. But no one blames Al. He made a gallant and gaudy campaign against tremendous odds, and he went down to defeat with every flag flying and the band playing on deck. He was, is, and will remain a man. There are not many in public life in America. They are so few, indeed, that the American people have got out of the habit of looking for them, and of following them when found. The standard-model statesman of today is a far more limber and politic fellow. Avoiding ideas as dangerous—which they un-questionably are—he devotes himself to playing upon emotions and sentimentalities. He may be himself an ignoramus, like Harding, or he may be a bright lad with a pushing spirit and an elastic conscience, like Hoover. In either case he has immense advantages over any frank, earnest, candid and forthright man.

I incline to believe that Hoover could have beaten Thomas Jefferson quite as decisively as he beat Al. He could have knocked off Grover Cleveland even more dramatically. His judg-ment of the American people was cynical but sound. Whenever he fed them it was with the mush that is now their pet fodder. He let Al bombard them with ideas, confident that ideas would only affright and anger them. Meanwhile he did business behind the door with all the professional boob-squeezers, clerical and lay. His victory was a triumph of technique, of sound political engineering. It did credit to his gifts as a politician. But Al hogged all the glory as a statesman and a man.

There is a certain fine irony in the plea of the vanquished that the victor be given whole-hearted support. Al is well aware that Hoover will need it, if his administration is to escape wreck. No President, not even McKinley, has ever gone into office burdened with worse supporters, all of them clamoring for reward. They range from professional vote-buyers so bold and shameless that even the majority of Republican leaders shrink from them to religious fanatics so frantic that the world has not seen their like since the Middle Ages. They all labored mightily for Herbert, and they all know what they want.

His agents spread the hint that he will ditch them when he is safe in the White House—in other words, that he will prove his rectitude by welching on his accomplices. It is not probable. More, it is not possible. He can no more get rid of those rogues and mountebanks than Harding could get rid of the Ohio Gang. His victory was quite as much theirs as his own, and they know it, and everyone else knows it. Especially does Washington know it. Some of them—notably the bosses of the Anti-Saloon League —are already on the ground, making lordly announcements of what they demand and what they propose to do. All the rest will be dug in long before March 4.

A President can combat such prehensile followers only by open war, and open war is the last thing that Dr. Hoover is capable of. He will continue to take refuge in platitudes, in the future as in the past. And Washington will continue, as ever, to lean the way the prevailing winds blow. No Methodist bishop, descending on the town to cash in, will have to wait in an antechamber. No broker in colored votes from Florida or North Carolina will have to introduce himself. The gang of miserable slaves that constitutes the real government of the United States is stupid, but it is not so stupid that it cannot read the election returns. Those returns show that Hoover was elected, but they also show that the Anti-Saloon League was reëlected. Already, in Washington, every prudent man leaps to open doors for Ma Willebrandt, and not even the most reckless traffic cop would want to offend the editor of the *Fellowship Forum*.

The President-elect's proposed tour of South America is characteristic, and not without its melancholy humor. His first official act is to turn his back upon the multitudinous problems that confront him, and go off on a windjamming expedition.

There will be dozens of banquets and hundreds of speeches. They will all repeat the blather loosed by the Hon. Charles Evans Hughes at Havana last winter. The Latin-Americans are familiar with such blarney, and do not take it seriously. They know very well that the course of the United States south of the Rio will be determined hereafter, as in the past, by Americans of highly enlightened self-interest, and they know that these Americans sweated hard for Hoover and will not let him forget it.

Coming home, he will find the Anti-Saloon League on his doorsteps. How will he handle it, inflamed, as it now is, by victory, and full of a sadistic frenzy to punish its opponents? My guess is that he will handle it by yielding to it. That course will be shrewder than resistance, and Hoover is surely shrewd. If the whole business of enforcement is turned over to the witch-burners, they will go slambanging to disaster, with Bible in one hand and whip in the other. They can no more make Prohibition a reality than they can make their Zulu theology a reality. They could not enforce it in even the dryest of States. It is definitely dead as a practical measure of reform; it remains in being only as a device to inflame morons against honest men.

Its damages widen and multiply. It has corrupted the police almost everywhere; it has prospered and encouraged criminals; it has brought religion into politics; it has sowed bitter and relentless hatreds. The Federal courts, once remote and impeccable, already show its smirches: under Hoover they will be blackened still more. No new judge will mount the bench without the Anti-Saloon League rubber stamp upon him. Will Hoover resist? It seems unlikely. And if he does, then certainly the Senate will not, for it will be filled with Goldsboroughs who owe their very seats to the limberness of their knees and necks.

But let us resign Hoover and his troubles to the will of God. We are in for four years of high-sounding and meaningless words, and four years of scandal and uproar. It will be a good show, and it will be very instructive. I see no reason why even morons should not take in some of its lessons. Hoover will probably find things harder in 1932 than they were in 1928. Al uncovered some of his weaknesses, but not all. They will begin to reveal themselves when he undertakes the appalling job of maintaining a reasonable decency and decorum among his friends.

The opposition, at the moment, wabbles all over the place. The Democratic party is down with boils. But it will recover, and I presume to predict that it will recover with renewed and augmented vigor. Despite the desperate raid of the political parsons it still holds the heart of the South, and in addition it has made appreciable gains in the North. Under handicaps never paralleled, its candidates polled 14,000,000 votes. A change of view in one-sixth of the voters of the country would put it on top.

Its danger lies in the weakness of many, if not most, of its leaders. Being politicians, they are cowards, and, what is worse, fools. They will counsel compromise, especially on such explosive issues as Prohibition. They will try to make terms with its traitors. But I believe there is ground for hope that these trimmers will not be on the quarter-deck in the next great battle. The future of the Democracy lies in following the furrow plowed by Al. As a feeble imitator of the Republican party it has no chance. But as a party of progress and enlightenment, dedicated to common sense, common rights and common decency— as a refuge for all men and women who tire of government by frauds and fanatics, exploiters and hypocrites, theologians and corruptionists, clowns and knaves—as the complete anti-Hoover party it faces opportunities. Can it win? Maybe. But, win or lose, it can at least carry on a brave and uncompromising war against the rabble of Babbitts and Gantrys which now afflict the country.

THE MEN WHO RULE US

May 19, 1930

That the Hoover administration has come a cropper seems to be the general feeling from end to end of the Republic. True enough, the greasers in attendance at the White House continue to anoint its august denizen with vaseline, butter, oleomargarine and *Putz-Pomade*, but anyone can see that their operations lack the fine frenzy of yesteryear, and some of them begin to show plain signs of dubeity. The rest of the country has apparently made up its mind that Lord Hoover is a flop. There are many who cling to the hope that he will do better on some vague tomorrow, but there would seem to be precious few, even among his Wesleyan friends, who believe that he has done well so far. The evidence to the contrary is too massive and too obvious.

In all this there is probably some injustice, for it is hard to make out how Dr. Hoover, coming into office as he did, could have done much better than he has. Few Presidents have ever entered the White House under a heavier burden of political debts, or owing them to worse varieties of politicians. Whether it was due to the hon. gentleman's innocence or to his craft I don't know, but the fact remains that his outfit, both in the primary fights and in the general campaign, was composed largely of highly dubious persons. Some of them were professional politicians and some of them were not, but over all of them there lingered the same cadaverous and unpleasant scent. In all my days I have never seen a fouler gang than that which showed up at Kansas City to make Dr. Hoover the Republican nominee. Ranged beside them, the Tammany braves who labored for Al at Houston smelled like roses.

Now that he is in office, the beneficiary of their ministrations has them on his hands, and getting rid of them seems to be beyond his power. They are apparently responsible for all the blunders that have made the plain people suspect him—the selection of the egregious Wickersham to head the prohibition commission, the Hughes and Parker appointments, the Claudius Huston business, and so on. In all these high matters he simply played politics according to the programme of his backers. But the public forgets the backers, and sees only the President. Let him fall for evil counsel a few times more, and he will be so far ruined that even his renomination in 1932 will begin to be doubtful.

As I say, there is some injustice in this, for it involves blaming Hoover the individual for a viciousness that has come to be inherent in the office he adorns. It is no longer possible for a man to be put into the White House by anything properly describable as the popular will. As Dr. Hoover himself discovered in 1920, even the most gaudy hero is helpless at a national convention unless he has previously made sure of a sufficiency of votes on the floor. Well, the only way to get those votes is to traffic with the vote-brokers. If one happens to be a Republican, one must do business with the Ohio gang, the Indiana gang, the Pennsylvania gang, and all the rest of them, and, above all, with the herders of Aframerican delegates from the South.

That is precisely what Dr. Hoover did—very reluctantly, let us hope, but none the less certainly. The job before him was to wrest the nomination away from such adept professionals as Jim Watson and old Charlie Curtis, the perfumed Indian, and the only way he could do it was on the time-honored basis of promising favors ahead for favors in hand. And once he had the nomination the job was to get elected—by sheer merit if possible, but in any case to get elected. Was it in human nature for a man so situated to spurn the help of Bishop Cannon, the Baptist mullahs, the Ku Klux Klan, and all the rest of that shabby indecent crowd? I believe it must be confessed, however sadly, that it was not.

Here is where public opinion tends to be unjust. On the one

hand it condones and even insists upon a political system which makes it a sheer impossibility—save, of course, by miracle—for a man to get into the White House without involving himself in hopeless obligations to rogues. And on the other hand it holds him, once he has got there, to a standard of conduct which amounts, in the last analysis, to repudiating and forgetting most of the men who put them there. Most Presidents, confronting that unhappy dilemma, show a great deal of distress, but none show more distress than those whose experience of practical politics has been relatively slight. Dr. Hoover, as he stands, is a pitiable object. He seems to be trying to play the game according to the rules and trying to convince himself that these rules are fair and honorable, but all the time it is plain that he is ashamed of them.

The chief problem before him, at the moment, concerns his relations to the accomplished and unconscionable politicians, clerical and lay, who run the Anti-Saloon League. If he continues, as in the past, to pay off his heavy debt to them by playing to their lust for oppression and corruption he will undoubtedly roll up more and more unpopularity. And if, venturing upon revolt, he turns upon them, they will probably retain sufficient hold over their dupes to give him serious trouble in 1932. Thus he roasts between two fires, and his situation is anything but comfortable.

How, in this department, his private inclination runs I do not know, and neither does anyone else. One of the lessons that he learned, when he resolved to go into politics as a business, was the old one to the effect that what a candidate neglects to mention he need never explain away. Thus we face the curious spectacle of the head of the state remaining silent upon the chief issue before the people. No one knows whether Dr. Hoover believes honestly in Prohibition, and no one knows whether he believes honestly that it can be enforced. All we have had from him is a series of platitudes, and a series of official acts that prove nothing save his willingness to repay the Anti-Saloon League for its high services in 1928.

It would be pleasant, in such a situation, to see a greater show of resolution in the White House. What the presidency needs, above all things, is character. But character is precisely the thing that, in these later years, we have bred out of our Presidents. It takes a complaisant man to come within even the remotest hailing distance of the chief magistracy today, and by the time a candidate has actually attained it, he has quite forgotten that there is any such thing in the world as self-respect. If, now, we behold a President who knuckles under to intriguing fanatics, and throttles the indignation that every decent man must have for them, then let us console ourselves with the thought that in the near future we'll probably have a President willing to submit his neck to men even worse.

There is consolation too, and of a measurably better variety, in the fact that, whatever its feebleness at the top, the government somehow goes on, and that its folly and futility seldom reach the intolerable. In many ways, indeed, it shows something of the blind, indomitable vitality of a living organism. Theoretically, nothing could be worse than a state ruled by Bishop Cannons and Claudius Hustons, with an irresolute President to do their bidding, but after all men and women manage to live under it, and most of them are only dimly aware of its deficiencies. Perhaps the very lack of character that it reveals is the chief source of its strength, for some of the most violent revolts of history have been raised, not against weak and stupid rulers but against strong and intelligent ones.

Certainly there is nothing either very strong or very intelligent about the present government of the United States. The head of the state shows almost complete incompetence to rule: he is unable to resist either the seductions of his friends or the onslaughts of his enemies. The Cabinet shows little more talent. It consists mainly of political hacks of the third rate, with the usual admixture of bad lawyers. The government leader in the Senate is Jim Watson of Indiana, a mountebank so puerile and preposterous that beside him even such a figure as Goldsborough of Maryland looks almost dignified. And the leader of the opposition is Borah of Idaho, a revolutionary with an unparalleled capacity for getting under cover whenever election day rolls 'round.

These are the leaders. On lower levels one encounters men so dreadful that it would be painful to describe them realistically. Nevertheless, the government goes on. There is some disorder, but not enough to be uncomfortable. A certain amount of money is wasted, but not enough to bankrupt us. The laws are dishonest and idiotic, but it is easy to imagine them worse. How are we to account for this? I can conjure up but two plausible theories. One is to the effect that the country is actually under the special protection of God, as many clergymen allege every Fourth of July. The other is that the hated and reviled bureaucracy must be a great deal more competent than it looks.

4

Roosevelt
Minor

THE CAPTION FOR THIS SECTION IS SUGGESTED BY Mencken's habit of distinguishing between the two Roosevelt presidents as Roosevelt Major (Teddy) and Roosevelt Minor (FDR). But the reader will please note that in the pieces collected under this title—running from December 8, 1930, through January 2, 1934—Mr. Mencken passes along many generous compliments to Franklin Roosevelt. Not until later does he take up the lance in earnest against FDR and the New Deal.

As we begin the section that follows, Mencken is once again raising his political periscope to see what he can spot in the way of fragile or sturdy barks bent on sailing toward the presidential nominations of 1932. At the moment, Hoover's prestige, already weakened by the rigors of the depression, has just suffered another serious blow. Not unexpectedly, the Republicans lost many seats in Congress during the fall mid-term elections of 1930, though when the returns were finally footed up they still appeared to control Congress by the slim margin of 220 to 214. But fate played an unsuspected role in the drama that followed.

Between the November elections and the organization of the Seventy-second Congress, in March, 1931, so many Republican congressmen died who were replaced by Democrats that the Republicans lost control of the House, and the Democrats organized the committees and elected their own speaker. Complicating Hoover's political leadership still more was the loss of eight Republican Senate seats, leaving the Senate divided with 48 Republicans, 47 Democrats, and one Farmer-Laborite who held the balance of power.

In the light of these serious setbacks, Mencken's judgment about Hoover's prospects for the future seem a bit bizarre. "Mr. Hoover is almost as sure of re-election next year," he writes as late as July 27, 1931, "as he was in 1928." And after juggling some electoral votes away from Hoover that he carried in 1928, Mencken insists that a Hoover victory in 1932 should still be as obvious as that "2 and 2 equal 4." Moreover, he confesses his inability to understand why everyone feels that Hoover would be beaten as badly as Taft was in 1912. Maybe we can charge Mencken's judgment here to a reluctance to follow the experts (he had no time for the pollsters and after the 1948 election he delighted in beginning his column like a merry mortician: "How could so many wizards be so thumpingly wrong?"). But even if he had talked with the Hoover inner circle at the time he would have found deep pessimism over Hoover's chances for a second term.

Somewhere along the line the joyous war whoops that Mencken let out for Smith in the 1928 campaign seemed to have been kicked under the rug as 1932 comes rushing up. And here Mencken the professional trooper shows up rather lamely when we recall that what he is now denying was precisely what he was praising Al for just a few short years and months before.

What everybody seems to have forgotten he tells us in 1931 was that "Al already was on the downgrade in 1928." And now he would have us believe that Smith made a "dreadfully pianis-

simo and inept campaign," whereas, before, he exulted in reporting that Al, though losing, had "fought a good fight," and that
no one blamed Al. "He made a gallant and gaudy campaign,"
and what really moved Mencken about Al in 1928 was that he
went down to defeat "with every flag flying and the band playing
on deck." But now his memory seems to have stalled. He speaks of
coming home from Al's campaign tours "Full of gloom," because
Al didn't throw any fast curves slightly on the demagogic side.
Had he forgotten how Al could reach for a high one and how he
was applauded at Nashville. Smith "wowed" the "Assembled
anthropoids," with a "brilliantly executed polemic," he had
written after one campaign into the South—one of many he
seemed to enjoy.

Admittedly, now that Al was no longer speaking of the wire-
less as the "raddio," and reputedly favored a morning coat over
the brown derby, Mencken was a bit bothered, as apparently
were others. But this hardly seems sufficient cause to retread
the past.

As always in Mencken's wide-ranging swings, he manages to
toss in a shiny thought about people that shows real insight.
Social psychologists have labored diligently and painfully to
lay out the theory of interactional leadership, but Mencken goes
a long way toward compacting it for us within the compass of a
single sentence. In summing up Teddy Roosevelt he tells us:
"*Life fascinated him and he knew how to make his doings fascinating to others.*" How true and how simple, for who can deny
that this was a skill that Roosevelt "Major" could play up to
the hilt, whether it involved drawing a bead on a hippo or
firing a postmaster whose organizational loyalties were beginning to be troublesome?

Here and there Mencken pauses to grapple wth a serious in-
stitutional problem in his own inimitable and amusing way. Like
the political scientist, he still wondered what we ought to do
with unsuccessful candidates for the presidency. But his solu-

tion seems a bit drastic—"that they be hanged," lest "the sight of their grief . . . have a very evil effect upon the young" (said possibly with a nod to a popular perversion of a remark by Johns Hopkins' Sir William Osler, a statement, of course, that he never made.

Not included in the articles that follow, but implied in some of Mencken's remarks, are his two-fisted blows at the farmer—a popular target of his during the early thirties. Mencken found the "windy pieties" eulogizing the farmer particularly offensive, and he usually swings from the floor in discussing this subject. A brief quote from "Bauernkrieg," a dispatch pounded out August 29, 1932, gives us a lively example:

> "One hears constantly," he writes, "from politicians with a gift for *Service* that the farmers of the land have a special claim upon the general consideration—that inasmuch as they labor in the heat of the day to raise our victuals, we ought to think of them as public benefactors, and even as altruists—in brief, that they should not be ranked with ordinary workmen and business-men, but with doctors, bishops, and perhaps even war heroes."

Twenty years later he crawled out of political retirement (as a reporter) to nail another postscript onto the same theme. Disgusted by the wild pitches to farmers from partisans of both major parties, he mourned that public office-seekers were now promising such outrageous prices to the farmer that soon we would all "be reduced to eating once a day."

The section of Mencken's writings before us closes with some observations on Franklin Roosevelt, written January 2, 1934, not quite a year after FDR had entered the presidency. Interestingly, Mencken still looks upon him in a favorable light—as a gentleman, "honest, gallant, and mellowed"—a mood, as we shall see, that shifts quickly a few months later. But that is a later story.   M. M.

LOOKING AHEAD

Eighteen months and two weeks from today a gang of wise and patriotic men and women, white and black, will meet in a hot hall in some great city of the Republic and proceed by ballot to nominate a Republican candidate for the Presidency—maybe Lord Hoover and maybe another. Two weeks later another gang, this time unanimously Caucasian, will meet in another hall in some other city and nominate a Democratic candidate— maybe Governor Ritchie and maybe not. How time does fly! It seems only last week that I sat in Kansas City and saw Jim Watson and old Charlie Curtis fight Hoover to the last ditch, and only yesterday that I sat in Houston and saw the Pope beat Bishop Cannon. But now the convention rolls round again, and pretty soon, if I am spared as I hope, I'll be packing my 14-year-old Corona and starting off to tell the old, old story once more.

I confess that national conventions always entertain me immensely. They constitute a very welcome quadrennial interlude in my habitual meditations, which have to do with grave questions of æsthetics, moral science, canon and constitutional law, dietetics, theology and *Weltpolitik*. I love to see the clans gather and to watch them at their monkeyshines—boozy, bawdy and full of hellment. It somehow delights me to behold dry United States Senators far gone in bad gin, and to observe scientifically how little the lady politicians resemble Clara Bow. I rejoice in the scandals, the combats, the imbecilities, the obscenities. There is excellent exercise for the diaphragm at a national convention: the laughing is as free and hearty as at a Methodist conference, and far more innocent.

For a long time past my associate in such sports has been Henry M. Hyde. Counting out archbishops and labor leaders, Hyde is probably the most dignified man now extant in America. Ribaldry is wholly foreign to his nature. Yet when the Hoover mercenaries, white and black, began to gather at Kansas City, with the trembling Andy Mellon at their head and the survivors of the Ohio Gang bringing up the rear, Hyde discharged such vast peals and salvos of mirth that he almost lifted the roof. And when the Pope and Bishop Cannon locked horns at Houston I began to fear seriously that he would bust.

I am surely no prophet, but it seems quite safe to predict that the next Democratic convention will nominate a wet. The chances are at least 1,000,000 to one that he will not be a Catholic, and probably two or three to one that he will not be from New York, but it is practically certain that he will be a wet. This, of course, is because of the two-thirds rule, peculiar to the Democrats. Under it, one-third of the delegates can prevent the nomination of any man they are really set against—and a good many more than one-third will be teetotally and irrevocably wet. So no dry can hope to get past them.

The drys, I believe, will have no such power of veto. No doubt they will be able to show, on the first ballot, a strength appreciably beyond one-third, but I doubt seriously that they will hold it. Too many of them, as always, will be full of convention booze—drys for home consumption only. Too many will be thinking of the cataclysm of November 4, 1930. So they will be even more ready to wobble than their predecessors were at Houston in 1928, and when the final ballot comes enough of them will be over the fence to beat the Anti-Saloon League again. But no wet will wobble. All the passion that once marked the dry side is now on the wet side. The wets are out for blood, and they will get it.

My guess is that the Anti-Saloon League will give up the Democratic party as hopeless long before the convention meets, just as it has already done in New York, Massachusetts, New Jersey, Maryland, Illinois, Ohio and a dozen other States. It will be possible, no doubt, to keep the South in line, and maybe also the more backward parts of the Middle West, but that will not be enough to win with; it will not even be enough to have a serious nuisance value. If Bishop Cannon is alive and still frocked, he will be on hand as usual, damning the Pope and glaring like a furnace-door, but the bishop's best days, I fear, are behind him. At the Houston convention the Democrats defied him. At the next one they will laugh at him.

On the other side, his chances will be far better. Dr. Hoover, as everyone knows, is now perched precariously on the fence, waiting to see what the Wickersham committee has to report, and how the country takes it. He got into office by playing with the Anti-Saloon League, but no one knows what he actually thinks about Prohibition, and the common report in Washington is that he is, in secret, more or less damp. But my guess is that, when the time comes, he will do business with the Anti-Saloon League again. If he turned wet he would split his party, drive the drys away from the polls (as the late Mr. Tuttle drove them away in New York), and run a grave chance of being heaved out of the White House. But if he continues to play dry the Anti-Saloon League and the Federal jobholders, mustering all the camp-meeting and hookworm States against the States of big cities, may be able to pull him through.

In any case, he will probably have a close squeak, for after nearly two years in office he seems to have no personal following whatever, and the general feeling is that he is a dreadful botch as President. On his merits alone it is plain that he would have no chance at all; they would be insufficient even to get him a re-nomination. That renomination, I suppose, the Federal job-holders will be able to manage for him, as they have always been able to manage it for Republican Presidents, even Taft; but in order to be reëlected he will need something more. I see no way

of getting that something more save from the Methodist bishops
and the rest of the dry outfit. If, in fact, they still have the
peasants of the country under their heels, then they may be able
to return the hon. gentleman to the White House in 1933. But
if, as begins to seem probable, even the peasants are tiring of
them, then he is in for a beating.

It will depend very largely upon the man the Democrats
nominate. If they are as foolish as they were in 1928, and name
a candidate as vulnerable as Al Smith, it will be excellent news
for Dr. Hoover. But if, showing sense for once, they put up a
man who has no inconvenient strings tied to him, and is of
pleasing personality, and knows the tricks of national politics,
then Dr. Hoover had better take a new lease on his old home in
London, and prepare to reënter the mine stock business.

So far but three aspirants of any genuine dignity have ap-
peared on the Democratic side. One is Governor Franklin D.
Roosevelt of New York, another is Governor Ritchie of the
Maryland Free State, and the third is the Hon. Owen D. Young,
LL.D. Of the three, it seems to me that Dr. Ritchie, at the
present writing, has the best chance.

The objections to Dr. Roosevelt are many. His name is a
source of strength in some areas, but probably a source of weakness in other and larger ones. The country began to grow tired
of Roosevelts even before the death of Theodore I, and its old
fondness has certainly not been restored by the mountebankeries
of Young Teddy. Dr. Roosevelt is damaged even more by the
awful name of Tammany. He is against the Wigwam and the
Wigwam is surely not in love with him, but the country in general connects the two, and will grow suspicious and uneasy as
Tammany rocks with scandal after scandal. Finally, Dr. Roosevelt waited a bit too long to come out as a wet, and the more
earnest wets, in consequence, do not trust him.

As for Dr. Young, he can be thought of only on the theory

that the country, having swallowed Andy Mellon and Dwight
W. Morrow, is now ready to swallow Wall Street *in toto*, stock-
tickers and all. He is not a senile country banker like Andy,
and hence presumably innocent, nor a penitent who has shaken
the sinful dust of Wall Street from his feet, like Morrow, but an
active and important officer in a long list of great corporations,
many of them engaged openly in grabbing the natural resources
of the country. I doubt seriously that such a candidate would
go down. Dr. Young is a man of many talents, and my agents
tell me that his private virtues are manifold, but he is simply in
the wrong business. He could no more inspire and enchant the
plain people than a hangman could inspire and enchant them.

This leaves Dr. Ritchie, Governor and Captain-General of the
Saorstat Mareann. On an early day I hope to discourse upon
his chances, and to offer some advice to his true friends.

LITTLE RED RIDINGHOOD

December 29, 1930

Once more the alibi boys of the White House gang are trying
to depict the Hon. Mr. Hoover, their patron and pattern, as a
political innocent, beset by sinful and designing men. Now it is
the Hon. Robert H. Lucas who has deceived, betrayed, embar-
rassed and undone him. A little while back it was the Hon.
Simeon D. Fess, A.B., A.M., LL.D. Before that it was the Hon.
Claudius H. Huston, B.S. And before that it was Colonel Mann,
Bishop Cannon, Ma Willebrandt, the Emperor Simmons and a
long line of other such wicked virtuosi, reaching back to the
Original Hoover Man. Always it appears that Dr. Hoover is
greatly amazed and chagrined when one of them is found out

and put to flight. And always it is hinted that he marvels that such gentry should ever get into places of honor and puissance in the party he heads and adorns.

I wonder how many people take such blather seriously? How many really believe that Dr. Hoover is as innocent politically as his whitewashers try to make him look? Probably not many. There was a time, no doubt, when their excuses and protestations were swallowed pretty widely, but that time is no more. The country has now taken the measure of Dr. Hoover, and knows him for what he is: a politician of a highly practical sort, eager for the main chance, and anything but squeamish. When it comes to choosing men he chooses bad ones almost infallibly, whether it is for places at the public trough or posts in the Republican organization. And when they depart in scandal, which is often, he plainly deserves to be held to account.

The notion that Huston was wished upon him is sheer nonsense. It was he who wished Huston on the Republican National Committee. The fellow, indeed, was an almost perfect specimen of the Hoover man, and had been a member of the intimate Hoover circle for years. He was in the Department of Commerce when Dr. Hoover was Secretary, and sat upon his right hand. In 1927 and 1928 he was in charge of the Hoover pre-convention campaign in a large sector of the Bible country, and helped to round up the blackamoors, the Ku Kluxers and the Methodist clergy. He was a towering figure at the Kansas City convention, and afterwards he led the embattled evangelists of Tennessee against the Pope.

It would be impossible to imagine a hero nearer to the Hooverian ideal. He not only measured up to it magnificently in a purely political way: he also measured up to it in every other way. He was what they call, in the Hookworm Belt, a sterling Christian business man. That is, he divided his time (forgetting politics) into two halves, and devoted the one-half to money-getting on a big scale, and the other half to saving and uplifting his fellow-men on an even bigger scale. He ran an oil company, a wheel-barrow factory and a furniture company; he was vice-president of a trust company and of a bank; he was president of the Chattanooga Manufacturers' Association and of the Chattanooga Chamber of Commerce, and, as the Senate investigation committee discovered, he often played the stock market. And on the other side he was chairman of almost every Y.M.C.A. drive that came along, an ardent supporter of prohibition and a consecrated Presbyterian.

This is precisely the sort of man that Dr. Hoover seems to admire. Whenever he has a choice between a politician who is also hot for the Y.M.C.A. and one who is not hot for the Y.M.C.A he always chooses the former. And whenever he has a choice between one who is what is called a Babbitt and one who is not, he picks the former again. Huston met his specifications perfectly. The common run of politicians are suspicious of Christian business men, but Dr. Hoover prefers them. So Huston, as Hoover's man, was forced upon the Republican National Committee—with what result readers of the Washington scareheads will remember.

There followed Dr. Fess, a Methodist pedagogue who had got on in the world and jimmied himself into the United States Senate by eager and doglike services to the Anti-Saloon League. Rather curiously for a fellow of his kidney, Fess was acutally religious and had a tender conscience, and one day it led him to blurt out a somewhat disconcerting truth, to wit, that he was a liar. This confession, made on the floor of the Senate, appalled the other Senators, for it is not etiquette among them to admit anything. But Hoover apparently had no aversion to liars, for presently he was slipping Fess into the place vacated so unwillingly by Huston. Now Fess is about to be canned by acclamation, and the next in line is the Hon. Raymond Benjamin, of California.

Of Benjamin the chief thing known is that he is the author of the California Anti-Syndicalist Act, perhaps the most drastic, cruel, disingenuous and nonsensical statute ever passed in America. He thus qualifies as a Babbitt of the most malignant sort, and, *per corollary,* as a 100% Hoover man. With thousands of Republican lawyers to choose from, some of them learned, and all of them willing, Dr. Hoover chose without hesitation the one whose chief claim to fame is that he launched the foulest blow ever delivered at the Bill of Rights and so opened the way to railroading scores of foolish and harmless men and women to prison.

Nevertheless, Dr. Benjamin is at least above the Hoover average. He may be, in his public aspect, a Babbitt of the most implacable and blood-sweating type, but in private life he is an Elk, and that is at least a fair indication that he has never taken any money from the Anti-Saloon League. The Elks, in general, are almost as wet as bankers, movie actors, newspaper editors or university presidents. Dr. Benjamin is not only a member of the order, he was once its Grand Exalted Ruler, with the rank and uniform of a field marshal. The fact is somehow reassuring. It may even mean that Dr. Hoover is preparing to turn damp.

But somehow I doubt it. His principles in this area, of course, are conveniently vague. He has never come out flat-footedly for the Noble Experiment. I believe that, if he thought it would re-elect him in 1932, he would turn himself into a thumping wet tomorrow. I go farther: I believe that he would turn Moslem or Single Taxer or New Humanist to the same end. Here I do not sneer at him: I simply call attention to the fact that he is President of the United States in this melancholy year 1930. It takes a very resilient and open-minded man, things being what they are, to get and keep that pretty job. But there is no sign that turning wet would help Dr. Hoover in the slightest; on the contrary, it would only split his party and insure his defeat. So there is every reason for believing that, no matter what the

Wickersham committee reports, he will keep on good terms with the Methodist bishops and the Anti-Saloon League.

He will, in fact, need the brethren far more in 1932 than he needed them in 1928. The Pope will not be in front of him next time, and so the Ku Klux idealism will not help him. Nor will there be a united party behind him. If he is to keep enough yokels in line to offset the bitter enmity of the cities, he must do it on the issue of prohibition, and there his principles must be in strict accord with those of Bishop Cannon, the very pattern and archetype of the Christian business man. How far the bishop will be forced to compromise remains to be seen, but you may be sure that Dr. Hoover will not compromise any more. Thus I look for many successors to Messrs. Huston and Fess. More judges of the caliber of the Hon. Richard J. Hopkins will go upon the god-forsaken Federal bench, and more visionaries of the type of the Hon. Mr. Lucas will supply copy for the sweating Washington correspondents.

Why Presidents of the United States, in these later days, should prefer such associates I don't know, but there is the fact. There was a time when the White House was frequented by interesting and amusing persons, notably during the reign of Roosevelt, but of late it is only a hangout for trash. The daily list of visitors reads like the roll call of a third-rate oyster roast, and Dr. Hoover fills his camp at the week-ends with the same dull and preposterous folk who used to snore with Dr. Coolidge on the *Mayflower*. In Harding's time it was even worse.

A President of the United States, if he has the taste for it, has access to the best society in the country. Very few men would refuse an invitation to visit him, and not many more would decline his call to the public service. But with 125,000,000 people to choose from Dr. Hoover almost always finds his man, not among the best million, but among the worst. When there is a Federal judge to be appointed he does not commonly canvass the leaders of the bar and choose a sound lawyer and an honorable man; he canvasses the dope-sheets of the Anti-Saloon League and gets a dub. So when God lays upon him the solemn duty of selecting managers for his tattered and demoralized party almost always he fixes upon candidates so dubious that they are in trouble the instant they take office.

Viewed in the most humane light imaginable, this habit is surely most unfortunate. One hates to think of a President of the United States seeking his associates and intimates in such circles. But the facts are the facts, and the historian cannot evade them. Perhaps on some doomed and distant tomorrow it will become the custom, when news arrives that this or that man has been invited to the White House, to throw him out of all decent clubs.

THE HOOVER BUST

May 18, 1931

That Dr. Hoover will be renominated by his party next year is as nearly certain as anything human can be, and that he will be reëlected at the ensuing plebiscite is highly probable. The first is true because a sitting President, at least if he be a Republican, can easily make sure of a majority of the delegates to a national convention, and at a Republican convention a majority is sufficient to nominate. He can make sure of them because most of them are Federal jobholders, and the rest, with few exceptions, are men who hope to be. Even the preposterous Taft, with Roosevelt in full rebellion against him, yet managed to be renominated in 1912, though Roosevelt, running as an independent, got more votes in the election following.

Hoover will have a much easier time of it next year. There is no Roosevelt to challenge him, and the rest of the Progressives are not likely to set up a formidable opposition. Borah, as usual, will shut off his wind-machine and put on the party collar well before the convention meets; he is always the first to give up. Nor is it likely that young Bob La Follette will make any greater pother than he made at Kansas City in 1928: he will have much to lose and very little to gain by putting on war paint. As for the rest of the Progressives, they may make some noise, but that is probably as far as they will go, for they know very well that Hoover is an easy mark, and they want him to shoot at between 1933 and 1937. A better man—and almost any conceivable man would be better—would only incommode their stroke.

The Hoover brethren are already rounding up delegates, and with unbroken success. The Hon. Walter F. Brown, Postmaster General and political agent, has just returned from the South with the Aframerican delegates in his pocket: they are always ready to do business with anyone who has jobs to dispense. Nor is there much danger to Dr. Hoover in the big States of the North —Pennsylvania, New York, Illinois and so on. Their delegations, as always, will be heavily loaded with jobholders, and the caveats of such Bolsheviki as Dr. Nicholas Murray Butler will go unheeded. Maryland will send its traditional delegation— eight jobholders and eight perfumers—and it will vote docilely for Hoover.

On the Tuesday following the first Monday in November, 1932, the hon. gentleman will face greater difficulties, but it is not likely that they will suffice to unhorse him. If the Democrats could be trusted to nominate a really strong candidate and to go into the campaign with a united front they might imaginably win, but it is highly improbable that they will do either thing. Their principal candidates, Franklin D. Roosevelt and Owen D. Young, are both full of holes, politically speaking, and they can't nominate any of their second-line men—for example, Ritchie or Cox—without a bitter fight, and a crop of very sore heads.

The trouble with them is that they do not constitute a party at all, but consist merely of a loose alliance of two desperate and naturally hostile gangs, each of which dislikes the other much more than it dislikes Republicans. The one gang is made up of big city men and women, chiefly in the East, who tire of the Methodist hegemony, and long to see it upset at any cost. The other gang is made up of peasants who are its main stalwarts, and view any attack upon it as an attack upon God. What that difference amounts to in practice was shown brilliantly in the last campaign. The big cities supported Al Smith with fanatical devotion, but the dung-hills were even more fanatically against him, and so, despite the 15,000,000 votes cast for him, he was beaten by 5,000,000.

My private belief is that the majority against him was actually much larger—that Hoover, if he had not been counted out, would have carried the whole South. Certainly he got a rough count in Alabama, Mississippi and South Carolina. In North Carolina—as I heard an eminent local statesman say in October, 1928—the local wizards were prepared to shave 50,000 from his vote, and probably did it. Unluckily, he rolled up a majority that seems to have been more than 100,000, and so he had to be let through by 60,000. What his majority was in Alabama no one will ever know, but it must have been huge, for the best the Democratic brethren could do was to count Smith in by 7,000. Davis carried the State in 1924 by 68,000, and Cox in 1920 by nearly 90,000.

I see no reason to believe that the Methodist-Baptist blood lust will be any the less fiery next year than it was in 1928, or that Dr. Hoover will be less disposed than he was the last time to put it to his uses. True enough, the Democrats are not likely to renominate Al or to name any other Catholic, but the fact will remain that they nominated a Catholic in 1928, and that will be sufficient for the pastors. Already, indeed, a movement seems to be under way to convict Governor Ritchie to taking orders from the Pope, and no doubt evidence against Dr. Roosevelt, Dr. Young or whoever else is nominated will be forthcoming at the proper time.

The pastors, having tasted blood and liked it, will certainly not keep out of next year's campaign. They had a gaudy time in 1928, and emerged from the rumpus full of a sense of power and bursting with malicious animal magnetism. No man in this world ever renounces power voluntarily. Thus I expect the rev. brothers to give another show in 1932, and look for it to be quite as gorgeous as the last one. They will lack the advantage of having an actual Catholic to shoot at, but they will have the advantage of having a sitting President, and not a mere candidate, to help them. That Dr. Hoover will help them all he can goes without saying.

I see no danger to the holy cause in the downfall of Monsignor Cannon. On the one hand, that downfall is still very far from an accomplished fact, and on the other hand there are plenty of Methodist bishops left. If Dr. Cannon is disposed of, then one of these others will take his place, with the ardent aid and comfort of the Hoover camorra of political blacklegs. But Cannon is yet full of consecrated steam, and I have every confidence that he will beat all his enemies, both within and without the fold. Those Wesleyan rebels—a small and stupid body— who now mouth charges against him are in a very weak position, for they were prudently silent at the time he was campaigning for Hoover. Nor is there any reason to believe that they would denounce him publicly if he campaigned so again. The great bulk of the faithful are with him, and will remain with him so long as he can draw blood.

The country knows Dr. Hoover far better today than it knew him in 1928. It has begun to believe that the holy war against Al was waged with his full knowledge, and probably with his active connivance. He could have stopped it easily, but the most that could be wrested from him was a feeble protest against one small detail of it. He knew very well what the Willebrandts, the Manns, the Cannons and the rest were up to, and he was quite willing to profit by it. He will be willing again, I believe, in 1932.

The more the hon. gentleman exposes his inward nature, the more it appears that he is sadly devoid of what is commonly called, for want of a better name, a sense of honor. If he has any principles, then he keeps them very liquid. I gather he is willing to say anything, or do anything, or believe anything that promises to keep him in office. His apparent weakness and irresolution are deceptive; only too often they are simply concealments for shrewd and shameless politicking. Whenever it looks feasible, he tries to get a leg over each side of the fence. Even his Methodist friends—for example, Bishop Mouzon—have been amazed and disgusted, at times, by his trimming.

In the big cities he has become the most unpopular President ever heard of. Both the babbitti and the proletariat have revolted against the legend of the Great Engineer: to mention it today, in any place large enough to have a policeman, is to provoke a howl of derision. But in the sticks he is still a hero, and there, thanks to the grotesque set-up of the Electoral College, he counts on vindication next year. To be sure, there have been murmurs against him even in the sticks, mainly because of his devious course in the recent famine. But famines come only now and then, whereas the war upon the accursed city man goes on year after year. Once the pastors resume whooping for him the yokels will fall in line, full of the old frenzy to rowel and punish their betters. It will surely not be a walk-over, but unless the Democrats are helped by a miracle, it will be victory, and we shall have four years more of bogus morality and shyster politics.

Well, the United States probably deserves it.

HOOVER IN 1932

July 27, 1931

Barring acts of God of a revolting and unprecedented character, Mr. Hoover is almost as sure of reëlection next year as he
was of election in 1928. To be sure, he will probably lose Maryland and Virginia, which he carried three years ago, and he may
also lose North Carolina, Tennessee, Texas and Florida, but he
won't need them. Altogether, they have but 70 electoral votes,
and in the last Electoral College the hon. gentleman had a
majority of 357. He could also lose New York, with its 45, and
still be as safe as a cop in a speakeasy. He could throw in Massachusetts, and not miss it. He could add Missiouri, Connecticut
and Oklahoma. He could even add Rhode Island. But still he
would beat the unfortunate heir and assign of Al Smith.

All this should be plain to anyone able to add and subtract.
It is as obvious as that 2 and 2 equal 4. Yet one constantly
hears easy prophesies that Hoover will be beaten as badly
as Taft was beaten in 1912, and even predictions that he
will lose the Republican nomination. This last is really too absurd to be discussed seriously. Is it so soon forgotten that even
Taft got himself renominated in 1912, despite the fact that his
political creator, Roosevelt, was openly in the field against him,
whooping and howling like a Comanche?

The fact is that a sitting Republican President can no more
fail of renomination, if he wants it, than a dry Senator can resist a drink. Beating him in the convention is simply a physical
impossibility. He goes into it with at least two-thirds of the
delegates irrevocably in his pocket, and a mere majority is
enough to nominate. These two-thirds are not only his for the
asking; they are his by an inescapable and irresistible natural
law, as potent as the law of gravity; they are his by the very
nature of things. For all of them are Federal jobholders—and

a jobholder always favors the boss who is in power against any conceivable boss who only may be. His sole aim and object in life is to hold on to his job—and the best way to hold on to it is to vote diligently for the man who gave it to him.

Since the moment the returns came in on that fateful night in November, 1928, Dr. Hoover has been devoting four-fifths of of his time and energy to making sure that his delegates will be safe next year. It is, in these latter days, the chief business of Presidents, and none other has ever pursued it more ardently than the innocent Wonder Boy. All of his operations, whether at home or abroad, have been shaped to that single end. Over and over again, in his appointments, he has sacrificed the public good to it, boldly and unashamed. And to the same end he has surrounded himself with a gang—some of whom are political thugs and harpies unparalleled in recent history—men so brazen and unconscionable that even the more tender professionals of his own party have more than once gagged at them.

Every delegation that goes to the convention save maybe one or two from the radical Cow States, will be constituted exactly as the Maryland delegation will be constituted. That is to say, it will be made up of a small minority of perfumers—mainly fat cats counted on to contribute heavily to the campaign fund —and a large majority of docile Federal jobholders, headed by the local Hoover patronage agent—a United States Senator, or what not. The Cow State uplifters will be permitted to do their stuff for an afternoon or so, and then there will be a vote. It will show that the jobholders are for their patron and hero to a man.

And so he will be renominated with loud hosannas, and the Democrats, who commonly hold their convention a week or two later, will confront the task of finding a candidate to beat him at the polls. Will they be able to do it? My sad and reluctant guess is that they will not. And for a plain reason: they have no hero, and seem to be unable to find one. They have plenty of aspirants, and some of them are very worthy ones, but they lack a man of really heroic mold—they have no one capable of capitalizing melodramatically the popular disgust with Hoover, no one able to make the public heart leap and pant, no one sufficiently gaudy and inflammatory to set the public hair on fire.

Not even Al. Al has been ruined, I greatly fear, by associating with rich men—a thing far more dangerous to politicians than even booze or the sound of their own voices. He has thrown away his brown derby and bought him a morning coat. He no longer says raddio. The end of his cigar no longer blinds his left eye. What is forgotten is that Al was already on the downgrade in 1928. He made a dreadfully *pianissimo* and inept campaign. The plain people turned out to hear him skin Hoover—in other words, to be thrilled and set to whooping—and he gave them a series of school-boyish declamations on the tariff, conservation and other such depressing subjects, by his staff of intellectuals out of the *New Republic*.

I had the honor of accompanying him on one of his tours, and I came home full of gloom. He had failed utterly to grab his opportunity. Obviously, his only chance of winning was by demagoging it. The Hoover orators—Ma Willebrandt, Bishop Cannon, Col. Mann and the rest—were demagoging to beat the band, and so it was fair to strike back. Moreover, Hoover himself was quite as vulnerable as Al, and probably more so. Was Al marked with the brand of Holy Church? Then what of the British coat-of-arms on Hoover's forehead? But Al kept on doggedly with his pale, preposterous *New Republic* stuff, and when the Electoral College met he had 87 votes and Hoover had 444.

If he is resurrected next year he will probably be still worse, for politicians never learn by experience. It is only the amateur who learns—and Hoover is still an amateur according to the rules, though he knows more than all the professionals. His next campaign, I believe, will be as dirty as his last. He will call in the same old gang of political parsons, with their consciences of sole leather, and he will have the aid of more and worse politicians than he had the last time. It may be that it will be impossible to pin the Pope on the Democratic candidate again, but if the Pope fails them then some other hobgoblin will be invented. Dr. Hoover is quite devoid of squeamishness in such matters, and the only way to beat him will be by an attack equally unsqueamish—in other words, by open and unlimited demagogy. But the Democrats have no one able and willing to make it.

My guess is that their nomination will go to the Hon. Franklin D. Roosevelt, if only because he is palpably less squeamish than the rest. He is a former dry who turned wet for political purposes, and is now apparently ready to go a bit dry again. The fact that the Southern professionals favor him, despite his more than amicable relations with Tammany, is damning testimony against him. They can be for him only on the ground that they are convinced of his pliability. They are against Ritchie because they believe that he will stand pat on his States' Rights platform, and they are against Owen D. Young for much the same reason. But they believe that they can do business with Roosevelt.

Perhaps they can. If so, he will get the nomination. But nominating him will be one thing, and electing him quite another. He is, in point of fact, a very poor campaigner—cautious, undramatic and not a little pedantic. At the San Francisco convention in 1920, when he was put up to do the first hot howling for Al, he made a long and dismal speech on the achievements of the Navy in the war. Running him against Hoover would simply be running one pussyfooter against another, and in the combat the odds for frankness would really be in favor of Hoover, for he has at least come out publicly and flatfootedly in favor of the Eighteenth Amendment, though in private he has let it be known that he has some doubts.

The belief that the name of Dr. Roosevelt will make millions of votes for him is probably illusory. Did it make any votes for Young Teddy in New York in 1924? As a matter of fact, the country tired of even the original Teddy long before he died, and in 1912 he carried but six States. Roosevelt is too feeble a man, both physically and temperamentally, to make the loud, raucous, ruthless, stop-thief, knock-him-down-and-drag-him-out campaign that offers the only colorable chance of beating Dr. Hoover next year. He is as incapable of it as Owen D. Young would be. Or, for that matter, Dr. Ritchie, who is too much the legal scholar—and, perhaps I should add, the statesman—to qualify as a gladiator. What is needed is rough stuff. But all that Roosevelt has to offer is a kind of equivocation at which Hoover is greatly his superior. One powder puff cannot harm another.

For these reasons I labor under the melancholy conviction that we'll have four more years of Herbert. In politics, as Mr. Kent is so fond of saying, it is impossible to beat something with nothing. The prospect is gloomy, but there are the facts. It is not prudent to cherish chimeras.

IMPERIAL PURPLE

August 17, 1931

Most of the rewards of the Presidency, in these degenerate days, have come to be very trashy. The President continues, of course, to be an eminent man, but only in the sense that Jack Dempsey, Lindbergh, Babe Ruth and Henry Ford are eminent men. He sees little of the really intelligent and amusing people of the country: most of them, in fact, make it a sort of point of honor to scorn him and avoid him. His time is put in mainly with shabby politicians and other such designing fellows—in

brief, with rogues and ignoramuses. When he takes a little holi-
day his customary companions are vermin that no fastidious
man would consort with—dry Senators with panting thirsts,
the proprietors of bad newspapers in worse towns, grafters
preying on the suffering farmers, power and movie magnates,
prehensile labor leaders, the more pliable sort of journalists,
and so on. They must be pretty dreadful company. Dr. Harding, forced to entertain them, resorted to poteen as an analgesic;
Dr. Coolidge loaded them aboard the *Mayflower*, and then fled
to his cabin, took off his vest and shirt, and went to sleep; Dr.
Hoover hauls them to the Rapidan at 60 miles an hour, and
back at 80 or 90.

The honors that are heaped upon a President in this one
hundred and fifty-sixth year of the Republic are seldom of a
kind to impress and content a civilized man. People send him
turkeys, opossums, pieces of wood from the Constitution, gold-
fish, carved peach-kernels, models of the State capitols of
Wyoming and Arkansas, and pressed flowers from the Holy
Land. His predecessors before 1917 got demijohns of 12-year-
old rye, baskets of champagne, and cases of Moselle and Burgundy, but them times ain't no more. Once a year some hunter
in Montana or Idaho sends him 20 pounds of bearsteak, usually
collect. It arrives in a high state, and has to be fed to the White
House dog. He receives 20 or 30 chain-prayer letters every day,
and fair copies of 40 or 50 sets of verse. Colored clergymen send
him illustrated Bibles, madstones and boxes of lucky powders,
usually accompanied by applications for appointment as collectors of customs at New Orleans, or Register of the Treasury.

His public rewards come in the form of LL.D.'s from colleges
eager for the publicity—and on the same day others precisely
like it are given to a champion lawn-tennis player, a banker
known to be without heirs of his body, and a general in the Army.
No one ever thinks to give him any other academic honor; he is
never made a Litt.D., a D.D., an S.T.D., a D.D.S., or a J.U.D.,

but always an LL.D. Dr. Hoover, to date, has 30 or 40 such
degrees. After he leaves office they will continue to fall upon him.
He apparently knows as little about law as a policeman, but
he is already more solidly *legum doctor* than Blackstone or
Pufendorf, and the end is not yet.

The health of a President is watched very carefully, not only
by the Vice-President but also by medical men detailed for the
purpose by the Army or Navy. These medical men have high-
sounding titles, and perform the duties of their office in full uniform, with swords on one side and stethoscopes on the other.
The diet of their imperial patient is rigidly scrutinized. If he
eats a few peanuts they make a pother; if he goes in for a dozen
steamed hard crabs at night, washed down by what passes in
Washington for malt liquor, they complain to the newspapers.
Every morning they look at his tongue, take his pulse and
temperature, determine his blood pressure, and examine his eye-
grounds and his knee-jerks. The instant he shows the slightest
sign of being upset they clap him into bed, post Marines to
guard him, put him on a regimen fit for a Trappist, and issue
bulletins to the newspapers.

When a President goes traveling he never goes alone, but
always with a huge staff of secretaries, Secret Service agents,
doctors, nurses, and newspaper reporters. Even so stingy a
fellow as Dr. Coolidge had to hire two whole Pullman cars to
carry his entourage. The cost, to be sure, is borne by the taxpayers, but the President has to put up with the company. As
he rolls along thousands of boys rush out to put pennies on the
track, and now and then one of them loses a finger or a toe, and
the train has to be backed up to comfort his mother, who, it
usually turns out, cannot speak English and voted for Al in
1928. When the train arrives anywhere all the town bores and
scoundrels gather to greet the Chief Magistrate, and that night
he has to eat a bad dinner, with only ginger-ale to wash it down,
and to listen to three hours of bad speeches.

The President has less privacy than any other American. Thousands of persons have the right of access to him, beginning with the British Ambassador and running down to the secretary of the Republican county committee of Ziebach county, South Dakota. Among them are the 96 members of the United States Senate, perhaps the windiest and most tedious group of men in Christendom. If a Senator were denied admission to the White House, even though he were a Progressive, the whole Senate would rise in indignation, even though it were 80% stand-pat Republican. Such is Senatorial courtesy. And if the minister from Albania were kicked out even the French and German Ambassadors would join in protesting.

Many of these gentlemen drop in, not because they have anything to say, but simply to prove to their employers or customers that they can do it. How long they stay is only partly determined by the President himself. Dr. Coolidge used to get rid of them by falling asleep in their faces, but that device is impossible to Presidents with a more active interest in the visible world. It would not do to have them heaved out by the Secret Service men or by the White House police, or to insult and affront them otherwise, for many of them have wicked tongues. On two occasions within historic times Presidents who were irritable with such bores were reported in Washington to be patronizing the jug, and it took a lot of fine work to put down the scandal.

All day long the right hon. lord of us all sits listening solemnly to quacks who pretend to know what the farmers are thinking about in Nebraska and South Carolina, how the Swedes of Minnesota are taking the German moratorium, and how much it would cost in actual votes to let fall a word for beer and light wines. Anon a secretary rushes in with the news that some eminent movie actor or football coach has died, and the President must seize a pen and write a telegram of condolence to the widow. Once a year he is repaid by receiving a cable on his birthday from King George V. These autographs are cherished by

Presidents, and they leave them, *post mortem*, to the Library of Congress.

There comes a day of public ceremonial, and a chance to make a speech. Alas, it must be made at the annual banquet of some organization that is discovered, at the last minute, to be made up mainly of gentlemen under indictment, or at the tomb of some statesman who escaped impeachment by a hair. A million voters with IQ's below 60 have their ears glued to the radio: it takes four days' hard work to concoct a speech without a sensible word in it. Next day a dam must be opened somewhere. Four dry Senators get drunk and make a painful scene. The Presidential automobile runs over a dog. It rains.

The life seems dull and unpleasant. A bootlegger has a better time, in jail or out. Yet it must have its charms, for no man who has experienced it is ever unwilling to endure it again. On the contrary, all ex-Presidents try their level damnedest to get back, even at the expense of their dignity, their sense of humor, and their immortal souls. The struggles of the late Major-General Roosevelt will be recalled by connoisseurs. He was a melancholy spectacle from the moment the White House doors closed upon him, and he passed out of this life a disappointed and even embittered man. You and I can scarcely imagine any such blow as that he suffered in 1912. It shook him profoundly, and left him a wreck.

Long ago I proposed that unsuccessful candidates for the Presidency be quietly hanged, as a matter of public sanitation and decorum. The sight of their grief must have a very evil effect upon the young. We have enough hobgoblins in America without putting up with downright ghosts. Perhaps it might be a good idea to hand over ex-Presidents to the hangman in the same way. As they complete their terms their consciences are clear, and their chances of going to Heaven are excellent. But a few years of longing and repining are enough to imperil the souls of even the most philosophical of them. I point to Dr.

Coolidge. He pretends to like the insurance business, but who really believes it? Who can be unaware that his secret thoughts have to do, not with 20-year endowment policies, but with 1600 Pennsylvania Avenue? Who can fail to mark the tragedy that marks his countenance, otherwise so beautifully smooth and vacant, so virginally bare of signs? If you say that he does not suffer, then you say also that a man with cholera morbus does not suffer.

On second thoughts, I withdraw my suggestion. It is probably illegal, and maybe even immoral. But certainly something ought to be done. Maybe it would be a good idea to make every ex-President a Methodist bishop.

THE MEN WHO RULE US

October 5, 1931

For his harangue to the learned brethren assembled for the reopening of Columbia University, on September 23, Dr. Nicholas Murray Butler chose the title of "Midgets in the Seats of the Mighty," and in the course of his remarks he indulged himself in some very sad reflections. The world, he said, and especially that part of it which prefers democratic government, is now run mainly by obvious third-raters. How many Presidents of the United States, since the first group of four, have fairly represented "the flower of the nation's intellect and character"? Probably five out of the twenty-six, and possibly six: Dr. Butler is not quite sure. And how many of the Prime Ministers of the Third French Republic—forty-nine in all—"will survive the same test of excellence"? "Perhaps," answers Dr. Butler, "not more than five."

Which Presidents he would nominate as superior if the police

got him into a back room at headquarters and proceeded to
loosen his tongue with lengths of rubber hose filled with **BB** shot
—this I can only guess. Most Americans, I suppose, would
agree upon Abraham Lincoln, and four out of five would add
Andrew Jackson. That makes two. The contenders for the third
place would be Cleveland, Roosevelt and Wilson, and probably
all three would get a majority of votes. We now have five. What
of the possible sixth? I search the list in vain. John Quincy
Adams? Hardly. Van Buren? Grant? McKinley? Taft? All are
plainly impossible. Coolidge? Harding? Hoover? The quest becomes ridiculous.

My suspicion, indeed, is that Dr. Butler is a good deal too
generous. Grover Cleveland undoubtedly had the "intellect and
character" that he speaks of, and I suppose we must throw in
Lincoln whether he had it or not, for he has become one of the
national deities, and a realistic examination of him is thus no
longer possible. But what of Roosevelt and Wilson? The first
was a politician long before he was a statesman, and if he were
running for the Presidency today, under the conditions that
Lord Hoover faces, there is every reason for believing that he
would take the same hopeful view of the Noble Experiment. His
Progressive world-savers, in fact, were always ready to flirt
with the Prohibitionists. As for Wilson, he was simply a pedagogue thrown up to 1000 diameters by a magic lantern, and he
never got over the shabby opportunism of the campus. If his
campaign in 1916 was honest and honorable, then honesty and
honor are words quite without meaning.

Intelligence has been commoner among American Presidents
than high character, though Grant ran against the stream by
having a sort of character without any visible intelligence whatever. He was almost the perfect military man—dogged, devoted
and dumb. In the White House he displayed an almost inconceivable stupidity. Whatever was palpably untrue convinced
him instantly, and whatever was crooked seemed to him to be

noble. If the American people could have kept him out of the Presidency by prolonging the Civil War until 1877, it would have been an excellent investment. A more honest man never lived, but West Point and bad whiskey had transformed his cortex into a sort of soup.

Very few Presidents have had IQ's as low as Grant's: even Harding was appreciably brighter. Among them, in fact, there have been some extremely sharp fellows—for example, Van Buren, Johnson and Arthur. Arthur was a Broadway character on the order of Jimmie Walker—fond of good living, full of humor, but with no more character than a Prohibition agent. He made, on the whole, a good President—certainly a better one than Garfield would have made. He was too intelligent to attempt any great reforms, and so the country got on very well during his term, and when he died at 56—the youngest ex-President, save one, to become an angel—he was sincerely regretted, especially by bartenders and philosophers. Washington, in his time, was gayer than it has ever been since. The old-timers there still talk about his parties.

Why some ribald historian doesn't do a book on the Arthur administration I can't make out, and often wonder. Washington swarmed with rogues returning after the scare they got at the end of Grant's second term, and every sort of graft prospered. After four years of Hayes' depressing Methodism, with prayer-meetings in the White House, the town was itching for a rough-house, and Arthur was the boy to provide it. It was his theory, as it is Jimmie Walker's that public office is a private bust. But he was no village guzzler like Harding: he preferred vintage wines to hard liquor, and permitted only the best to lave his tonsils.

There is also room for a study by some competent psychologist—if one exists—upon the character of Roosevelt. He was, by long odds, the most interesting man who ever infested the White House, not excepting Jefferson and Jackson. Life fascinated him, and he knew how to make his own doings fascinating to others. He was full of odd impulses, fantastic ideas, brilliant phrases. He was highly intelligent, and, for a politician, very widely read. Instead of consorting with the dull jackasses who seem to satisfy Lord Hoover he made contact with a great variety of able and entertaining men, ranging from prize-fighters to metaphysicians, and managed to dredge a lot of useful knowledge out of them. The White House, in his day, was a sort of *salon.* Today it is more like a garage.

Unfortunately, Roosevelt's extraordinary mentality was not supported by character of equivalent voltage. He was, on occasion, a very slippery fellow, and he knew how to sacrifice principle to expediency. His courage, which he loved to display melodramatically, was largely bluster: he could retreat most dexterously when ballot-boxes began to explode. On many of the capital questions which engaged the country in his time he seems to have had no settled convictions: he was, for example, both for a high tariff and against it. He belabored the trusts publicly, but granted them favors behind the door. He was a Progressive for votes only, and had little respect for most of his followers.

Roosevelt's operations during the World War were shameless. His sympathy, at the start, naturally went to Kaiser Wilhelm, for the two men were very much alike, and he defended the German invasion of Belgium with great plausibility. But later on his yearning to get back into the White House inspired him to begin badgering Wilson, and toward the end he carried that badgering to extravagant and preposterous lengths. Poor Wilson, a pedagogue and hence full of vanity and pomposity, bore the racket very badly, and it drove him into extravagances of his own. In the end, of course, he won the bout. Roosevelt passed from the scene in the melancholy rôle of a politician out of a job—and mourning for it with heavy sobs. When he died in 1919 Wilson was almost an archangel.

Coming down to Harding, Coolidge and Hoover, one finds the word character losing all intelligent meaning. Did Harding have it? Then so has any other serf of the Anti-Saloon League. Did Coolidge? Then so has a cast-iron dog on a lawn. As for Hoover, it is perhaps too soon to judge him, but certainly it is fair to say that he has shown few signs of genuine character so far. The thing we look for in men who indubitably have it—the assurance that they will act in a certain way in any new situation, and that it will be an honest, resolute and unselfish way—this excessively rare and valuable something is simply not in him. The word principle seems to have no meaning to him. The only thing he appears to think of is his job.

His intelligence, I suspect, has been vastly overrated. He belongs to a class of shiny, shallow go-getters who were much esteemed during the late Golden Age. They swarmed in the country, and were everywhere mistaken for master-minds. But now their essential vacuity is plain to all. Facing genuine difficulties, they have gone to pieces unanimously—with Hoover leading the pack. If medical men were as generally incompetent and fraudulent as these busted wizards, then all of us would be down with smallpox, cholera and yellow fever. If lawyers were as bad, then the wizards themselves would all be in jail. Hoover, like the rest of them, is a brisk and successful salesman—but it will be a long time before there is another seller's market.

What is the remedy? Dr. Butler casts a somewhat trembling eye toward a dictatorship. Experience shows, he says, that it brings "into authority and power men of far greater intelligence, far stronger character and far more courage than the system of elections." But I fear we are not yet ready for the change. The common people still have a great fear of their betters. Even Hoover is a shade too fancy for them. Before we get rid of the democratic imposture at last, we must first go through a file of sub-Hoovers and worse-than-Hoovers. Some day, I believe, a marveling world will see a Charlie Curtis, a Puddler Jim Davis, a Jim Watson, maybe even a Cole Blease in the White House. Then for the whirlwind!

THE IMPENDING CARNAGE

May 2, 1932

Six weeks from tomorrow, in the great city of Chicago, the national conventions will begin. Of the first of them, that of the Republicans, it may be predicted confidently that it will go through with all the grace, ease and dispatch of a wedding, a tonsillectomy or an electrocution. Lord Hoover already has a majority of the delegates in his corral, safely knee-haltered and with rings through their noses, and before the gavel falls he will have at least ninety-five per cent. What patriots, precisely, will represent the Maryland Free State is not yet known, but you may be sure that all of them will be persons of high Christian character who have convinced themselves, by long prayer and meditation, that Hoover is one of the massive intellects of modern times, and that he should thus be continued in office *ad infinitum.*

One hears prophecies in the illicit wineshops that the convention will see a gaudy row over Prohibition, and that the wets will try to frame the platform, but in this I take no stock. The wish is only too palpably the father to the thought. Whatever row there is will go on behind closed and puttied doors, and long before the gathering is called to order. By the time the platform is ready to be reported by the resolutions committee all factions will be strongly in favor of it, and it will be adopted with a whoop. For the Republicans never do any serious fighting in public. If Prohibition were a minor issue they might conceivably spat over it on the floor, but it is far too dangerous to be let loose, and so they will settle it in camera.

My guess is that the platform will both praise Prohibition as a great moral agency, and leave the way open to jump from under it. No doubt the straddle will take the form already proposed by the more astute drys. That is to say, it will admit the principle of a referendum, but suggest a kind of referendum— say by a four-fifths vote of the States—that will give the dry side a vast advantage. Most of the wets will be fools enough to fall for this. But whether they are fools or not they will have to submit when word comes from the White House. For practically all of them will be Federal jobholders, and no one ever heard of a Federal jobholder bold enough to resist the fiat of a sitting President.

There is a good deal of wild talk about the increasing dampness of Lord Hoover, but I can see no sign of it. He is plainly quite willing today, as he was willing when the California wine growers tackled him, to trade with the wets behind the door, but he is far too shrewd a politician to change barrels on his way over Niagara Falls. If he turned wet tomorrow he would set all the drys against him without winning any considerable number of wets. Archbishop James Cannon, Jr., head of the State church, has already warned him formally of the hazards of any such caper, and he has heard that voice before, and knows that it means what it says.

No, Hoover will stick to the dry side, at least publicly, until election day. The party platform, at best, will be a disingenuous compromise, with the wets getting the worst of it. What will keep them in line, if they are actually kept in line, will not be any overt solace from the White House, but a reassuring whisper. That whisper, in fact, is heard already. It is to the general effect that Hoover will remain faithful to the Methodist Book of Discipline until the Tuesday following the first Monday in November, but that if he is reëlected on that day he will see a great light and come to the reluctant conclusion that Prohibition is a flop.

It certainly seems reasonable. For one thing, it is well known that the right hon. gentleman, in his private capacity, is more than a little wet, and always has been. For another thing, it is also well known that he is tired of dancing to Monsignor Cannon's piping, and would be glad of a chance to kick his Grace in the pantaloons. For a third thing, and most important of all, he will be safe from reprisal if he is reëlected, and may thus indulge himself, for the first time since he entered the Harding Cabinet, in the thrilling luxury (so rarely vouchsafed to an American statesman) of integrity. The drys themselves plainly believe that he is meditating some such wicked step. They show a great nervousness, and keep their snouts close to the White House keyhole. More than once they have made threats that reveal how sadly their old complete confidence in the Wonder Boy has decayed.

In theory, they have already lost the Democratic convention, but that is only in theory. In fact, they will be on hand with their drums beating, and the chances are very good that they will be able to stage a gory bout on the floor. The Democrats, unlike the Republicans, always do their fighting in public, and seem to like nothing better than a prolonged and implacable combat, with both sides reduced to tatters. They even fight desperately when there is no serious issue. But this time there will be a serious issue, and I see no way, short of divine intervention, to compose it.

The truth is that the Democratic party, as I have often pointed out in this place, is no party at all, but simply an illogical and uncomfortable compound of irreconcilable factions. Between the urban wets who constitute its chief voting strength and the rustic drys who still intimidate its councils there is no more possibility of peace than there is between cats and rats,

Babbitts and *intelligentsia*, or the Sacred College and the Ku
Klux Klan. The two sides hate each other with a hatred that is
bitter and incurable. Each on occasion has gone over to the
Republicans, openly and with loud hosannahs, to beat the other.
Neither would hesitate to do it again tomorrow.

I see no way to compromise the differences between these
factions over platform and candidate. They are at the opposite
poles, and will remain there. To be sure, they always manage,
after a week or so of brutal combat, to put together a platform,
and after another week of even worse mayhem and battery, to
nominate a standard-bearer, but a full half of them go home
convinced that the standard-bearer is a fraud and a scoundrel,
and virtually all of them are strongly against the platform. No
one ever heard of a Democrat who actually believed in Democracy. He always keeps on protesting after the vote has been
taken, and he usually tries to upset its verdict. And if he can't
do it by fair means, then he is always willing to try foul. The
history of the party is one long record of ambushes, treasons
and kidnappings. It has always turned upon its own leaders,
and it has always deserted and made a mock of its so-called
principles.

At the moment the Hon. Franklin D. Roosevelt, LL.D., seems
to have the edge on the other Democratic aspirants, but the
returns from Massachusetts and Pennsylvania show that he still
has a heavy fight on his hands, and we may have every confidence that that fight will be carried on in a berserker and
suicidal fashion. No one, in fact, really likes Roosevelt, not even
his own ostensible friends, and no one quite trusts him. He is a
pleasant enough fellow, but he has no more visible conscience
than his eminent kinsman, Theodore Dentatus. His chief
strength at this moment does not lie among people of his own
place and kind, but among the half-witted yokels of the cow and
cotton States, and these hinds prefer him, not because they have
any real confidence in him, but simply because they believe he

can split New York, and so beat Al Smith and the Pope. That beating Al and the Pope will also, in all probability, involve losing New York altogether, and maybe most of the other essential Northern States with it—that fact, since they are Democrats, does not concern them for an instant.

Whether Al and his friends can stop Roosevelt at Chicago, and force the nomination of Governor Ritchie or some other more seemly candidate, is something that no one knows at this writing. But one thing is pretty sure: that whether Roosevelt wins or Ritchie wins or some third man wins, the row will end with sore heads on both sides, and the chosen candidate will go into the campaign with a shattered and almost hopeless party behind him. If Roosevelt is nominated the big cities will cut him, for they see him flirting with the dry witchburners, and so distrust his wetness. And if an honest wet is nominated, then the Southern lynchers and Middle Western revivalists will vote for Hoover—perhaps not in as large numbers as they did in 1928 but at any rate in numbers sufficient to reëlect him. Hoover will be renominated by the Republicans, but if he is returned to the White House it is Democratic votes that will return him.

I see no way out save for the Democratic party to throw overboard all its half-civilized country jakes, whether Southern or Middle Western, and start off anew as the party of the big cities. If it did that it would attract millions of Republicans instantly, and thus gain more than it lost. Moreover, it would acquire a coherent and plausible platform, and be free to develop competent and honest leaders. At one stroke it would get rid of all its Bryans, McAdoos, Roosevelts, Heflins and Huey Longs, and at the same stroke it would force the Republicans irrevocably into the arms of the yahoos. Not only would the party itself escape those yahoos, but the country as a whole would escape them.

What chance is there that anything of the sort will happen? I see next to none. The Democrats seem to be committed irretrievably to fraud and imbecility. They will keep on making an indecent spectacle of themselves until they bring their party down to ruin, and maybe the nation with it.

WHERE ARE WE AT?

July 5, 1932

There is no disguising the fact that beating Lord Hoover and the Injun with Roosevelt Minor and the Texas Bearcat is not going to be easy. The betting odds tell the story quite as well as long argument. At the time when the Allies seem to be prevailing, the Chicago sports offered 5 to 1 that Governor Ritchie, if nominated, would defeat Hoover. But when the nomination went to Roosevelt they began offering 10 to 1 that Hoover would win. Bookmakers, of course, sometimes err, just as the other varieties of mathematicians err. But in this case their guess is also the guess of the majority of practical politicians.

Mr. Roosevelt enters the campaign with a burden on each shoulder, and neither is a light one. The first is the burden of his own limitations. He is one of the most charming of men, but like many another very charming man he leaves on the beholder the impression that he is also somewhat shallow and futile. It is hard to say precisely how that impression is produced: maybe his Christian Science smile is to blame, or the tenor overtones in his voice. Whatever the cause, the fact is patent that he fails somehow to measure up to the common concept of a first-rate man. Moreover, there is his physical disability. He struggles against it in a most gallant manner, and will certainly never let it down him, but all the same it would be idle to say that he is as fit as a normal man.

The burden on his other shoulder is even heavier. It is the

burden of party disharmony. As I have so often noted in this place, the Democrats are really divided into two parties, and each distrusts and dislikes the other more than it distrusts and dislikes the common enemy. No man can become the Democratic standard-bearer without leading one faction against the other, and then having to face the losing faction's lust for revenge. At Houston, four years ago, the beaten Bible students from the South and Middle West walked out on Al Smith, holding their noses. And at Chicago last week the beaten Al Smith men from the big cities walked out on Roosevelt, to the sinister tune of Bronx cheers.

There were, of course, plenty of sincere Roosevelt men in the convention, but they fell far short of the strength needed to make the nomination. It would probably be safe to say that they numbered no more than 200 altogether. The rest of the necessary votes came from delegates who were not primarily Roosevelt men, but simply anti-Smith men. Some of them were Ku Kluxers who revolted against Al in 1928, and were eager only to smash him again. Others were more seemly fellows who believed honestly that he had caused enough trouble for the party, and ought to retire. Together, these factions probably mustered 400 votes, divided God knows how. The 200 really sincere Roosevelt votes, added to them, made 600, leaving the nomination still in the air. It was achieved by the flop of the slippery McAdoo, who hated Smith even more than the frank Ku Kluxers, and was full of a yen to ruin him.

That this ruin was accomplished I verily believe. It was due in part to the strength and ferocity of the factions thus lined up against poor Al, but even more to his own folly and ineptitude. From the moment he arrived in Chicago he made only blunders. First, he insisted idiotically that he could get the nomination himself, and announced that he would fight for it to the last ditch. Then, when it became plain that he could halt Roosevelt only by stepping down and organizing and leading the Allies, he approached the job so clumsily that they quickly deserted him and turned to former Senator James A. Reed. And finally, after letting it be known that if the worst came to the worst he would take to the platform and destroy Roosevelt utterly with a brutal and unanswerable speech, he fled from the hall in silence, his tail between his legs.

What has happened to Al I do not know. But that he is no longer the resilient and indomitable leader of yesteryear must be plain to everyone. The Happy Warrior has been transformed by some black magic into an ill-humored and ineffective fellow, bent only upon a melodramatic vengeance. He may get it in November, but if so it will do him no good. For he is almost as dead, politically speaking, as John W. Davis or James M. Cox. When he walked out of the convention nearly 200 delegates were still faithful to him, but no such number will ever vote for him again.

If, however, his defeat disposes of him, it does not rid the party of his ghost. That ghost will walk on election day, and its operations, I suspect, will be painfully visible in the old Smith territory, which is to say, in the big cities of the East and Middle West. Roosevelt will probably carry all the Southern States that Al lost in 1928, despite the difficulties that the repeal plank is bound to raise in some of them, but he will certainly lose New York, and there is little chance that he will carry Massachusetts and its tributaries. He may win nevertheless, but if he does it will be by a kind of miracle.

Almost any of the other candidates before the convention (I except, of course, Al) would have stood a better chance, if nominated, of beating Hoover. This is especially true of Governor Ritchie. He showed a very high degree of political skill while the Smith-Roosevelt combat was on, and though he failed to get on the ticket in the end he at least came out with many new friends and greatly enhanced prestige. Hundreds of delegates went home regretting that he had not been nominated. He would have been strong precisely where Roosevelt is weak—in the big cities of the Northeast—and it would have been easy for him to conquer the South.

But Roosevelt won, and now the party begins the campaign with a candidate who has multitudes of powerful and implacable enemies, and is in general far too feeble and wishy-washy a fellow to make a really effective fight. Soon or late the voters of the country are bound to ask themselves two questions. The first is, In what way precisely is he better than Hoover? And the second is, what has he ever done to justify making him President? These questions are going to be hard to answer. Ritchie might have answered them, but not Roosevelt. He got the nomination without adequate reason, and that lack of reason will haunt the campaign.

The downfall of Smith brought back a whole flock of political cadavers, some of them resident in the boneyard for four, eight and even twelve years. If it was astonishing to see William G. McAdoo return to the fray, it was even more astonishing to see Josephus Daniels and A. Mitchell Palmer. I confess that I almost fainted myself when I discovered that Palmer, as Roosevelt's agent, was writing the platform. He got a dreadful beating on his Prohibition plank, which was rejected ignominiously by the really wet wets, but he played an important part in the proceedings otherwise, and if Roosevelt is elected he will no doubt return to Washington, and resume his patriotic assault upon the Bill of Rights.

It is a good measure of Roosevelt that Palmer is his friend and supporter. Try to imagine an honest Progressive resorting to such company! I often wondered, during the grotesque agonies of the convention, what the Hon. Thomas J. Walsh thought of it, but I was too discreet to ask him. It was Walsh, in the closing days of the Wilson Administration, who put an end to the Palmer reign of terror, and yet here the two of them were lying down in the same bed! But that, alas, is always the fate of Democrats. Either they must lie with their natural enemies, or they must go without sleep at all.

My guess is that Roosevelt, before the campaign proceeds very far, will try to pull some of the teeth of the repeal plank. He essayed a preliminary yank in his speech of acceptance, by denouncing the saloon. The really wet wets are not against the saloon: they are in favor of it, and they hope to see it restored —if not under its old name, then under another. But the biblical scholars from the South and Middle West will have to do a great deal of yowling against it to placate their pastors and the ladies of the W.C.T.U., and they will demand some aid and comfort from the standard-bearer. Everyone will recall how long he kept silent about Prohibition when repeal first became a serious issue. But this time silence will not be enough: he will have to say something. If what he says is uncompromisingly wet, he will be in trouble in the Hookworm Belt, and if what he says shows the slightest dryness his ruin will be complete in the Babylons.

Altogether, the right hon. gentleman is on a hot spot. I shall vote for him as in duty bound. Anything to get rid of Hoover and his camorra of Republican blacklegs! I'd vote for a Chinaman to beat them, or even a Methodist bishop. But I greatly fear that there will be insufficient Americans of like mind to reëstablish and perpetuate the Roosevelt dynasty.

THE HOOVER BUST

October 10, 1932

The collapse of Dr. Hoover is one of the most curious phenomena ever seen in American politics. In mid-July, with both national conventions over, he seemed to have an easy victory

ahead of him. His own party had made a limber straddle on
Prohibition, and was appealing with some apparent success to
both wets and drys. The Democrats, having gone the whole hog,
could appeal only to the wets, and in that quarter they faced
the bitter discontent of the Al Smith men, who were strongest in
the big cities, precisely where votes were most needed. Moreover,
the Democrats, as usual, were also split on other issues, and not
a quarter of them were really in favor of their candidate, Dr.
Roosevelt. It looked like a walkover for Hoover, and the betting
odds on him went up to 5 to 1.

But now they are running the other way and it is manifest
to everyone that if he squeezes through in November it will be
by the narrowest of margins. His own party, as an organization, remains behind him, but he has suffered great losses among
the rank and file, and those losses appear to be increasing. All
the straw votes are against him, save only in New England.
Even Pennsylvania, the Republican Gibraltar, begins to show
signs of wabbling. Beginning with the returns from the Maine
elections, nothing but bad news has reached Republican headquarters, and in consequence the strategy of the campaign has
been revised two or three times, and Dr. Hoover himself, who
had planned to sit in Washington and let Roosevelt do all the
hollering, has been forced to take to the stump.

What effect his stumping will have remains to be seen. His
opening speech at Des Moines, like his speech of acceptance,
was very fair hokum, as hokum goes in politics, and it may have
won back a few waverers. He is still a bad speaker, but he has
begun to hire competent rhetoricians to compose his state
papers, and they are thus much better stuff than they used to
be. A really good orator might have made a lot of the Des
Moines speech. There were some fine spots in it for eye-rolling,
breast-beating and breath-catching, and even for a moderate
shedding of tears. But Dr. Hoover rolled it off in his customary
dull way, and it is unlikely that it was much more moving in the

actual hall than it was by radio. He is the sort of man who, if he had to recite the Twenty-third Psalm, would make it sound like a search warrant issued under the Volstead act.

The Hoover apologists, who still survive, though in rapidly decreasing numbers, try to make it appear that the right hon. gentleman is suffering unjustly at the hands of the plain people —that he is being blamed for calamities that he is no more responsible for than the policeman on the beat. This, of course, is true, though only with qualifications. A President naturally has to take rather too much of the blame when things go badly, just as he naturally gets far too much of the credit when they go well. If the Coolidge prosperity had continued, Hoover would be basking in it today, and asking for and getting votes on the strength of it. Thus it is no more than the fair trade risk of his job for him to be damned somewhat excessively for the present Depression.

Indeed, he deserves to suffer much more of that damning than any ordinary President would have had to face, for he was elected in 1928 on the representation that he had far more than the average skill of American politicians in economic matters, and that electing him was thus a sort of insurance against trouble in that department. His sponsors certainly did not advertise him as an ordinary politician, eager only for the job. They advertised him as a master mind, and he himself let it be known that he was loaded for any kind of economic bear that might come down from the woods. But when the bears actually appeared he turned out to be quite helpless before them, and his friends are finding it hard today to show that his panicky shots have really drawn any blood.

In his Des Moines speech he boldly claimed credit for every measure that has been taken to combat the Depression, but it would not be hard to show that he had little to do with most of them, and that he opposed some of them violently. One or two examples will suffice. First, the German moratorium. He not only did not invent it; he actually fought it off for months, and agreed to it only after it was too late to do much good. Again, there is the matter of reducing Government expenses. The time for that reduction was back in 1930, but Hoover did not come to it until the last session of Congress, and the plan he then proposed was accompanied by so gross an overestimate of the Government's revenues that it was virtually useless.

Thus his Des Moines speech, despite its flowing periods, was largely compounded of hooey, and it seems unlikely that it made him any substantial number of votes. Those it convinced were simply those who were already eager for conviction. Even the farmers who heard it must have smiled at the statement that "the farmers of America are not selfishly interested in their own industry alone." Farmers as a class are a dumb lot, but they never forget which side of their bread is buttered. If, indeed, they have any other politics than their own self-interest, then no one has ever heard of it. Thus I can't imagine them being deceived by Dr. Hoover's tall talk about the benefits flowing to them through the current tariff. All they know is that under that tariff they are poorer than ever before—and that is enough.

But the election is not going to be decided by a debate over farm relief. Everyone save the farmers themselves has been long aware that no conceivable juggling with the tariff can do them any good. If they are ever to get their business back upon a paying basis they must first reorganize it in a rational and efficient manner, and that is something they seem incapable of. In all probability better times for farming will not come until practically all of the existing farmers are starved out and converted into wage slaves, and more competent men take over the sad tickling of the soil. Meanwhile, only politicians looking for office talk of farm relief, and only the stupidest sort of farmers pay any heed to them.

The real issue in this campaign is something else again.

Unless I greatly err, that issue is Prohibition. It is dry votes that will have to save Dr. Hoover, if he is really to be saved, and it is wet votes that, far more probably, will elect Dr. Roosevelt. Politicians always try to duck Prohibition, for most of them, at some time or other in the past, have been burnt by it. But this time, I venture to suspect it will not down, for a clear majority of the American people have made up their minds to get rid of it. They know by experience that Depressions may be endured, but they also know by experience that Prohibition is completely intolerable. For every vote that Roosevelt gets by piling Ossa on the Pelion of Hoover's nonsense about saving the farmers, he will get a dozen votes, and maybe even a hundred, by being really wet.

I believe that it is in this direction that Hoover's real weakness is chiefly to be found—that the plain people have turned against him, not because he did not perform miracles, but because his dealings with the Prohibition question destroyed their confidence in his *bona fides*. When he went into office they thought of him as a sort of super-politician, even as a sort of anti-politician, and they trusted him to handle Prohibition in a more frank and competent manner than the professionals. He seemed to be doing so when he appointed the Wickersham Commission, but when its report came in and he leaped into the arms of the Anti-Saloon League it was seen by everyone that he was simply a mountebank like the rest. From that moment he became a suspicious character to multitudes. He remains a suspicious character today, and it is in that rôle that he seems doomed to ignominious defeat in November.

Like most other politicians, Hoover greatly underestimated the public fury against Prohibition. He believed that the Anti-Saloon League would hang on for a long while, and he was very fearful of offending its grand goblins. So he pigeon-holed the Wickersham report, his confidential agents deliberately misrepresented its contents, and he prepared to run for reëlection as an uncompromising dry. When the Republican National Convention met at Chicago he discovered suddenly that this was bad medicine, and undertook his celebrated flop and straddle, but it was too late. All he achieved by it, in fact, was to turn most of the honest drys against him, and to make the wets more suspicious of him than ever before. His whole course, once it was examined calmly, was seen to be disingenuous, devious and unconvincing. The people had a right to hear the candid opinion of their President, but all they got from him was a string of discordant and preposterous false pretenses.

No wonder they distrust him now. They have sized him up, and got his measure. They know by hard experience that he is not to be trusted. Instead of the competent and conscientious administrator who asked for their votes in 1928 they see before them only a shifty and shabby politician, his back to the wall. If he is beaten in November, as seems certain, he will be getting only what he deserves. No American President ever went into the White House with better opportunities, and no President has ever failed so ingloriously to meet the reasonable demands of his high and formerly honorable office.

PRE-MORTEM

October 24, 1932

The Republican grand goblins, having given up hope of reëlecting Lord Hoover on November 8, now devote themselves *con amore* to concocting what, on less exalted levels, would be called his alibi. He will go to the block, they say, as a sacrifice to the public's notorious incapacity for cerebral functioning. He will be butchered at the polls, brutally, melodramatically and against all justice and reason, because it blames him for the Depression, and pants to punish him. All this, we are told, should be deplored by every right-thinking man, whether Republican or Democrat, Christian or heathen, white or colored, for the right hon. gentleman really had no more to do with bringing on the Depression than Babe Ruth or Aimée Semple McPherson, and all his magnificent talents have been consecrated for months past to trying to get rid of it.

In this there is some sense, but not much. Without question, Dr. Hoover is receiving rather more blame for the present discontents than he deserves, just as he would be receiving a great deal more credit than he deserved if prosperity still raged among us. But the plain people, after all, are not quite such fools as his apologists try to make them out. They do not, in fact, blame him for causing the Depression, or even for neglecting to take measures against it; they simply blame him for failing so miserably to cure it. And in so blaming him they are on ground that is surely solid enough for all practical purposes, for he was sold to them in 1928 as a wizard who could keep the ball of plenty in the air forever, and when he let it fall at its first wobble, and it cracked his head, and then knocked him down and rolled him out as flat as a pancake, they had every support in logical science for concluding that he was actually a dud, and had got their votes by false pretenses.

Dr. Hoover did not go into office as an ordinary American politician (*Blatta sapiens*). His agents did not represent him to be the usual and familiar amalgam of knave and imbecile, so natural and normal to public life under democracy. On the contrary, they represented him to be a most extraordinary and even miraculous character, politically speaking. They said that he had a genuine genius for public affairs, perhaps unparalleled in the world, and especially for public affairs of an economic nature. They said that his brain was an organ of astounding virtuosity, and could grasp and solve any conceivable problem with almost supernatural speed and accuracy. And they said, finally, that he was a man of peculiar and lofty rectitude, a hater of shams and dodges, a life-long adherent of the true, the good and the beautiful, a sturdy individualist, the captain of his own soul—in brief, the complete antipolitician.

Alas, all of these specifications turned out to be bogus. Hoover failed on every count, publicly, grossly and abjectly. No wonder the plain people are sore.

If he were Harding, I suspect, their soreness would fever them a great deal less, but they know, by long experience, what to expect of ordinary politicians. But Hoover came in as the antithesis of Harding, and when it began to appear that he was not only quite as bad but even rather worse there was a burst of natural indignation. I say worse advisedly. Harding brought a gang of political blacklegs to Washington, but Hoover has fetched in a larger gang, and a more impudent one. Harding played with the Anti-Saloon League and other such indecent organizations, but Hoover has played even more ardently. Harding often sacrificed the public interest, especially in his appointments, to his private political advantage, but Hoover has sacrificed it oftener, and more shamelessly. Harding, confronting public problems of grave importance, met them like an idiot, but Hoover has met them like two idiots.

There has never been, indeed, a more incompetent President, or one whose *bona fides* were more painfully in question. The public distrust of him is wholly justified by his record. It is impossible to imagine a really honest man making some of his appointments—for example, that of the Anti-Saloon League hireling to the Federal bench in Kansas. And it is impossible to imagine a really sensible man mauling and manhandling anything as badly as he mauled and manhandled the scotching of the bonus morons. Over and over again he has failed in intelligence, and over and over again he has failed in good faith. The reasonable public expectation is that a President, facing the business of his office, will bring to it, at the least, the prudence, the sagacity and the integrity that one looks for in a traffic cop. But Hoover, half of the time, has acted like a not too bright schoolboy, and the rest of the time he has acted like a Prohibition agent or a Methodist bishop.

No, the plain people do not prove that they are fools by doubting him. They proved that they were fools, four years ago, by trusting him. He had sat for eight years in the stench of the Harding-Coolidge Washington without uttering a sound of protest, or even making a face. His campaign was carried on in a brazen and disgraceful manner, and his agents raised up hatreds that we'll be a generation living down. He was surrounded by the worst politicians ever heard of. Yet the country swallowed him, and he won. I only hope that those who vote against him on November 8 will remember, if they voted for him four years ago, how much they are themselves responsible for the evils they denounce.

My guess is that the thing which really finished the right hon. gentleman was his singularly disingenuous and unconvincing dealing with Prohibition. Like most other politicians, he greatly underestimated the importance of the question. In so far as he thought of it at all, he apparently thought that the Anti-Saloon League was dug in so securely that it would last for a long while, and that the best way to grease the way for 1932 would be to play dry. But to play dry openly was not the Hoover way of doing things. He simply could not come out frankly, laying his cards on the table. Instead, he entered into friendly dealings with the dry bosses in secret, and tried to stall off the wets by appointing the Wickersham Commission. The drys ran the Prohibition Bureau and got their agents on the Federal bench. The wets could wait.

It seems to me that a fair reading of the record indicates that Dr. Hoover expected the Wickersham Commission to bring in a dry report. There were, to be sure, several wets on it, but the chairman, as the event showed, could be trusted, and so, apparently, could a majority of the other members. Every hint that issued from official quarters while the commission was sitting pointed to a report satisfactory to the Hoover-Anti-Saloon League combination. Unluckily, there were honest men among the members, even on the dry side, and their investigation convinced them that Prohibition was not only a failure, but also a public nuisance. So they said so in their report.

Everyone will recall what painful scenes that report produced at the White House. On the appointment of the commission it had been the public understanding—and it was a fair inference from everything that Hoover had ever said openly on the subject—that its recommendations would be followed. But instead of following them Hoover permitted his office to send out a false version of the report, representing it to be dry in tendency, and then hastened to announce loudly that he was still dry himself, and unalterably opposed to any abandonment of the Eighteenth Amendment. The professional drys rejoiced, but the country coughed behind its hand. There was plainly something tricky about the whole business.

No further discussion of the question came from the White House. The American people debated it furiously for months, but the President of the United States was silent. Obviously, he thought that the wet movement would soon blow over. The dry imperial wizards, seeing him behind the door, reported to their customers that he was still satisfactory to them. This went on until the week before the Republican national convention. Then, of a sudden, it dawned upon him that the country had really gone wet. The delegates, rolling in from all points of the compass, reported that Prohibition was dead. At once the dry plank that had been prepared was scrapped, and a straddle was quickly concoted. But the country only laughed, and when, two weeks later, the Democrats went the whole hog the November 8 débâcle was already in the making.

How can anyone believe that Dr. Hoover's dealings with this

grave problem have been candid and honest? How can anyone believe, reading his speech of acceptance, that he spoke his true mind when he repudiated the Wickersham Report? What evidence was before him in August of this year that was not before him in March, 1930? If he favors resubmission now, why did he fight it so implacably and so long, while the proofs that Prohibition was bankrupt mounted around him on every side, convincing every sensible man? And if, favoring resubmission, he still hesitates to advocate repeal, then how, precisely, does he figure that resubmission without repeal will do us any good?

The American people have been giving a great deal of thought to these questions, and to others like them. Their answer is that they are tired of Hoover, and want no more of him. He had a magnificent chance, but he muffed it. He muffed it because there is something in his character that makes it impossible for any rational person to trust him.

A TIME TO BE WARY

March 13, 1933

Mr. Roosevelt's appeal to the American people, in his inaugural address, to convert themselves into "a trained and loyal army willing to sacrifice for the good of a common discipline," and his somewhat mysterious demand, immediately following, that they "submit" their *lives* as well as their property to "such discipline"—this appeal and demand, as everyone knows, have met with a hearty response, and almost all of us are now looking forward confidently to that "larger good" which he promised in the same breath. Only the war heroes have done any conspicuous holding back, and for that, perhaps, both the President and the country will forgive them, for they got horse-doctor's doses of training and loyalty in 1917-18, and it is thus no wonder that they are somewhat shy of those elixirs today.

But just what the eminent speaker meant by his mention of lives is not clear. Can it be that he proposes to seize and hang some investment bankers? If so, there are plenty of likely candidates for his gallows. My private belief, long ago set forth in this place, is that it would be an excellent idea to hang half a dozen such idealists every year, in good times as in bad, along with a like number of judges, the whole current corps of Prohibition agents, and maybe 10,000 or 15,000 head of lawyers. (I reserve the clergy for the lions and tigers of the arena, as the intelligent Romans did.) If I have never pushed this sanitary scheme with any fire and fury it is only because I have always feared that the wrong candidates might be chosen, to the sorrow of judicious men. In a plebiscite, indeed, democracy being what it is, the six best investment bankers would probably run quite as much risk as the six worst, and the first nominees among the judges would be Mr. Justice Brandeis and Mr. Justice Holmes.

But if the great masses of the plain people, in such grave and difficult matters, are apt to err, there is no evidence that the statesmen who ride them so dashingly are much better. We have had two dictatorships in the past, one operated by Abraham Lincoln and the other by Woodrow Wilson. Both were marked by gross blunders and injustices. At the end of each the courts were intimidated and palsied, the books bristled with oppressive and idiotic laws, thousands of men were in jail for their opinions, and great hordes of impudent scoundrels were rolling in money. The natural consequences of the Wilson dictatorship still afflict us—for example, in the form of Prohibition. Thus I hesitate to go with Dr. Roosevelt all the way. My property, it appears, is already in his hands, but for the present, at least, I prefer not to hand over my life.

This, of course, is not because I have any doubt about the

right hon. gentleman's *bona fides.* On the contrary, I have the utmost confidence in his good intentions, and I believe further that he has carried on his dictatorship so far with courage, sense and due restraint. But it is always well, when anything of the sort is set up in a presumably free country, to scrutinize it very carefully and even biliously, lest it get out of hand. Who can forget what happened when Wilson was turned loose in 1917? He too was a Liberal, and he began with sweet talk about feeding orphans, putting down tyranny, and saving humanity. But he ended with A. Mitchell Palmer's spies roving the land, with every avenue for the exchange of honest opinion barricaded, with the press paralyzed and the people cowed, and with thieves more prosperous, and safer, than they had ever been before in American history.

Dr. Roosevelt, it seems to me, is a far better man than Wilson, and on all counts. He is not an inflated pedagogue with a messianic delusion, but a highly civilized fellow, and there is a good deal of humor in him. Thus there is not much likelihood that he will run amuck as Wilson did. But Roosevelt, let us remember, is only one man, and he can't do everything himself: he must depend upon others—some of them close to him and under his eye, but most of them pretty remote. The danger lies in what those others may do, once a dictatorship is really in effect. Who believes that they will always act prudently, moderately, sensibly? Certainly no one who has any acquaintance with the course of dictatorships in the past, whether in this country or elsewhere.

Always they resolve themselves into huge bureaucracies, and a bureaucracy is a public menace in direct ratio to its power. In normal times it annoys us devilishly without doing us much serious damage, but when it has Authority with a big A behind it it invariably puts on a circus in the grand manner. The bureaucrat begins, perhaps, by doing only what he conceives to be his sworn duty, but unless there are very efficient four-wheel brakes upon him he soon adds a multitude of inventions of his own, all of them born of his professional virtuosity and designed to lather and caress his sense of power. Here my figures of speech may be mixed, but my meaning should be clear. The only good bureaucrat is one with a pistol at his head. Put it in his hand and it's good-by to the Bill of Rights.

Thus I presume to hope, if such hopes are licit in these unhappy days, that Congress will go very slowly in making further grants of its constitutional powers. They will all be made, in form, to the President, but they will be made in fact to a great army of jobholders, some of them intelligent but most of them fools. The banks are already being run by telegrams from Washington, each bearing an eminent signature but all of them in truth anonymous. It may be necessary, as I believe it is, but let us not delude ourselves into thinking that it is altogether safe. That right to be wrong which Liberals demand for all men is one of the inalienable perquisites of bureaucrats, and they habitually exercise it in a manner which makes the efforts of other men seem puny.

The best that can ever be said of them, looking at them in the most friendly light, is that they are not quite so bad as party politicians. This, in fact, is what everybody is saying today; it is the most often heard rationalization of the general belief that Congress has been throttled at least, and its howling mountebanks put in their places. We know by bitter experience just what would be happening if the ordinary constitutional processes were in operation. In the Senate all the Borahs and Huey Longs would be in full blast, and in the House there would be the immemorial manœuvering for position, popularity, party advantage. It would be going too far, perhaps, to say that the most absurd plan for dealing with the emergency would certainly win, but everyone will agree that the best plan would certainly not go through without long delays and serious emasculation.

We get rid of this danger by taking the whole business out

of the hands of the Borahs and Huey Longs, the Raineys and Snells, and putting it into the hands of the President, which is to say, into the hands of a vague group of financiers, economists and other more or less dubious "experts" revolving around his Secretary of the Treasury, the handsome and dashing Dr. Woodin. Everyone believes, at the moment, that they are disinterested, and everyone hopes that they are competent. But the only way to make sure that they, or their successors, are either or both is to keep alive a sufficient suspicion that they are not.

In brief, all bureaucracies will bear close watching, and none more so than that which comes into power on a wave of popular enthusiasm, and with the avowed purpose of saving the country from ruin. I suggest, as a practical measure in the present case, that the able corps of Washington correspondents give some scientific attention to the gentlemen constituting Dr. Woodin's cabinet of advisers. Among them there seems to be at least one gentleman whose economic studies in the past have been largely confined to speculating in Wall Street, and perhaps there may be others. If it turns out that they are all altruists, then no harm will be done by establishing and publishing the fact. But if it turns out that some of them have axes to grind, then it will be valuable to know it.

What I here suggest is by no means a general walk-out on Dr. Roosevelt. He is tackling the problem before him in a very vigorous manner, and he seems to be moving toward its solution. He is obviously not infallible, but it is certainly refreshing to behold his courage and enterprise after four years of the pathetic mud-turtle, Lord Hoover. There has probably been no President since Cleveland who was better worthy of the immense and almost singular powers now put in his hands. But even the best dictatorship ought to have clearly defined limits, and its end ought to be kept in sight from its beginning. If the American people really tire of democracy and want to make a trial of Fascism, I shall be the last person to object. But if that is their mood, then they had better proceed toward their aim by changing the Constitution and not by forgetting it. And they had better remember that Fascism means not only rough usage for crooked bankers but also rough usage for multitudes of far better men.

THE TUNE CHANGES

March 27, 1933

So far Mr. Roosevelt has been giving us things, and getting in return a deafening acclaim. First came his swift and resolute effort to clear up the bank situation, then came his onslaught upon the bogus war veterans, and then came beer. His beer honeymoon has still some weeks to run. Barring the members of the hate-your-neighbor sects, now very low in mind and beginning to have grave doubts that prayer really works, the whole country is stimulated and enchanted by the scents bursting from the breweries. At midnight on April 7 the right hon. gentleman will be the most popular President in American history, and it will be worth anyone's life to hang his portrait upside down.

But all honeymoons have to end, and this one is like the rest. The dulcet cooings and twitterings of poetry give way to the harsh croak of prose. Taxes follow beer. So far no one has paused to figure out what the whole Roosevelt programme will cost us, but it will be a plenty, you may be sure. Are we to save $20,000,000 a year, or maybe $50,000,000, by getting rid of the Prohibition black legs, and their attendant spies and snoopers? Then we are to pay at least $100,000,000 for the boon of beer, and perhaps, when all the States and cities have got their bits, $250,000,000. And are the bogus heroes to be cut

$500,000,000? Then the farmers will make off with $1,000,-000,000.

The farmers, of course, we have with us always. They are chronic and incurable mendicants. No matter what other issues may fever and lather the country, to them there is only one issue, and that is "What is in it for us?" How much they have got out of the public treasury since the war no one seems to know, but certainly it has run to two or three billions. This money was all wasted; they are poorer today than ever before. But they still believe that the way to get rich is to steal money from the rest of us, and to that end their agents in Washington prepare the usual crop of bills. One of those bills, embodying three separate plans to pillage us, seems to have the approval of the White House. I herewith predict formally, signing my name with a great flourish, that if it becomes law it will mulct the Treasury in the sum of at least $1,000,000,000 a year, and that after three years of it the farmers will be quite as hard up as they are today, and howling as ever for more.

The provisions of this measure are really almost incredible. It ought to be entitled A Bill to Encourage Thieves and Give the Taxpayer a Headache. Consider, for example, what one of its three sections says to the farmer in the Corn Belt, as Mark Sullivan reduces the thing to plain English:

> Last year you planted 100 acres in corn. This year we want you to plant only 90. To make it worth your while the Government will rent 10 of your acres at a fair rental. The rent you get from the Government will be as much as the profit you can expect from planting the 10 acres in corn. You will be saved that much labor. Also, by this plan the quantity of corn on the market next Fall will be reduced and the price should be higher.

I submit this offer to a candid world. Think of the chances it offers the farmer to get something for nothing! First, he will lie monumentally about the amount of corn he grew last year—

and every other farmer for miles around will step up as a witness for him. Second, he will demand (and get) a rental for his idle acres that is based, not upon his profit last year, but upon his potential profits next Autumn. And third, the Government promises him categorically that those profits next Autumn will be higher than they could possibly be in a normal open market —in other words, that you and I will be robbed every time we buy a pound of cornmeal.

The other sections of the bill are even worse. One of them proposes to use your money and mine to bribe cotton-planters to reduce their acreage, and at the same time to sell them the cotton now in the Government's hands (as a result of the last farm bill) at 7 cents a pound, so that they may make a speculative profit when it goes up. That cotton cost the Government more than 7 cents a pound, of course, but just how much more I don't know. Whatever the difference, you and I paid part of it when we paid our income-tax installment on March 15, and we will pay the rest on June 15, September 15 and December 15. And if cotton duly goes up, then we will pay the difference all over again—that is, if we have any money left to buy an occasional shirt.

The third section has to do with the wheat farmers. Its general effect is to lay a heavy tax on flour, and to use the money to reimburse the farmers for raising less wheat. The net result of it will be that you and I will pay more for bread.

I have hinted that the farmers are not to be trusted to make honest returns of the acreage they planted last year. Is this a libel on them? If you think so, then consider what happened when the Government, a year or so ago, began lending them money to buy seed, on the theory that they were too poor to buy it themselves. At once thousands of them began putting in large orders, and soon afterward they were reselling the seed for whatever they could get for it. At this very moment the Government is spending more millions trying to run down these swindlers and put them in jail. I do not know how many have been nabbed so far, or at what cost, but in one small Southern county it was discovered that nearly 50 per cent of the farmers engaged in the swindle. In the Middle West, where the ethical influence of the late General Robert E. Lee is not felt, the number participating probably ran close to 100 per cent.

The troubles of the farmers, in fact, are largely due to their own incurable knavery. Every effort to get rid of their crop surpluses by the voluntary reduction of acreages has failed because only a few parties to the compact could be trusted. In Maine, where potatoes are the chief crop, the farmers agreed several years ago to cut down their planting—and instantly nearly every farmer planted more. Now the Government is expected to accomplish what coöperation has always failed to accomplish. Who believes that it will succeed? Who believes that the farmers will actually reduce their acreage? Or that they will report it honestly? Or that the political hacks sent out from Washington to watch them will really make them toe the mark? Or that, after getting rent for their idle land and high prices for their wheat, corn and cotton (all at your expense and mine), they will be satisfied at the end of the year, and shut down their immemorial howling for more?

If any such optimist survives in the world, I shall be glad to embalm his name and address in this place. And to give him a signed photograph of the late Ananias of Jerusalem (Acts V, 1-11).

The farmers, of course, will have first place at the trough, for it belongs to them by ancient usage, but there will be plenty of other candidates for the swill. Washington at this moment swarms with visionaries whooping up gaudy schemes to succor the depressed and lay on new taxes, and some of them are in high office. I point, for example, to the lady uplifter, the Hon. Frances Perkins, A.M., the new Secretary of Labor. She has already launched a scheme to put 250,000 more men on the

Government pay roll, and presently she will be launching others, to the same glorious end. As a set-off, according to the Associated Press, she has "discontinued the posts of 55 special immigration inspectors"—chiefly, it appears, because the appropriation to pay them has run out.

There is, indeed, no genuine disposition among American public officials, or indeed among public officials anywhere, to reduce public expenses. As I have pointed out in this place a hundred times, they always try to lay on at least $2 every time they "save" $1. The saving gets brilliant headlines in the newspapers, but the new waste is disguised as a scheme to end the Depression, or even as a scheme to reduce taxes. This last dodge is now being worked again, and before our very eyes. The Federal Government has already laid a heavy and senseless tax on beer "in order to relieve the taxpayers," and the State and municipal governments, as everyone knows, have made brave efforts to get bites at the same cherry. If, in Maryland, those efforts fail it will surely not be the fault of the politicians. As always, they have tried their level damndest to give the taxpayer one more squeeze, and so find more money for the quack pedagogues, the endless inspectors and nuisances, the political contractors and promoters, the long files of useless jobholders, and all the other harpies who now beset him.

The politicians, in brief, have yet to learn and believe that the people are really tired of being rooked. They still go through the dumb-show of reducing budgets—and then propose gayly to load us with new Bath street viaducts, new Philadelphia roads, new Chesapeake Bay bridges, new imposts on beer, gasoline and what not. They will go on in this happy, innocent way for a year or two more. And then there will be an explosion, and some very talented stump-speakers will go flying through the air.

VIVE LE ROI!

May 1, 1933

The abdication of Congress is certainly not as overt and abject as that of the German Reichstag or the Italian Parliamento; nevertheless, it has gone so far that the constitutional potency of the legislative arm is reduced to what the lawyers call a nuisance value. The two Houses can still make faces at Dr. Roosevelt, and when a strong body of public opinion happens to stand behind them they can even force him, in this detail or that, into a kind of accounting, but it must be manifest that if they tried to impose their will upon him in any major matter he could beat them easily. The only will left in the national government is his will. To all intents and purposes he is the state.

We have thus come to a sort of antithesis of the English system, under which Parliament is omnipotent and the King is only a falseface. It would be rather absurd to call the change revolutionary, for it has been under way for more than a hundred years. Since Jackson's first election, in fact, Congress has always knuckled down to the President in times of national emergency. After 1863 Lincoln ruled like an oriental despot, and after 1917 Wilson set himself up, not only as Emperor, but also as Pope. In 1864, as antiquaries familiar with *Ex parte* Merryman will recall, the Supreme Court undertook to bring old Abe to book, but as the same antiquaries know, it had to confess in the end that it could do nothing.

There is no likelihood that it will intervene in the present situation. For one thing, there seems to be no public demand that it do so. For another thing, judges as a class are naturally sympathetic toward arbitrary power, for their own authority rests upon it. Thus there seems to be every probability that Dr. Roosevelt will continue to operate as an absolute monarch, at

least for some time to come. If the schemes of salvation con-
cocted by his Brain Trust, *i.e.*, by the King in Council, appear
to be working, then no one save a few touchy Senators will want
to depose him. And if we continue wandering in the wilderness,
with our shirtails out and the hot sun scorching our necks, then
most Americans will probably hold that it is better to go on following one leader, however bad, than to start scrambling after
a couple of hundred of them, each with a different compass.

My gifts as a constructive critic are of low visibility, but the
state of affairs thus confronting the country prompts me to
make a simple suggestion. It is that a convention be called under Article V of the Constitution, and that it consider the de-
sirability of making Dr. Roosevelt King in name as well as in
fact. There is no constitutional impediment to such a change,
and it would thus not amount to a revolution. The people of
the United States are quite as free, under Article V, to establish
a monarchy as they were to give the vote to women. Even if it
be held, as some argue, that the Bill of Rights is inviolable and
cannot be changed by constitutional amendment, it may be answered that there is nothing in the Bill of Rights requiring that
the national government shall be republican in form.

The advantages that would lie in making Dr. Roosevelt King
must be plain to everyone. His great difficulty today is that he
is a candidate for reëlection in 1936, and must shape all his acts
with that embarrassing fact in mind. Even with a docile Congress
awaiting his orders he cannot carry on with a really free hand,
for there remains a minority in that Congress which may, soon
or late, by the arts of the demagogue, convince the public, or a
large part of it, that what he is doing is dangerous, and so his
reëlection may be imperiled. To meet and circumvent this peril
he must play the demagogue himself, which is to say, he must
only too often subordinate what he believes to be wise to what
he believes to be popular.

It is a cruel burden to lay upon a man facing a multitude of appalling problems, some of them probably next door to insoluble. No other man of genuine responsibility under our system of government is called upon to bear it. It lies, to be sure, upon Congressmen, but Congressmen, after all, are minor functionaries, and no one has expected them, these hundred years past to be wise. We try to lighten it for Senators, who are a cut higher, by giving them six-year terms and so postponing their ordeal by ballot, and we remove it altogether for Federal judges by letting them sit during good behavior. But the President has to go on the auction block every four years, and the fact fills his mind and limits his freedom of action from the moment he takes the oath of office.

I am not a Roosevelt fanatic, certainly, though I voted for the right hon. gentleman last November, and even printed a few discreet pieces arguing that he might be worse. But it must be manifest that, in any situation as full of dynamite as the present one, it is a great advantage to have a leader who can devote his whole time and thought to the problems before him, without any consideration of extraneous matters. Yet that is precisely what, under our present system, a President cannot do. He is forced, at every moment of his first term, to remember that he may be thrown out at the end of it, and it is thus no wonder that his concern often wobbles him, and makes him a too easy mark for the political blackmailers who constantly threaten him.

If his term were unlimited, or limited only by his good behavior—in brief, if he were in the position of an elected King —he would get rid of all this nuisance, and be free to apply himself to his business. I believe that any man, under such circumstances, would do immensely better than he could possibly do under the present system. And I believe that Dr. Roosevelt, in particular, would be worth at least ten times what he is worth now, for he is a good enough politician to know that his current high and feverish popularity cannot last, democracy being what it is, and that the only way he can save himself in 1936 is by forgetting the Depression once or twice a day, and applying himself to very practical politics.

What this division of aim and interest amounts to is shown brilliantly by some of his appointments. He has made a plain effort to surround himself with men in whose competence and good faith he can put his trust, but he has been forced by the exigencies of his uncomfortable situation to give a number of important posts to political plugs of the most depressing sort. These plugs were too powerful to be flouted, and now that they are in office they are even more powerful than before. If they remain they will disgrace the administration soon or late, and if they are turned out they will imperil it in 1936. An elected King could rid himself of them at once, and they could do him no damage, now or hereafter.

The objections to monarchy are mainly sentimental, and do not bear up well under inspection. I shall rehearse some of them at length in a future article, and try to show how hollow they are. Suffice it for the moment to glance at a few of them. One is the objection that a King, once in office, can't be got rid of. The answer is that Kings are got rid of very often, and usually very easily, and that the same constitutional convention which provided one for the United States might also provide for his ready impeachment and removal, and even for his lawful and Christian execution.

Another objection is that the problem of the succession is hard to solve, and that any King that we set up would probably want his son to succeed him, and would root for that son exactly as a President in his first term now roots for himself, and in his second term for some favorite in his entourage. Well, why not? I believe that a Crown Prince, brought up in his father's office, is likely to make at least as good a King as any other fellow. Moreover, is it so soon forgotten that Dr. Roosevelt himself came in as a sort of Crown Prince?—though I should add that he was challenged by a Legitimist party led *de jure* by the

Young Pretender, Prince Theodore Minor, and *de facto* by Princess Alice. If His Excellency's name were Kelly, Kraus or Kaminsky would he be in the White House today? To ask the question is to answer it. Despite the theory that Americans fear and abhor the hereditary principle they have elected one President's son to the Presidency, one President's grandson and one President's cousin, and in at least two other instances they have made motions in the same direction. This is five times in thirty-one times at the bat, or nearly one in six.

But the succession is really a minor matter. I see no objection to letting the sitting King nominate three candidates, and then choosing between them, by plebiscite, at his death. His nominations, at worst, would be far better than any that professional politicians could or would make, and three nominees would give the voters sufficient choice. There remains the problem of starting the ball rolling. But that problem, as I have sought to show, is already solved. We have a King in the White House at this minute, and he is quite as much of the Blood Royal as George V. All that remains is to call a constitutional convention, and, as it were, make an honest woman of him.

ROOSEVELT

January 2, 1934

About some of Dr. Roosevelt's schemes to save us all from ruin, revolution and cannibalism there are rising doubts, but the popularity of the man himself continues, and if he suffers a combat with Congress this winter he is pretty sure to have the public on his side. In part this is due to his sheer skill as a politician, or as one would say if he were not President of the United States, as a demagogue, but probably in larger part it is due to a widespread and not irrational confidence in his intelligence and courage. We have had so many Presidents who were obvious numskulls that it pleases everyone to contemplate one with an active cortex, and so many who hugged their corners that it is stimulating to have one who leaps out into the ring, and can give as well as take.

The contrast with Hoover is very striking. I pass over Hoover's long and preposterous efforts to deny that there was any Depression, and point to his almost incredibly incompetent dealing with Prohibition. He was too stupid to see that the vast majority of the people were sick of it, and too cowardly to risk the crumbling fangs of the Anti-Saloon League, and in consequence he hung on to the Eighteenth Amendment at least two years too long, and when he turned on it at last he seemed a traitor rather than a hero. Centuries ago some wise man said that though many welcome treason, no one loves a traitor. Poor Hoover discovered the truth of this on the Tuesday following the first Monday in November, 1932. With both drys and wets distrusting and disliking him he went down to ignominious defeat.

The course of Dr. Roosevelt was much more shrewd, candid and bold. He saw clearly back in 1929, when he was a candidate for Governor of New York, that Prohibition was on its way out, and he got upon the wet bandwagon forthwith. In the past he had been more or less friendly to the dry delusion, but he had studiously avoided incurring any debt to the Methodist bishops, and his conversion was thus free of the smell of treason. In the Presidential campaign he spoke out unequivocably, promising the immediate return of beer and the immediate resubmission of the amendment in case of his election. Elected by a huge majority, he straightway undertook to make good on both promises. His resurrection of beer, in fact, was so swift that it lifted the wets to heights of joy from which they have not yet descended, and when repeal followed almost at once they were still sailing the stratosphere, and throwing down tons of roses on Dr. Roosevelt.

He showed his mettle again in the matter of lynching. At the time of the last public butchery on the lower Eastern Shore he was heading for Chestertown, which is on the upper Shore, to receive an honorary degree, an attention inspired by a pedagogical itch to get some free notice and prestige out of him, but the sort of thing that a President can hardly avoid. Obviously, it would have been an indecorum if he had denounced lynching in his address of thanks, for he was in the position of a guest, and could not question the common decency of the neighbors of his hosts. But when the California obscenity followed he was not incommoded by any such obligation, and what he had to say was said quickly, plainly and forcefully. The Eastern Shore assassins, if they have any sense left, now know what he really thinks of them, and what all civilized men think of them.

Hoover was also heard on the subject of the San José civic pageant, but he spoke only as a very private citizen, and after four years of dense silence in the White House. During those four years there were scores of lynchings in the Bible country, and more than one delegation of Aframericans had at him with demands that he denounce the sport, but he said nary a word. It was not difficult to surmise reasons for his holding his tongue. He had carried a large part of the South in 1928 through the efforts of the evangelical Ku Kluxers, which is to say, through the efforts of convinced and habitual lynchers, and he was in hopes of carrying it again in 1932. It is possible, of course, that he had some nobler reason, but if so it did not appear. The colored brethren believed, and still believe, that he was afraid of offending his homicidal friends, and so believing, they voted for Roosevelt.

It took no courage for Hoover to denounce Governor Rolph a few weeks ago. Having learned a lot since 1932, he knows very well that he can never collar another elective office in this life, and so the enmity of bucolic and barbaric evangelical sects is now nothing to him. But it may mean a very great deal to men who are still in politics, as the recent earnest silence of the Maryland jobholders has demonstrated. Not a word has come out of the Goldsboroughs, or out of any other professionals of their class. The local Roosevelts have been few, and when I have mentioned Governor Ritchie, Attorney-General Lane, and the Secretary of State, Mr. Winebrenner, I can think of only two or three others. The rest, like Warden Martin of the City Jail and President Ames of the Johns Hopkins, have been extremely careful not to offend the lynchers.

I suspect that a large part of Dr. Roosevelt's hold on the plain people is that they recognize him to be what is called, for a lack of a better word, a gentleman. Most of them, I suppose, would have difficulty defining the term, but all the same they know what it means. A gentleman is one who is somehow superior to the common run. He will fight longer, and he can be trusted further. There is a point, perhaps, at which he, too, will turn and run, and another at which he will sell out his friends to his own advantage, but both points lie far out in space, and much beyond the spot at which an ordinary politician will be ready and even eager to barter his grandmother's false teeth for a job.

The very superiority of such a man causes him to be viewed with a certain uneasiness, for some of his processes of mind are incomprehensible to his inferiors, and he commonly strikes them as a bit stiff and pedantic. He may be, in the ordinary relations of life, what they call a good fellow, and very often he is, but he nevertheless keeps up a considerable dignity, and is never quite a swine among swine. This dignity is resented increasingly as one goes down the scale, and on the lowest levels it encounters an implacable hostility, shot with envy, no doubt easily explicable on Freudian grounds. When a gentleman, by any chance, gets into politics, and especially if he arises to any sizable office, the vermin at the bottom feel uncomfortable in his presence, and are always ready, when it seems safe, to fall on him.

Here, perhaps, we may find a clue to some of the adventures of Governor Ritchie. It is pretty generally recognized that he is superior, in tradition and character, to the common run of Maryland politicians, and this superiority has probably had quite as much to do as his mere political skill with keeping him at Annapolis. The more reflective sort of people have confidence in his fundamental decency. They may believe that he is unwise on occasion, but they do not believe that he is knavish. There are obviously things that he will not do, even to continue in office. But all his qualms and points of honor are bound, soon or late, to alienate the low-down variety of politicians, who have no more notion of honor than so many street-walkers, and with them go the simian half-wits who are their customers. It is useful, in politics, to be decent, if only because it is so rare, but only up to a point. After that it is hazardous, as Grover Cleveland discovered.

Whether or not Dr. Roosevelt will hang on to his *principia* as long and as tenaciously as Dr. Cleveland, and pay for it in the end by going out of office unthanked and unpopular—this remains to be seen. He is a Roosevelt, and hence, by American standards, a gentleman, and he shows plain signs of being aware of the obligations that go with the character. But as a Roosevelt he is also—a Roosevelt, and that means a born politician. Some of his appointments have certainly involved little apparent sacrifice of political advantage to the public interest. But in this field, perhaps, it is imprudent to ask too much, for a President is elected for four years only, and on the day he takes office he has to begin laying his plans to be reëlected. The persons he must rely upon to achieve that end need not be as dreadful as Hoover's evangelists, but at best they are likely to be pretty bad.

So far, though he has made some lamentable concessions to

them, Dr. Roosevelt has kept the whip-hand over the whole outfit, including both the professional politicians and the Brain Trust. He knows how to get rid of men when they become too manifestly liabilities, and he does it without any vain gurgle of apologies. More than any other President since Cleveland, he is his own man. The well-heeled yearners who put up the money for his campaign have all been taken care of, but they have been taken care of in such a way that they have done a minimum of damage to the public interest, and some of them are already on their way out. So with the Brain Trust. Its members have rolled and hollered in the catnip of publicity, and will never be fit for flogging sophomores again, but it must be evident by now that they are not running the White House. All orders still come from the front office, and not infrequently they leave the Brain Trust looking silly.

On this fact we must pin what remains of our trust. The science of government is really very simple, else the world would have gone to pot long ago. The country will remain safe enough for all practical purposes so long as it is in the hands of a man of character, honest, gallant, and mellowed and moderated by a sense of humor. Most Americans, I take it, still believe that Roosevelt answers to these specifications. He will have a free hand while he can keep them thinking so.

The Burden of Omnipotence— Roosevelt & Alf

5

Long before the year 1936 made its debut, Mencken and the man who won his vote for the presidency in 1932 had come to a parting of the ways. Increasingly he stepped up his attacks against Franklin Roosevelt and the "Braintrusters." And this time his cannonading did not sound quite the same as it did in the twenties, nor did it by any means have the same reception. James Bone, the celebrated London editor of the *Manchester Guardian,* who knew Mencken well, remarked on the death of his friend that one of Mencken's great contributions was that he "did much to make Americans realize that their country was great enough to laugh at itself while pursuing its destiny." This, of course, Mencken managed superbly, but the winged jeers against democratic government that flew from his typewriter in the twenties when the nation was living riotously now had a wholly different impact on 130,000,000 Americans who had undergone the harrowing experience of the Great Depression.

Unmistakably the blows that Mencken struck at the New Deal, though they appeared to have little effect, seemed to be fired with greater muzzle velocity and personal conviction than those he aimed in the twenties. If Mencken moved into the attack like a roaring bulldozer in the twenties, it was frequently the attack of a bulldozer wearing mittens. For he had a way of softening the blow, a kind word or two even for the mediocrities or those he appeared to find the most obnoxious. But with Roosevelt and the New Deal the barbs were planted deeper. Roosevelt's concept of government, he gibed, was that of "a milch cow with 125,000,000 teats," and Roosevelt's appeals, he scoffed, "were not addressed to the cortex but to the midriff."

That the rebel of the twenties should now become a spokesman of the conservatives of the thirties, that the man who voted for the reformer LaFollette for president in 1924, should now appear to be in league with the Committee to Defend Constitutional Government, the Liberty League, and other organizations of the political Right came as a shock to many of Mencken's admirers. And Mencken himself, though taking to the press box quadrennially to report national conventions (his last was the Progressive Party Convention at Philadelphia in 1948), left domestic politics pretty much alone after 1936 and turned his creative talents to other channels.

As the preconvention campaign heated up in 1935 with everyone wondering whom the Republicans would nominate to oppose Roosevelt, Mencken in company with many political writers of the day underestimated Roosevelt's tremendous popularity. So much did he lean in this direction that he even expressed doubt about the applicability of the old political maxim "you can't beat something with nothing." He also questioned whether the Republicans really needed to find "an impeccable hero." But soon Mencken's pieces began to show a trail of unsteady conviction about the chances of unhorsing Mr. Roosevelt. On December 21, 1935, just four months after he opined that it was possible to beat "something with nothing," he was asking: "Where is the Republican grand and gaudy enough to polish off Mr. Roosevelt on election day?"

Whatever Mencken's hatred for Roosevelt and the New Deal,

his pieces leading up to the 1936 conventions and subsequent campaign are interlarded with some pithy judgments. He protested that the New Deal objectives seemed to be to provide everyone with "free mayonaise mixers," among other consumer goods, but he also correctly saw that the Republican platform promised "tickets to the Rendezvous with Destiny at cut rates," or "as good a show as the Brain Trust but at much less cost."

Mencken, though aware of the limitations of the Republican nominee, Alfred Landon, had a genuine affection for him that reveals itself as the campaign progresses. He worried at the outset about Landon's voice—"his loudest shout, and faintest whisper," he complained, "were probably no more than two decibels." And he finally despaired that even the professionals were wrong in believing "that his flat colorless voice might be teased and tortured into something resembling a Kiwanis Baritone, with maybe even some dulcet overtones of tenor. . . ." But as the campaign wore on Mencken defended Landon against charges that he was a stooge of publisher William Randolph Hearst. And when Landon showed particular courage in denouncing laws requiring schoolteachers to take oaths of loyalty to the Constitution in a speech at Buffalo and one in Pennsylvania, Mencken let forth a real war whoop. This for Mencken showed real muscle meat, and he appears again as a critic longing for the days of the giants—for one more swift swish of the club to strike against midget minds that believed in thought control.

Unaccountably again—no doubt to even the more hardy variety of Republican rustics—Mencken wonders at the close of this action if "some other hero" could have defeated Roosevelt in 1936. And incredibly his answer is "yes." But here once more, as we have seen earlier, Mencken's radar equipment was stubbornly resistant to the real facts of public opinion at the time. Even the true "spine rattler" that Mencken was hopefully seeking could hardly have turned back the tide of a triumph that swept every state but Maine and Vermont into the Democratic column.

M. M.

Up to six months ago it seems to have been generally believed in Washington that the Hon. Mr. Roosevelt would have a walk-over at the polls next year, but now there are sneaking doubts of it on both sides of the fence. His renomination, of course, is still a certainty—to the extent, at any rate, that anything can be certain in this most irrational and non-Euclidian of worlds. The national convention of the party in power is always saturated with Federal jobholders, and they are for the sitting President to a man. Even the Hon. Mr. Taft was able, in 1912, to get a renomination, though many of the master-minds of his party, including Roosevelt Major, were violently against him, and hardly anyone believed that he could be reëlected. But to control the political apes and peacocks who dominate a national convention is one thing, and to fetch the voters at the ensuing plebiscite is quite another.

It must be manifest to even the meanest understanding that Dr. Roosevelt is no longer the demigod that he was a year ago. He has lost his halo and his shining armor, and fast becomes, in the common sight, simply a politician scratching along. His infallibility has dropped from him as one after another of his vast and cocksure schemes for bringing in the millennium has blown up, and the assumption of his lofty altruism has been considerably corroded by his constant and transparent politicking. In brief, he has shed most of his erstwhile splendors, and begins to be viewed realistically. To be so viewed is immensely dangerous to a statesman under democracy. The plain people, once they start to put two and two together, are very apt to change their minds quickly and cruelly.

The sad cases of Roosevelt Major and the Hon. Woodrow

Wilson, Ph.D., will be recalled. Both enjoyed, in their days, the sort of veneration that is ordinarily reserved for the Holy Saints; both were spoken of familiarly as the full peers of Washington and Lincoln. But both died rejected and almost forgotten, and neither, in his last years, amounted to a hill of beans politically. Dr. Wilson, in 1920, expected his party to offer him a third term; instead, it gave a cadet of the Roosevelt house second place on the ticket as a sort of final, brutal fling at him. As for the elder Roosevelt, he went down to death with none so poor to do him reverence, though at his peak he had been Cæsar, Demosthenes, Aristotle and both Gracchi. I need not add the case of the Hon. Mr. Hoover, 22 (LL.D.). Within the short space of four years he ran the whole gamut from immortality to infamy. Indeed, he did it in two years.

It has been frequently observed by metaphysicians that in politics you can't beat something with nothing, and this fact is supposed to stand in the way of beating Dr. Roosevelt next year. The Republicans, so far, have failed to flush a really popular candidate. There is sound objection to all of the gentlemen so far mentioned. The Hon. William E. Borah is 71 years old, and will be 77 by 1941; moreover, he has curled up on so many noble causes that no one trusts him any more; yet more, he is a Prohibitionist, and hence, by the prevailing *mores*, an enemy to society. The Hon. W. Franklin Knox (he used to be plain Frank, but is now Franklin) owns a newspaper, and is thus a suspicious character, comparable almost to a dog-catcher. The Hon. A. H. Vandenberg is another, and for the same reason. The Hon. Henry P. Fletcher was once in the Diplomatic Service, and so lies open to the fatal charge that he wears spats and uses a broad *a*. The LaFollette boys are too far to the Left, and the Wadsworths, Ham Fishes *et al.* are too far to the Right. And so on.

But is it really necessary for the Republicans to find an impeccable hero, completely satisfactory to every patriotic and red-blooded American? Is it really a fact that you can't beat something with nothing? There are days when I find myself doubting it. The Republicans beat Cox and Roosevelt with two nothings in 1920, and they beat the Hon. John W. Davis, of Wall Street, W. Va., with considerably less than nothing in 1924. And with what did the Democrats score their stupendous triumph in 1932? If it was not with nothing, then it was certainly with something that had been precipitated from the void, like the nebulæ in the remotest heavens, only a short while before.

The truth is that Dr. Roosevelt seemed a feeble and even hopeless candidate to the Democratic statesmen gathered in Chicago three years ago. They had let him be nominated, not because they wanted him, but because Jim Farley had rounded up a majority of the delegates, and they couldn't help it. He was hardly popular, even among the delegates who voted for him, and he got much less applause on the floor than Al Smith or Governor Ritchie. When he flew out to the convention hall, and made his ringing (if belated) promise to bring back beer, the Southerners and Middle Westerners went home to the Bible Belt sick at heart, convinced that they faced another Armageddon like that of 1928. And when, simultaneously, Al stalked out of the hall, his veins running quinine and castor oil, the Easterners rolled up their eyes and prayed.

What these Democratic statesmen didn't grasp, at that unhappy time, was the extent of the collapse of Prohibition. They believed, like poor Hoover, that there remained in it at least one more victory at the polls, and they looked forward gloomily to seeing Hoover score it. But when, with the convention over and Congress adjourned, they got back to their constituencies and listened to the talk going on, they found that they were wrong. The plain people, it turned out, had decided suddenly that the Prohibition obscenity had gone on long enough. What had moved them no one knew, but moved they plainly were. Hoover, grasping the fact, tried to straddle in his speech of acceptance, but it was in vain. The event proved that a Chinaman might have beaten him. Indeed, even Roosevelt beat him.

My belief is that this was an authentic victory of nothing over something. Dr. Roosevelt, in those days, certainly fell far short of the heroic proportions that counselors of perfection are now calling for in the Republican candidate. He had made so little impression as Dr. Cox's running-mate in 1920 that he was a stranger to the country when Al made him Governor of New York in 1928, and his two terms as Governor had surely not been filled with shining achievement. He got the nomination for two reasons, the first being that, with the artful aid of Dr. Farley and a large war-chest, he had rounded up a great many otherwise unattached and bewildered delegates, and the second being that the opposition to him was horribly mismanaged by Al.

But the dudgeon of the plain people against Prohibition was enough to elect him, and more than enough. They would have elected Al just as readily, or Ritchie, or Jack Garner, or John Smith. The beer issue was the only vital issue in the canvass. The country heard Dr. Roosevelt's gabble about the causes and cure of the Depression so inattentively that it scarcely noticed, after the election, the gross conflict between his campaign promises and his actual programme. The New Deal was hardly mentioned. The wizards of the Brain Trust were still flogging sophomores, raising chickens, and trying to drum up solvent customers for their non-constitutional brand of law.

It is my suspicion that the More Abundant Life may be just as dead, by the Tuesday following the first Monday of November, 1936, as the Anti-Saloon League was in the late Summer of 1928—just as dead, and just as offensive to the nostrils of the plain people. That they begin to sicken of it already is only too plain. Those who are on the dole bellow constantly for more and better handouts, and those who are hard at work and paying their own way have begun to figure what it will cost them when the bills confront them at last. By this time next year those bills will be coming in, and many a smile now radiating Washington will be coming off.

Such great shifts in public sentiment are always concealed in their early stages, and even when they begin to be visible politicians are commonly too stupid to detect them. The fact that the Rev. Charles Edward Coughlin, LL.D., blew up with a bang last Fall was not observed in Washington until a few months ago. Down to April or thereabout he was still being received with grave dignity on Capitol Hill, and dozens of Senators and Representatives were sneaking out to Royal Oak, Mich., to cultivate him. At the same time other Senators and Representatives were giving ear to Dr. Townsend, the Los Angeles prophet of Baal, though the Walls of his Jericho were already dust. It may be that the Republicans and Jeffersonian Democrats among them, when they tremble before the Führer, tremble before a banshee worn just as thin and diaphanous. In brief, it may be that, when the time comes, there will be so many votes against him that it will be hardly worth while to reckon up the votes for his opponent.

THE SHOW BEGINS

March 9, 1936

Those opponents of the New Deal who are depending upon the Hon. Al Smith to run it through the *kishkes* at the Philadelphia convention are leaning, I fear, upon a very fragile reed. Al, no doubt, will do some hollering, but that is probably as far as it will go. When the time comes to vote, the Federal jobholders wearing delegates' badges will vote unanimously for four years more of the Abundant Life, and so will an overwhelming majority of the other brethren. For, as the Hon. Mr. Tydings was arguing sensibly last Thursday night, the only thing that could be accomplished by turning Dr. Roosevelt out and nominating another would be to set up that other for a dreadful beating in November, which is something that no Democratic politician in his senses can contemplate without his blood turning to water. Roosevelt, at best, will certainly have no walkover, but he is the only Democrat who can conceivably win.

Al has been definitely out of politics since the Chicago convention of 1932. He landed there as the titular leader of the Roosevelt opposition, and at once performed such prodigies of political imbecility that he made Roosevelt's nomination certain. If there were any genuine gratitude in politicians he would be invited to the White House, not for an occasional dish of tea, but as a regular boarder, paying no board. It was obvious the moment he got to Chicago that he had lost all contact with the most elemental political realities. His talk was not that of a Tammany Ph.D., but that of an amateur in the baby class. In two days he was floored ignominiously, and in four days he was on his way home.

His speech before the Liberty League in Washington was another and massive proof of his loss of professional technic. Surely the Al of gaudy legend, with such a speech in him, would never have got himself up in long tails and a white tie and gone to a dinner of Palm Beach crocodiles and boa constrictors to make it. He would have worn his old brown derby, and loosed it before an audience of his ancient lieges—horrible, hairy, human. There would have been 1,000 New York firemen in the gallery armed with gongs and fire whistles, and down on the floor they would have been supported by 10,000 garbage haulers, white wings and cops in mufti, howling like hyenas at every pause in the flow of syllogisms. Such was the customary stage setting of the Al we all revered. But the Al of today wears a boiled shirt, prefers champagne to schooners, and plays golf instead of pinochle.

But though the Hon. Mr. Roosevelt thus runs no ponderable risk of disaster at Philadelphia, his chances in November continue to worry his partisans, and they show it by a considerable jumpiness. Two years ago the corn-doctors and snake-oil vendors he has assembled at Washington were so sure of themselves that they carried on like Asiatic despots, and the most they ever vouchsafed to a critic was an occasional wisecrack, full of lofty scorn. But of late they have begun to take the opposition much more seriously, and to bring up far heavier artillery against it. Indeed, it is now rare for one of them to make a speech without calling names plentifully, and alleging that Wall Street gold is behind every cavil.

It should be said for these great thinkers that, as the combat stands, they labor under a burdensome disadvantage. That disadvantage is that there is no master villain for them to concentrate their fire on. Every projectile that comes in their direction finds an easy mark, for there stands Dr. Roosevelt in the full glare of the limelight, and there stand the quacks themselves, grouped about him as chorus girls in red-white-and-blue pants used to be grouped about Lillian Russell in the old-time comic operas. But when they return the cannonade they have no definite target—at all events, none of any dominant conspicuousness.

This lack will be remedied when the Republicans meet in Cleveland and nominate a standard bearer. I suppose that all the Brain Trust boys are praying that they will name Hoover or Borah, for either would make a magnificent mark. But that is hardly likely. The Republicans, when such a situation as the present one confronts them, usually nominate a safe nonentity who has no known enemies, and has never said anything that can be used against him. Their ideal candidate was Harding, who came as near to being a vacuum as is humanly possible on this earth. And to support, sustain and succeed him they chose Coolidge, whose degree of rarification was only a trifle less.

At the present writing no such ideal wraith is visible. The Hon. Mr. Landon of Kansas has done a great deal of imprudent talking in the past, and the Hon. Frank Knox is doing some even today. As for the Hon. Mr. Vandenberg, he shares with Dr. Knox the handicap of being a newspaper proprietor, which means that the files of his paper, stretching back to the invention of printing, are available to refute and flabbergast him. If any of these gentlemen is nominated there will be happy days ahead for the Hon. Charles Michelson, LL.D., the No. 1 torpedo of the Democratic National Committee. Dr. Michelson performed dreadful execution upon the late Mr. Hoover, and he will do another good job if he gets the chance. But as things stand, he is hamstrung, for if he started a work-out on one of the three aspirants he would only help the other two, and if he tried to tackle all three at once his fire would be dispersed and none of them would be seriously hurt.

I daresay that he is praying, along with all the chief noodles in the alphabetical soup, for the nomination of either Hoover or Borah. He has the precise range of Hoover, and Borah would be a set-up for any scare-monger of reasonable gifts, let alone such a virtuoso as Dr. Michelson. But the Republicans may baffle him by naming the empty unknown aforesaid. Indeed, some of them are already talking darkly of one Chester C. Bolton, M. C. L., an Ohio Congressman whose chief merit seems to be that no one has ever heard of him, though he has been in the House since 1929, and is a war veteran, and is said to make a very good speech.

Unluckily, second thoughts will probably finish the boom of Dr. Bolton, for a quiet investigation that I undertook the other day discovered in ten minutes that he is a graduate of Harvard, a Son of the Revolution, a convinced Episcopalian and a member of the Racquet Club of New York, which last is almost as bad as belonging to the Liberty League or the League of Nations. I thus predict formally that Chester will not get very far. He would probably make a good President, but what the Republicans are looking for is not a good President, but someone able to beat Roosevelt.

That they will find what they seek I incline to believe, for they have usually managed to do so in the past. It would not be going too far, indeed, to argue that the powers and principalities of the air are ordinarily on their side. They were in a deadlock at Chicago in 1920 when some beneficent fairy sent them Harding. He was almost the ideal candidate. He had bushy eyebrows, he made a loud and impressive speech, and he had no fixed opinions on any known subject. Even more than Dr. Roosevelt, he was blessed with a mind that could think whatever he wanted it to think. Thus he mowed down the Hon. Jim Cox with ease, and also gave a setback to the career of Dr. Roosevelt, who was running on the Democratic ticket with Cox as an advocate of Law Enforcement, and enjoying the favor of the Anti-Saloon League.

After the nomination of Harding the Republican politicians assembled at Chicago and had a bad scare, for it was discovered by some Democratic polecat that the candidate was married to a divorced lady, and had been accused in open court of stealing her from her first husband. But this scare lasted no more than two weeks, for at the end of that time the Democrats assembled at San Francisco obligingly nominated Cox, who had also been through a divorce case. Thus x turned out to be precisely equal to y, and nothing was heard, in that campaign, of the sanctity of the American home. Every other great moral issue got attention, including Prohibition, but not that one. There was a kind of moratorium on it.

I have said that the Hon. Al Smith is hardly to be feared at Philadelphia, but that is not saying that no other hero will arise to gum the works and give Dr. Roosevelt and his faculty grief.

The Democrats, as everyone knows, always try to commit hara-kiri at their conventions. When they are unanimous on the candidate they quarrel over the platform, and vice versa. The reason thereof lies in the fact that they hardly constitute a party at all, but are simply two gangs of natural enemies in precarious symbiosis. One gang consists of big city antinomians, and the other of pious yaps. Once in a great while they lie down together peaceably, as in 1932. But not often. Their usual plan is to go into battle shooting one another from the rear. A lot of that sort of shooting will be done in November.

THE MORE ABUNDANT DIALECTIC

April 20, 1936

The joke is on those confiding folk who turned on their radios last Monday night, expecting to hear a trenchant discussion of the issues of the hour. Let them be warned against the next time. Nothing but hooey will issue from the Hon. Mr. Roosevelt for the balance of the campaign. He will make vague and gaudy promises in plenty, first to this group of horse-leech's daughters and then to that one, but if he ever descends to cases it will be a miracle indeed. The plain fact is that his mind does not run to facts and figures. He is not a scientist, but a sort of mixture of poet and evangelist, with overtones of the opera singer.

Certainly a statesman who sought to fetch the higher cerebral centers would not come out on a public platform with Hopkins on one side of him and Ickes on the other. The support of such comic characters gives away the true nature of the entertainment. It is not addressed to the cortex at all, but to the midriff; not to sensible men and women, but to boobs. Its one and only aim is to fill those boobs with such high and glistening hopes that they will flock to the polls in November, and keep the evangelical party at the trough. Once they have discharged that patriotic function, they will be handed over, as they have been handed over since time immemorial, to statistics and the devil.

I often wonder that no one has ever undertaken a formal history of demagogy. If I had the time I think I'd take on the job myself, but too many other jobs stand in the way, some spiritual and some secular. The notion that the thing is a modern imposture seems to be widely held, but is in error. It actually arose in the dark backward and abysm of history, and it has been throwing off renowned and even immortal practitioners for many, many centuries. Indeed, the thing we call history is to a large extent only a serial biography of such charlatans. But it would be a mistake to dismiss them as mere swindlers. Like the inventors of bogus religion, they have often convinced themselves of their own inspiration, and not a few of them have suffered martyrdom. The last to go to the stake, as connoisseurs will recall, was William Jennings Bryan, LL.D. He needed no executioner to set him afire. He was consumed by the natural heat of his own dreadful fury against his betters.

Aside from that fury, there is precious little to be discovered in the New Deal metaphysic. It is a puerile amalgam of exploded imbecilities, many of them in flat contradiction of the rest. It proposes to give people more to eat by destroying food, to lift the burden of debt by encouraging fools to incur more debt, and to husband the depleted capital of the nation by outlawing what is left of it. It heads in all directions at once, and gets precisely nowhere. No two of the Brain Trust wizards appear to agree, save of course upon the constant need for more money. They give at least as much time to brawling among themselves as they give to the actual promotion of their discordant and preposterous Utopias.

With a change of a few words, a large part of Dr. Roosevelt's harangue to the local come-ons might have been converted into the spiel of a quack doctor addressing yokels at a county fair. Its obvious purpose was to scare them into believing that something awful ailed them, and then to offer them an infinite series of sure cures. "If the first bottle doesn't relieve you, come back and we'll try another"—of course, for another 25 cents. Show me anything else in the speech, and I'll eat a copy of it soaked in one-hundred-proof strychnine. It was not only silly; it was shameless. There was no pretense of rational discussion. It was pure and unadulterated demagogy.

Consider, for example, the sonorous gabble about taking all persons below the age of 18 or above the age of 65 out of productive industry. The first part of this, I suppose, was a bone flung to the pedagogues and uplifters, who yearn to collar the whole population up to the age of 21, and even beyond. And the second part was only too palpably a bone for the Townsend racketeers, who still control plenty of votes along the lunatic fringe. How much sense was in either half? None whatever. If all the wage-earners below 18 were handed over to the gogues and uplifters, to be converted into incurable mendicants, and all those above 65 were handed over to the Townsend grafters, to be starved to death, the net increase in jobs at living wages for workers between 18 and 65 would not be five per cent.

There is, in fact, only one intelligible idea in the whole More Abundant Life rumble-bumble, and that is the idea that whatever A earns really belongs to B. A is any honest and industrious man or woman; B is any drone or jackass. On this proposition all the quacks clustered about the Greatest President Since Hoover are agreed, and on this proposition alone. Each and every one of their schemes, from the AAA to the TVA, is a scheme to convert the lubricous imaginings of the incompetent and unhappy into blissful realities—in brief, to put envy on a gold basis, substantially higher than that of the boloney dollar.

There is nothing in the New Deal save that, and there never will be.

All demagogy rests upon the same beautiful foundation. It is a device to organize the discontent of all those, who, under the prevailing rules of the game, are getting on less well than they think their talents and virtues deserve, and who spend most of their time yearning for the usufructs of those who seem to be getting on better. The demagogue argues (*a*) that the rules were made by wicked men, and (*b*), that if enough nickels are dropped into his hat he will be able to change them. The first part is false pretenses and the second part is fraud. There is nothing else whatsoever. To be sure, a given demagogue may sometimes convince himself that he is honest and even that he is a hero, but what he thinks is of no more validity than what he says.

His actual purpose is never concealed from the judicious. He is always after a job for himself, and if he talks loudly enough and foolishly enough he not infrequently gets it. There then begins an inevitable cycle of disillusion. His poor victims, reaching out for the moon, find to their disquiet that what he has really handed to them is only a cabbage. He must then begin to promise two moons, three moons, a dozen moons, with clusters of other gauds thrown in for good measure. They turn out to be onions, potatoes, wads of reconditioned chewing-gum, wet sponges. Presently the demagogue is chased away—and another rises to fill his room. This has been going on in the world since Hector was a blastocyte. It will go on until the last galoot's ashore.

The More Abundant Life brethren now face the first stirring of serious doubt in their customers. They have been assailed by naughty skeptics since the day of their emergence from primeval chaos, but persons of a congenitally believing turn of mind, which is to say, persons of normal human stupidity, have

hitherto gone along with them pretty docilely. But now they
find themselves confronted by rising dubieties, and it is necessary for them to do something to hold on to their soft and
glorious jobs. The half of what they do consists in shoveling out
more and more billions of the taxpayers' money. The other half
consists in beating the woods for new coveys and classifications
of suckers.

Dr. Roosevelt, in his Baltimore speech, made several separate
and distinct attempts in that direction. His somewhat crude
overture to the Townsend halfwits I have already mentioned.
They are his natural game, but Dr. Townsend has so far managed to keep them penned in a private preserve, and is apparently not eager to let out shooting rights to other huntsmen.
But mainly Dr. Roosevelt leveled his artillery at the large and
uncertain class of first voters. It may be that many of them are
suckers, too, so it seemed worth while to spread some bait for
them, and thus round up enough of them to make up for the old-
timers snared by Dr. Townsend.

In this theory there was and is a considerable plausibility.
The youngsters of this year's crop have passed through some
very demoralizing years, and it will not be surprising if large
numbers of them turn out to be *mashuggah*. Their woes, of
course, were considerably exaggerated by the right hon. gentleman in his harangue. It is not a fact that the door of hope is
wholly closed to them, and that they face a unanimously black
future. The smart fellows among them will get on just as smart
fellows have always got on, and a generation hence they will be
running the world in the same old way, and basking and frying
in the envy of the dubs.

But to the dubs the outlook is surely not very bright. Belabored for years by pedagogues gradually passing from panic to
hysteria, they enter upon adult life with their wits sadly addled.
Some of them, as everyone knows, have already gone Red, and
begin to argue boldly that their fathers ought to be hanged,

drawn and quartered. There must be many more who are equally upset, but do not venture to go so far. Properly wooed with more and more of the idiotic, alarming sort of rhetoric that they heard every day at school and college, they may be induced to cast their first votes for Hopkins and Tugwell, Ickes and Mother Perkins, Morgenthau and Wallace, the New Deal and glory hallelujah. But not, I fear, their second. By 1940 they will be in the full tide of *Katzenjammer*. And perhaps even in 1936 many of them will retain a sufficiency of faculty to refuse the cup of bathtub Peruna.

THE COMBAT JOINS

July 6,1936

I take my text from an article in the eminent *New Masses* by a Communist brother, Comrade Joseph Freeman:

> Anne O'Hare McCormick, writing in the New York *Times,* wants us to believe that the Republican party has been captured by Main Street. The Republicans want us to believe that, too. Actually, the Republican party is trying to capture Main Street.

I have praised Comrade Freeman in the past as a Communist appreciably less jackassical than the norm of the species, and it is a pleasure to unearth and broadcast this fresh evidence of it. He puts his finger on the truth with great precision. The Kansas Gang has been depicted in many of the public prints as a whale which went to Cleveland and swallowed all the Wall Street sharks. It is actually a minnow that was neatly threaded upon a hook. The hook is now cast, and it is the hope and prayer of the fishermen behind it that it will land sufficient honest trout and bass in the pellucid backwaters of the Republic to outweigh

the New Deal's great haul of alewives and catfish in the stag-
nant ponds and sewer outlets.

But we had better drop the metaphor, which grows compli-
cated. The essence of Comrade Freeman's idea, as I understand
it, is that the Republican brethren, convinced that the city
dole-birds and mendicant one-crop farmers are already in the
New Deal bag, are concentrating upon the folk of the small
towns, including, of course, the small-town folk (there are millions of them) who live in big cities. These small-town folk, in
the long run, will be the goats of the More Abundant Life, and
they begin to realize it. The money to pay for it will come out of
their pockets. It offers them nothing save a tawdry show, and it
takes everything. Their ears begin to prick up, and their breasts
to heave. They tire of wizardry.

So defined, they may appear to be sordid fellows, and it is in
that character, as everyone knows, that the New Deal apologists
describe them. They are depicted as idiot stooges of the Money
Power, as dupes of Hearst and the du Ponts, as clandestine
believers in the superiority of property rights to human rights.
They appear in the harangues of the Hon. Mr. Roosevelt as
congenitally deficient in the Christian virtues of faith, hope and
charity—indeed, as complete moral morons, comparable almost
to child-stealers, grave-robbers, or Darwinians.

But all that, of course, is only campaign hooey. These small-
town folk are actually idealists of the most virulent sort, and it
takes a swindle as gross as Dr. Hoover's Noble Experiment or
Dr. Roosevelt's Rendezvous With Destiny to shake their natural confidence in Utopias. They were crowding after all sorts of
world-savers, some political, some economic, some theological,
and some only Rotarian, at a time when Dr. Roosevelt himself
was actually a Wall Street werewolf offering to speculate (with
other people's money) in German securities. They were sitting
up all night sweating over the sorrows of the world in the days
when he was making careless whoopee on Vincent Astor's yacht,

with not a thought for the poor and downtrodden in his mind.

There is, however, a natural limit to idealism in this world, and it comes when the collector pulls the doorbell. Even Tugwell, I suspect, would be shaken in his heroic libido to "make America over" if he had to pay for his own pick and shovel, blueprints and cement. Even Wallace and Ickes, put to work earning taxes instead of spending them, would be measurably less eager to provide every hillbilly in the Tennessee Valley with free electric fans, mayonnaise mixers and permanent-wave machines. The idealists of the small towns are exactly like these consecrated men. They were hot for the New Deal before the bills began to come in—indeed, they were for it long before Dr. Roosevelt was for it, or ever heard of it. But now they begin to figure.

The Republican platform, it seems to me, is a neat effort to catch them coming and going, and deserves a great deal more praise from connoisseurs than it has been getting. It does not mock and put to scorn their natural and probably incurable belief in a Golden Age that is always just around the corner; on the contrary, it conjures up a vision of that Golden Age which is almost as enchanting as the purple dreams of Tugwell and Jim Farley, Ickes and Cactus Jack Garner, Ma Perkins and Old Joe Robinson.

But it promises, in addition, something that the framers of the Democratic platform, for all their genius, were too stupid to think of—it promises to bring on Utopia at an inside price—it promises tickets to the Rendezvous With Destiny at cut rates. In brief, it promises just as good a show as the Brain Trust's show, but at very much less cost. Instead of talking grandly about spending more and more money, it binds the Hon. Mr. Landon to spend less and less, and he himself has ratified that engagement. Instead of treating the taxpayer as a malefactor without any rights in law or equity, it treats him as a victim to be soothed and succored.

I consider this very smart politics, let the chips fall where they may. For the small-town American, whatever he may be otherwise, is always and primarily a taxpayer. Whether he lives in an actual small town, or in a big city, or on a selfsustaining farm, he is the sort of fellow who still practises and believes in the virtues hymned by Benjamin Franklin, the *Ur*-Coolidge. There is nothing of the horse-leech's daughter about him. He is willing and eager to pay his own way in the world, and nine times out of ten he manages to do it. He never buys anything that he can't pay for. He never borrows if he can avoid it. When misfortune overtakes him, he bears it without whining. When he is lucky, he ascribes 99% of his luck to his own merit—just as you do and I do, just as Dr. Roosevelt and the Brain Trust professors do. And when he has collared a dollar, he believes, and with considerable plausibility, that he ought to be consulted politely before any plans are laid to spend it. Taxes are his nightmare, for it is his experience that they are laid out by the politicians, in most cases, not to benefit him but to injure him.

I am not in the Hon. Mr. Landon's confidence, but it is my guess that this is the American he will address his canoodling to during the campaign. If so, he will be very well advised, for there stands the real Forgotten Man of William Graham Sumner. Everybody has been thought of by the young pedagogues save the poor fellow who, in the long run, will have to pay the bills. Every sort of misfit and lazybones has been taken care of, but not the man who takes care of himself. If Dr. Landon tackles him directly and on the one simple issue of economy, leaving all the poetry and other buncombe to Dr. Roosevelt, then the chances will be very good, it seems to me, that the Rooseveltian Rendezvous With Destiny will turn out, in November, to be a rendezvous with a bouncer.

I am reminded here of what happened, some years ago, in a town in Kansas. The place swarmed with reformers and idealists, and they had been maddening the voters for years with their projects for converting it into a New Jerusalem. Every imbecility hatched in the cow country had been tried, and all had failed, but the candidates for public office were always ready with more. At the time I speak of there was a mayoralty election impending, and seven candidates were in the ring, each with a programme longer than the platform of the Bull Moose of blessed memory.

Into this *mêlée* stepped the Hon. Jay Elmer House, an humble newspaper reporter. He was not a politician, but in his professional gambols about town he had noted that the respectable, hardworking, decent citizens were gradually getting tired of the uproar. In particular, they were increasingly against a scheme of general salvation that had been actually executed— the appointment of a policewoman. This dreadful virago had made herself an intolerable public nuisance. She snooped on the young folks when they necked and upon their elders when they boozed, and she kept the town jail full of prisoners and the town court full of vexatious and expensive litigation. But all the candidates for mayor were afraid to say anything against her, for she represented the first real triumph of the idealism they all whooped up.

At this point the Hon. Mr. House announced his own candidacy, and upon a platform of one plank, to wit, "If elected, I promise to fire the policewoman." He was elected almost unanimously, and his first act on being sworn in was to fire the policewoman. He is dead now, but in that town they still venerate him as the Romans venerate Romulus and Remus.

BURYING THE DEAD HORSE

August 17, 1936

Whatever the result of the plebiscite of November 3, we are in for four more years of grief and melancholy. If the Hon. Mr. Landon is elected it will take him the whole of his first term to clean up the mess that Dr. Roosevelt hands on to him, and if Dr. Roosevelt is reëlected we may expect it to be made much worse before any honest effort is undertaken to make it better. The right hon. gentleman's recent harangue to the prehensile idealists of Passamaquoddy Bay is enough to prove that. He is upset because Congress revolted against his crazy project to waste $100,000,000 of the taxpayers' money there, and he threatens plainly to push the thing through, Congress or no Congress. If he is reëlected he will undoubtedly try to do so, and in all probability $50,000,000 will be gone before he can be stopped.

Legal and constitutional impediments will hardly stay him. He has already advised Congress categorically to pay no heed to the Supreme Court, and he has himself often proceeded in open contempt of both the court and Congress. During his second term, if he has one, he will have the choosing of at least three judges, and perhaps of all nine, for the youngest of the sitting ones is beyond sixty, and searching the law is almost as hard upon the kidneys and arteries as it is upon the *gluteus maximus*. That he will appoint men who actually believe in the Constitution is hardly likely. It is immensely more probable that he will choose revisionists, and it is equally probable that they'll be advocates of the kind of revision that will greatly enlarge his own powers.

Thus his reëlection will set off the most violent attack upon the Constitution ever made, at least since the Hon. Abraham Lincoln adjourned it during the Civil War. He will waste no

time (and run no risk) trying to change it by the orderly process of amendment. Instead, he will simply set his juridic stooges
upon it, asking them only to make a thorough job. Are there
lawyers ready and willing to undertake that rapine? There are,
alas, plenty of them, and some of them are full of doubts about
the New Deal. But, as Thomas Jefferson observed long ago, the
moment the lust for public office enters a man's mind, there is a
subtle corruption in his character. Dr. Roosevelt himself offers
a monumental proof of the truth of that observation.

But though he will thus have a swell time for a year or two, it
is certain beyond the peradventure of a doubt that he will be
making very heavy weather before the end of his second term.
He has managed, so far, to finance his spree by borrowing, but
soon or late he will have to resort to forthright and brutal taxation, and when that time comes the discontent now getting under
way will come down upon him in earnest. If, as his customers
hope and pray, it is not quite strong enough in November to
unhorse him then, it will surely be strong enough by 1938 to
knock him galley-west.

That will be the year of the next midterm elections, and it is
an easy bet that he will lose the House, and probably also the
Senate. But even if he doesn't actually lose them, he will find his
majorities greatly reduced, and those of his serfs who escape
will begin to see a great light. His chief weakness, indeed, lies in
the fact that most of his supporters in Congress do not really
believe in the evangelical rubbish he preaches. They go along
because it has been the easiest way, so far, to hold their jobs.
The moment it ceases to be the easiest way they will be off the
reservation.

How the thing works was shown brilliantly in the case of
Prohibition. When Congress adjourned in the summer of 1932
there were large dry majorities in both Houses, and they included all the heaviest boozers of each. But when the election
returns came in in November those majorities vanished, and by

Christmas Prohibition was done for. All the driest drys were
converted overnight. The day before election day they were still
bowing their necks to the Anti-Saloon League, but two days
later they were howling for beer, and by the end of the year they
were also howling for whisky, gin and rum.

Such snappy conversions interest the psychologist, but do
not surprise him. The sort of politico who sits in Congress taking orders from outside, whether those orders come from the
White House, the Anti-Saloon League, Dr. Townsend, the Ku
Klux Klan, or what you will, is a naturally dishonest and dishonorable man, and may be trusted to prove it at the first
chance. Dr. Roosevelt has been supported since March 4, 1933,
by a preponderance of just such chiggers, and the moment he
shows signs of collapse they will turn upon him unanimously.

But if he is reëlected in November, they will not jump, of
course, just yet. It will probably take the inevitable upset of
1938 to move them, though the smarter among them will see it
coming long before. While they stay in the corral we'll be in
for a sharpening of New Deal activity, and hence for an unparalleled waste of money. The Brain Trust quacks will not
only assume that they have been given a mandate to do their
delirious damndest; they will also be panting for revenge upon
their enemies, to wit, the economic royalists, to wit, the taxpayers. And Dr. Roosevelt himself, who is a vindictive fellow,
despite his Christian Science smile, will be moved to fresh prodigies of pillage by the same motive.

Thus we'll be in for a saturnalia of spending in the grand
manner, with every wicked holder of an insurance policy or a
savings-bank book tracked down to his foul den, and forced to
disgorge. The threat to revive the Passamaquoddy scheme offers
a fair sample of what is in the cards. A hundred projects of the
same lunatic sort, and many a great deal worse, will emanate
from the incandescent brains of Tugwell and Ickes, Wallace and
Hopkins. Every professional uplifter in the land will bawl

hosannah and every one-crop farmer and other loafer who gets a dole today will get two doles. Is the taxpayers' money now being poured out to send gangs of ham actors about the country, playing Communist plays? Then each gang will grow to twenty, and along with every one will go a band of music, a truckload of free hot dogs, and another of bad beer, the true begetter of all radicalism.

Try to imagine what gaudy visions Hopkins will conjure up, once he is relieved of the fear of being sent back to work! Picture to yourself Tugwell in his studio with busts of Wat Tyler, Marx and Heywood Broun looking down upon him, and his racing pen scratching new stanzas for his famous hymn:

> I will roll up my sleeves;
> I will spit on my hands;
> I will make America over!
> Glory, glory, hallelujah!

And don't forget La Perkins, now said to be somewhat alarmed about her job. And the incomparable Ickes, prince of idealists. And Wallace the moon-calf. And the indefatigable Jim Farley, snouting endlessly for more and more jobs for those who vote right and have their hearts in the right place.

Even if the Hon. Mr. Landon and his anthropophagous royalists prevail in November, and all these jitney upyankers of the downtrodden are thrown out upon their ears, it will still cost a pretty penny to mop up the garbage. To be sure, Dr. Landon won't have to bother about Congress, for if he is elected even those New Dealers who escape the New Deal's collapse will be galloping down the road to Damascus by 6:30 A.M. of November 4. But he will quickly discover, as the Martyr Harding discovered in 1921, that it is one thing to admire the Old American System, and quite another thing to pry even the meanest jobholder from the trough.

The More Abundant Life charlatans, in fact, have got their

machine running at such velocity that stopping it will be almost impossible; it will have to run down. They have convinced millions of the lazy lowly that the taxpayer owes them a living— that every cent he earns by hard labor is, and of a right ought to be, theirs. They have brought up a whole generation that has been taught only one thing, and that is to hold out its hands. It will not be easy to dissipate such romantic notions. It will take a long time, and it may also require some rough stuff. But mainly it will take time, and while that time is running on the taxpayer will have a lot to think about.

In one direction, at least, Dr. Landon shows that he realizes all this. He makes no promise to chase the mendicant one-crop farmers away from the trough. Such an enterprise would make even Sisyphus throw up his hands. They are anchored there by chains of steel. For at least another thirty years every American who works for a living will have to give up a definite part of his income to them. They have learned how to scare politicians, whether Democratic or Republican, and so they are safe. They will be bawling for more and more help, and getting it, long after most of the voters who go to the polls on November 3 are penned up in Hell and moaning for Heaven, or *vice versa*.

AFTER THE NEW DEAL

September 28, 1936

In the slanging match between the White House secretariat and the Hon. William Randolph Hearst, LL.D. (Oglethorpe), the fortunes of war are plainly running with Dr. Hearst. He has produced plenty of evidence to support his charge that the Reds of the United States are rooting for Roosevelt, and that evidence has come, not from the du Ponts, but from such impeccable authorities as the Rev. Norman Thomas, Socialist candidate for the Presidency; the Hon. Upton Sinclair, a pink since before the Spanish-American War already; and the Hon. James Casey, until lately editor of the *Daily Worker*, organ of the so-called Communist party of America.

If the Hon. Mr. Hearst wants further proof he can find it by reading almost any book, pamphlet, magazine or handbill that the Reds have brought out during the last three months. They have been moving toward symbiosis with the Hon. Mr. Roosevelt ever since the two national conventions met in July. To be sure, they have occasionally denounced him, but so far as I can recall, they have never done so with anything even remotely resembling the venom they have shown against the Hon. Alf M. Landon. One and all, they recognize the fact that, compared to Landon, Roosevelt is their boy, and is heading their way.

Their hopes for the future have been often set forth at length. They believe that, if Roosevelt is reëlected, the old type of labor leader, typified by the Hon. William Green, will quickly fade out, and that the new type represented by the Hon. John L. Lewis will displace him. Lewis and Green are both for the New Deal, but it is easy to see that the New Deal wizards favor Lewis as against Green. He is, indeed, far more their kind of man. Green is a respectable Baptist, Odd Fellow and Elk, and if he had been born on the other side of the street he might have turned out a bank cashier, the operator of a chain of one-arm lunchrooms, or a college president. But Lewis is essentially a revolutionist. He does not dream, like ordinary labor leaders, of being invited to dinner at the Maryland Club, and there gorging on free terrapin, caviar and champagne; he dreams of liquidating the Maryland Club with the connivance of a Supreme Court packed with forward-lookers, of stripping all the members of their cushioned silk underwear and diamond stickpins, and of inviting them not too politely to take up picks and shovels in the mines and steel mills of Pennsylvania.

Lewis says that he is not a Communist, and there is no reason to doubt him. He is too hard-boiled a fellow to swallow the puerile rubbish that passes for dialectic among the Marxian intellectuals. But all the same he joins in some of their fundamental assumptions, just as he joins in those of the New Deal sorcerers. Especially does he join in the assumption of both outfits that the nation would be vastly benefited if its present scheme of government could be radically overhauled, and the safeguards now thrown about property eliminated, and all power and prerogative handed over to men of vision, sworn to serve and save the lowly.

Thus the young professors and the Red fee-faw-foh-fums are alike in favor of him, just as they both pooh-pooh the Hon. Mr. Green, who believes in all innocence in the present system. Lewis, if he beats Green, will help along the game of all uplifters, Utopians and magicians, of whatever wing. He will help the New Dealers by moving the country a step nearer the Planned Economy they advocate so poetically, and he will help the Reds by promoting the division of all Americans into classes, and opening the way for the organization of a labor party.

The Reds, as they admit frankly on frequent occasions, believe that this Labor party, once it is a going concern, will gradually edge in their direction, and in the end become Red itself. They realize that they are too little trusted by working men today for them to undertake its organization themselves, but they are confident that they will be able to seize it after it is organized by others, and by the familiar process of boring from within. In support of this confidence they point to the history of Labor parties in other countries, and especially in Germany, Italy, France and Spain. In England they came a cropper, but they hope for better luck in America.

Obviously, the election of the Hon. Mr. Landon would throw a number of monkey-wrenches into these benign arrangements. He is plainly in doubt that the launching of an open class war

would be a good thing for the country, and he is equally in
doubt that the Planned Economy of the young professors has
worked well enough so far to justify its unlimited extension. If
he is elected, it will take him all of his first term to wind up the
New Deal, and maybe most of his second term, but he may be
trusted, at the worst, to pull that way as fast as possible.

Thus he has no support among men of vision, and to most of
them he is anathema. In particular, he is anathema to the Reds,
who believe, and on sound ground, that if he makes a reasonably
good job of his scavenging, the country will quickly return to
something resembling normalcy, and that their own alarming
evangel will find fewer and fewer customers. Roosevelt, they
think, offers them a much better chance. He will keep the credulous hoping for miracles, and so long as they hope for miracles
it will be possible to feed them anything, including even Communism. So the Red brethren favor Dr. Roosevelt. When they mention Landon, it is to yell "Voilà l'ennemi!"

Roosevelt's repudiation of their support is no proof that he
abhors them, but simply that he disdains them. Their principal
ideas, in fact, are entertained by some of his chief aides and followers, not a few of whom are prominent members of the "I Am
Not a Communist, But ———" Club. Indeed, there are wizards
in Washington, and some of them in high office, beside whom
Stalin looks almost like a member of the Liberty League. But
the Communists, despite all the uproar they make, can actually
deliver very few votes, so it is smart politics to read them out
of meeting. Most of them may be trusted to vote right anyhow.

The Hon. Mr. Roosevelt's denunciation of the Hon. Mr.
Hearst is not to be taken seriously. If Hearst had kept on supporting the New Deal, he would be an angel today, and even the
Reds would be for him. The Reds are now against him, and have
made him the chief devil in their motley menagerie, simply because he has kept them jumping. And the More Abundant Life
quacks are against him for exactly the same reason.

The notion that the Hon. Mr. Landon is his stooge is complete nonsense. Hearst came out for Landon before any other considerable newspaper proprietor, and thus stole a march upon the rest, but when he did so the nomination of good Alf was already in the bag. It was in the bag because there was no other Republican candidate of any size in sight. The so-called Old Guard knew that it couldn't nominate one of its trusties, and the Western inflationists had no one to propose who could poll 100 votes in the convention. So the prize went by forfeit to the Kansas Gang, which took a middle-of-the-road position, and had a middle-of-the-road candidate in waiting.

Landon's Chautauqua speech was certainly not that of a Hearst stooge. He might have pleased Hearst immensely by denouncing Red propaganda, and at the same time made a great many votes, for an overwhelming majority of Americans are against it, and believe that it is much more dangerous than it is in fact. But he spoke out for free speech like a man, and left the denunciation of Reds to the White House secretariat. In brief, he left it to hypocrites, for even the White House secretariat must be well aware that the Reds are still for Roosevelt.

Roosevelt himself got into office with the active help of Hearst. He was in serious difficulties at the Chicago convention of 1932 when Hearst's stooges, led by the Hon. William Gibbs McAdoo, traded the Garner vote in California and Texas for the Vice-Presidency, and so gave him the nomination. If there was ever a bare-faced deal in American politics, it was that one. Hearst emerged from it a hero, and was invited to the White House as soon as Hoover cleared out. He'd be going there still if he had not revolted against the New Deal hooey. And without the change of a hair otherwise, he would be "eminent" instead of "notorious."

SHAM BATTLE

October 26, 1936

The campaign draws to a close without having developed a realistic and forthright discussion of its real issue, either in the newspapers or on the stump. The Hon. Mr. Landon's crusade for a return to what he calls the old American system has been incommoded by the fact that he has neglected to say precisely what he conceives that system to be; moreover, he has himself done violence to it, given any even half rational definition of it, by his advocacy of doles for lazy and half-witted pseudo-farmers. As for the Hon. Mr. Roosevelt he has confined himself to playing upon the innocent yearnings and hallucinations of morons of all species, and there has been precious little in his speeches to instruct, or even to entertain, the more enlightened moiety of his customers.

What the Hon. Mr. Landon really undertakes to advocate, I gather, is a return to the Jeffersonian doctrine that the only tolerable government is a relatively weak one. That doctrine, it seems to me, is still quite as sound as it was in Jefferson's day, and if it were put into practice it would probably make an end to many of the abuses and nuisances which now afflict the country. Unfortunately, only a small number of living Americans appear to believe in it, and the Hon. Mr. Landon not infrequently offers excuse for the suspicion that he is not one of them. On the metaphysical plane, to be sure, he may be a convinced Jeffersonian, but as a practical matter he is a Kansan, and in Kansas the notion that the Treasury was set up to pay the debts of clod-hoppers is as axiomatic as the notion that a horsehair put into a bottle of water will turn into a snake.

Thus there is no genuine debate of the question fundamentally at issue, and the campaign resolves itself into a furious flogging of irrelevancies. Soon or late, of course, a true conflict will have to be joined, but apparently the time is not yet. It may be, indeed, that the Rooseveltian or anti-Jeffersonian concept of the government as a milch-cow with 125,000,000 teats still has many years to go. Challenging it today, in the full glory of its heyday, is certainly not an enterprise that promises much of a harvest. Later on, after the cow has begun to go dry, it should be measurably easier, but there is not much chance that it will ever become anything properly describable as a cinch.

The reason is not far to seek. The great majority of men, living in a world that is very far from their heart's desire, discover early in life that they have no means within them to make it tolerable. They can neither conquer it by craft nor defy it by philosophy. Thus they are forced to seek help, and whoever offers them that help is their friend. It used to be the church, but in late years the church has gradually lost credit, partly by its own blundering and partly by the rise of competitors. Of all those competitors, the state is now the most formidable. In all kinds of countries, and in all kinds of forms, it is setting up shop as a universal savior.

Its qualifications for that office, at first glance, look very impressive. It has power of an extremely palpable and overt variety, flowing from the end of the policeman's espantoon. It penetrates to every nook and fissure of the national life, and so takes on an appearance of omniscience. It is staffed by men who are, by definition, eminent, and in that character are heard politely, even when they talk nonsense. Most of all, there is something mystical about it, something transcendental and even supernatural, so that simple people, thinking of it, slip naturally into the moony ways of thought that they employ in thinking about the awful enigmas of Heaven and Hell.

Its real nature thus tends to be concealed, and, in the long run, forgotten. That real nature may be described briefly. The state—or, to make the matter more concrete, the government—consists of a gang of men exactly like you and me. They have, taking one with another, no special talent for the business of government; they have only a talent for getting and holding office. Their principal device to that end is to search out groups who pant and pine for something they can't get, and to promise to give it to them. Nine times out of ten that promise is worth nothing. The tenth time it is made good by looting A to satisfy B. In other words, government is a broker in pillage, and every election is a sort of advance auction sale of stolen goods.

Government, of course, has other functions, and some of them are useful and even valuable. It is supposed, in theory, to keep the peace, and also to protect the citizen against acts of God and the public enemy. It performs, too, many lesser but still necessary services, such as, for example, maintaining the roads and carrying the mails. But it must be obvious that these operations seldom have any influence on the rise and fall of the men who constitute the governing camorra, and are very far from their principal concern.

What mainly engages them, and increasingly in late years, is the satisfaction of purely private wants. Their first business is to discover such wants, and their second is to meet them. They may be either spiritual or material. The have-not, B, may ask only a larger measure of power over the life and liberty of A; on the other hand, his yearning may be for a share of A's property. In either case, it is the chief present business of government, which is to say, of politicians, to give him what he wants. And in both cases it may be given to him only by taking away something that belongs to A.

There was a time when this forced transfer of goods lay quite outside the sphere of government, and was regarded with abhorrence by the prevailing governmental philosophers. To Thomas Jefferson, prohibition would have seemed as completely outrageous as the AAA, and for the same reason. He believed that the sole function of government was to protect citizens in the enjoyment of their lawfully acquired rights and goods, and that when it had gone so far it should shut down. But today its field of operation has been immensely widened, and its principal aim, in nearly all the great countries of the world, is to maintain itself in power by transferring rights and goods from those who oppose it to those who support it. The object vended is always somebody else's property. The consideration is votes.

This process goes on under various disguises, some of them of a high plausibility. In Russia the theory is that it is a rectification, by altruistic men, of the gross inequalities that existed under the czars; in the United States it is depicted as a measure of social justice, and spoken of as the New Deal or the More Abundant Life. But its true purpose is always the same, and likewise its true effect. That purpose is to keep a gang of politicians in control of the government, and that effect is to pillage unmercifully all persons who venture to challenge them.

How long this sort of thing can go on remains to be seen. There is, in the process, a considerable wastage, for the brokers take a heavy toll. When A is relieved of a dollar, not all of it goes to B—indeed, B seldom gets a half of it. The rest goes to the philanthropists who engineer the transaction. Even when the thing exchanged is not property but power—as, for example, in the case of prohibition—the ostensible beneficiaries find that most of it has stuck in the hands of the entrepreneurs, and that some of their own power has stuck there too.

At the moment, as I have said, there is no realistic discussion of this process in our great and glorious country. The Hon. Mr. Landon is opposed, in theory, to every such augmentation of governmental functions and prerogatives, but he is apparently willing to condone a great deal of it in practice. The Hon. Mr. Roosevelt is for it without qualification: the kind of government he seems to advocate would take the place of all other human agencies, and every man's goods, whether material or spiritual, would be held only by its license, and subject to its revocation of that license for contumacy to itself.

Obviously, not much is to be hoped for in the way of an amelioration of this scheme of things. It sets up so many vested rights, not only in its admitted beneficiaries but also and more especially in its operators, that it would be asking too much of human nature to expect them to consent to any whittling down. The thing must be obliterated in *toto*, or it will never be got rid of at all. The question before the house is, When and by whom will a forthright attack upon it be made? And will the fore-ordained revolutionist, if he ever appears, be realist enough to see that the only remedy that will really work is to make government weak, and to keep it weak? The chances, alas, are very good that his first measure will be to try to make it even stronger than it is today.

THE CHOICE TOMORROW

November 2, 1936

Nevertheless, and despite all Hell's angels, I shall vote for the Hon. Mr. Landon tomorrow. To a lifelong Democrat, of course, it will be something of a wrench. But it seems to me that the choice is one that genuine Democrats are almost bound to make. On the one side are all the basic principles of their party, handed down from its first days and tried over and over again in the fires of experience; on the other side is a gallimaufry of transparent quackeries, puerile in theory and dangerous in practice. To vote Democratic this year it is necessary, by an unhappy irony, to vote for a Republican. But to vote with the party is to vote for a gang of mountebanks who are no more Democrats than a turkey buzzard is an archangel.

This exchange of principles, with the party labels unchanged, is naturally confusing, but it is certainly not so confusing that

it goes unpenetrated. Plenty of Republicans who believe sincerely
in a strong Federal Government are going to vote tomorrow
for the Hon. Mr. Roosevelt, and plenty of Democrats who believe sincerely in the autonomy of the States and a rigid limitation of the Federal power are going to vote, as I shall, for the
Hon. Mr. Landon. Whether the shift that confronts us will be
permanent remains to be seen. But while it lasts it is manifestly
very real, and those who let party loyalties blind them to its
reality will be voting very foolishly.

The issue tends to be confused by a distrust of both Presidential candidates, inevitable under the circumstances. There
are those who believe that the Hon. Mr. Roosevelt, if he is re-
elected, will abandon the socialistic folderol that he has been
advocating since 1933 and go back to the traditional program
of his party, and there are those who believe that the Hon. Mr.
Landon, if elected, will quickly turn out to be only another
Harding, Hoover or McKinley. Both notions, it seems to me,
represent little more than a naïve sort of wishful thinking.
Landon, I am convinced, will actually stay put, and so will
Roosevelt. Roosevelt, to be sure, has flopped once, but he has
now gone too far down his new road to turn back again.

The defense commonly made of him is that he confronted, in
1933, an unprecedent situation, and so had to resort to new and
even revolutionary devices in dealing with it. There is no truth
in either half of that theory. The situation that he confronted
differed only quantitatively, and not at all qualitatively, from
others that had been confronted in the past. And of all the devices he employed in dealing with it the only ones that really
worked were those that had been tried before.

I am aware that there are many undoubtedly intelligent persons who believe otherwise. The fact, indeed, is not to be wondered at, for the intelligent, like the unintelligent, are responsive
to propaganda, and all the propaganda since 1933 has been
running one way. But it still remains historically true that all

the major problems before the country when Hoover blew up were intrinsically simple and familiar ones, and it still remains true that those which were not tackled in tried and rational ways still remain unsolved.

All the rest was quackery pure and unadulterated. The situation of the country was exaggerated in precisely the same way that a quack doctor exaggerates the illness of his patient, and for exactly the same reason. And the showy and preposterous treatments that were whooped up had no more virtue in them, at bottom, than his pills and liniments. We then and there entered upon an era of quackery that yet afflicts and exhausts the country. We'll not get clear of it until all the quacks are thrown out.

Whether that will happen tomorrow I do not know. The probabilities, as anyone can see, are largely against it. But soon or late the business will have to be undertaken, and the longer it is delayed the more difficult it will become. For people in the mass soon grow used to anything, including even being swindled. There comes a time when the patter of the quack becomes as natural and as indubitable to their ears as the texts of Holy Writ, and when that time comes it is a dreadful job debamboozling them.

The *bona fides* of the Hon. Mr. Roosevelt was pretty generally assumed in the first days of his Presidentiad. He was, to be sure, excessively melodramatic, but observers remembered that he was a Roosevelt, and that a talent for drama was thus in his blood. Even his closing of the banks—in retrospect, a highly dubious measure—was accepted without serious protest, even by bankers. The NRA, when it was first announced, seemed a plausible if somewhat violent remedy for admitted evils, and most of his other devices of those days got the same tolerant reception.

But as his administration closed its first year, and he gradually extended and elaborated his program, it began to be evident that he was going far beyond the borders of the reasonable, and that the theory underlying some of his major operations, as it was expounded by his principal agents, was becoming increasingly fantastic and absurd. Bit by bit, the purpose of restoring the country to its normal manner and ease of life was submerged in the purpose of bringing in a brummage Utopia, fashioned in part out of the idiotic hallucinations of the cow States and in part out of the gaudy evangel of Moscow. And simultaneously, the welfare of the American people as a whole began to be forgotten in a special concern for special classes and categories of them, all of manifestly inferior status and all willing to vote right for goods in hand.

In brief, the New Deal became a political racket, and that is what it is today—that and nothing more. Its chief practical business is to search out groups that can be brought into the Hon. Jim Farley's machine by grants out of the public treasury, which is to say, out of the pockets of the rest of us. To serve that lofty end the national currency has been debased, the national credit has been imperiled and a crushing burden has been put on every man who wants to pay his own way in the world and asks only to be let alone. The excuse that a grave emergency justified such pillage is now abandoned. The emergency is past, but the pillage goes on.

At tomorrow's plebiscite this grandiose and excessively dangerous Tammanyizing of the country will come to judgment, with the chances, as I have said, in favor of its ratification. That it will be supported heartily by all its beneficiaries goes without saying. Every dole-bird in the country, of whatever sort, will certainly vote for it. It will get the suffrages of all the gimme pseudo-farmers in the Middle West, of all the half-witted sharecroppers in the South, of all the professional uplifters and of all the jobholders on Farley's ever-swelling roll. It will be whooped up by every politician who lives and thrives by promising to turn loose A in B's cornfield. It will have the kindly aid of all other varieties of professional messiahs, ranging from

the fantoddish prophets of milleniums to the downright thieves.
Will there be enough of them to ratify it? Probably not. It
will meet also some support by honest if deluded men and
women. Thousands of them, I gather, are in the ranks of the
labor organizations. They have been told that the New Deal
saved them their jobs, which it didn't, and that it will prosper
them hereafter, which it won't, and large numbers of them have
believed. The actual fact is that they are not, and can never
be, the beneficiaries of any such carnival of loot; they can only
be its goats. In the long run the cost of the whole show will
settle down upon them. In the long run every man and woman
who works will have to pay for the upkeep of some Farley
heeler who has been taught that working is foolish and unnecessary and even a shade immoral.

The Brain Trust brethren, of course, still promise that all
the bills will be sent to the rich. Well, they were so sent in Russia,
and paid in full. But when they had been paid, more money was
still needed, and it is now being provided by the Russian workers. Living in filthy and miserable dens, and badly fed on poor
and monotonous food, they labor under a brutal stretch-out
system which yields them the equivalent of ten American dollars
a month. That is what Utopia always comes to in the end.

CORONER'S INQUEST

November 9, 1936

The Hon. Mr. Roosevelt's colossal victory in last Tuesday's
plebiscite gave him plenty of excuse to leap and exult, but if he
is really the smart politician that he seems to be he must be
entertaining certain stealthy, *pizzicato* qualms today. He now
carries all the burdens of omnipotence. There is no one to say

nay—that is, no one he is bound to heed. He has in his hands a blank check from and upon the American people, authorizing him to dispose of all their goods and liberties precisely as he listeth. The Congress that was elected with him will no more dare to challenge him than a pussy cat would dare to challenge a royal Bengal tiger, and even the nine old metaphysicians on Capitol Hill may be trusted to recall, if only subconsciously, that it is imprudent to spit too often into Cæsar's eye.

In brief, he has become a sort of chartered libertine, and it will be interestng to note how he reacts to his franchise. The great majority of his lieges believe firmly in the Utopia that he has been preaching since 1933, and they will now expect him to bring it in at last. He can no longer make the excuse that wicked men are hindering him, nor can he plead that he is navigating unmapped waters and must proceed cautiously. He has been engaged, for nearly four years, in exploring and mapping the way, and in that work he has had the aid of a vast band of transcendental engineers of his own choice. What everyone will look for now is full steam ahead. Either we must soon see the glorious shores of Utopia or the whole argosy will be wrecked.

For a year or two past, as everyone knows, it has been making heavy weather. Not one of its greater objectives has been attained. The rich continue rich, and many millions of the poor remain on the dole. Business has improved, but it has improved a great deal more for stockmarket speculators than for honest men. The one-crop farmers continue to bellow piteously for help. Labor is still torn between sweat-shop employers on the one hand and racketeering labor leaders on the other. For all these woes and malaises the right hon. gentleman must now find something colorably resembling remedies, and with reasonable dispatch. Either he is actually a wizard and knows how to cure them, or he is the worst quack ever heard of on earth.

Against his success in this great moral enterprise stand two inconvenient facts. The first is the fact that many, and perhaps indeed most of the woes and malaises aforesaid appear to be inherently incurable. The second is the fact that people in the mass are very mercurial, and especially the sort of people who believe in miracles. They are all with him today, but that is no assurance that they will be with him tomorrow. On the contrary, there is every reason to believe that they will turn on him, soon or late, as they have turned on all popular messiahs since the dawn of history.

The melancholy careers of Wilson, Roosevelt I and Hoover offer cases in point, to keep to recent times and the boundaries of this great Republic. Dr. Roosevelt himself, in truth, has already had a couple of warnings, and thus has good excuse for the qualms that I have surmised. After his great victory at the mid-term elections of 1934 there was a rapid descent in his popularity, and by the middle of 1935 he seemed headed for repudiation and disaster. In September, 1935, the very accurate poll of the Institute of Public Opinion showed that only a bare majority of the people canvassed were for him.

He recovered a bit toward the end of the year, and kept on gaining favor until the national conventions met last June. He then showed a headlong drop, and by the middle of July he was very near the low point he had touched in September, 1935. But when, on July 23, the speech of acceptance of the Hon. Mr. Landon was broadcast, there was a rise in the stock of the Hon. Mr. Roosevelt, and as the campaign developed it went on rising. Toward the very end, in all probability, there was another recession, but if so it was not sufficient to affect the result on election day. The hon. gentleman was reëlected by an unprecedented majority.

But it is not to be forgotten that 16,000,000 Americans voted against him. These may be trusted to stay put, and millions of those who voted for him may be trusted to begin suffering the pangs of *Katzenjammer* very shortly.

The immense improbability of the Hon. Mr. Landon's election was manifest from the day he made his first speech. It was, as such things go, a pretty good speech, and it was followed by many even better ones, but there was nothing in any of them to lift and frenzy multitudes, and there was nothing in the hon. gentleman's delivery of them to compensate for their ineffectiveness. He turned out, indeed, to be one of the worst public speakers recorded in the archives of faunal zoölogy. Over and over again, facing an eagerly friendly audience, he scotched its nascent whoops and reduced it to scratching itself.

I traveled with him on three of his four campaign trips, and witnessed his performance at close range. In all my life I have never encountered anything more depressing than his elocution. Most of his speeches were not delivered at all; they were simply recited. And what a recitation it was! If it was possible, by any device, however tortured, to stress the wrong word in a sentence, he invariably stressed it. If the text called for a howl of moral indignation he always dropped his voice, and if a sepulchral whisper was in order he raised it. The audience was never given a fair chance to applaud, and when it barged in notwithstanding it was cut off.

At Philadelphia and again at Pittsburgh the hon. gentleman started off with unaccustomed fire, and it seemed likely that he would make good speeches at last. But both times he subsided into his usual forbidding manner after a few minutes. Off the platform he is certainly not cold. On the contrary, he is a very amiable and charming fellow, and, what is more, a shrewd one. Sitting in his private car, he talked amusingly and persuasively, and often had something penetrating to say. But once he got before the microphone he became a schoolboy reciting a piece, and it was in that character that he appeared before the country. I can recall no audience that showed any sign of being genuinely aroused by him. And I encountered no radio fan, however willing, who got any kick out of his soughings.

Worse, the content of his speeches was often as ineffective as their manner of delivery. There was only one way to beat Roosevelt, and that was to attack him with horse, foot and dragoons, denouncing his mountebankeries in a voice of brass and allowing him no virtue whatever. Above the level of the dole-birds, at the start of the campaign, there was a great deal of doubt about the New Deal, and if the opposition candidate had belabored its Father Divine in the grand manner, keeping him constantly on the defensive, there might have been a different tale to tell last Tuesday.

But the Hon. Mr. Landon, it quickly appeared, was quite incapable of that sort of war. He was too mild a fellow for it, and, perhaps I should add, too candid, too conscientious. He conceived it to be his high duty, not to flog and flay Roosevelt, but to submit his own ideas to the country, and the more he submitted them the more it became evident that some of them, and not the least important, were indistinguishable from the fundamental hallucinations of the New Deal. When he came out for more and bigger bonuses for mendicant farmers he simply surrendered to the enemy, and from that time on his campaign was dead.

In a word, the Republicans nominated the wrong candidate. They got an honest man, and one who, if he had gone to the White House, would have made a diligent, reliable and courageous President, but the majority of them took him unwillingly, and never agreed with the notions he expounded so laboriously and so futilely. The old-time professionals of the party, when they reached Cleveland last June, found themselves hamstrung. The stench of Hoover was so strong upon them that they were clapped into quarantine instantly; indeed, many of them went there voluntarily. The Western Progressives, save for the old moo-cow, Borah, were *non est*; they had gone over to the New Deal in a body, bellowing "Glory, glory, hallelujah!" This left the show to the Kansas Gang, an unearthly combination of former stooges of the Anti-Saloon League, county chairmen from the Dust Bowl and irresponsible amateurs out for a lark. It was only this Kansas Gang that had a presentable candidate ready, and he was nominated by default.

Could some other hero have won? I am inclined to believe that it was possible. Roosevelt, skillfully and relentlessly bombarded, would have got into difficulties quickly, for he was vulnerable in front, in the rear and on both flanks. But Landon's earnest homilies upon the issues of the hour left him unscathed. Until the last week of the campaign he did not even bother to answer them. All his radio time was devoted to the intoning of mellifluous dithyrambs, with music by dulcimers and accordions.

GLOSSARY

INDEX

Glossary

Allen, Henry J.: United States Senator (Rep.) from Kansas (1929–1930). Allen was an unsuccessful candidate for re-election to the seat he had been appointed to fill. A newspaper writer, editor, and publisher, he was chairman of the board of the Wichita *Beacon*.

Ames, Joseph S.: Distinguished physicist and researcher in electrodynamics. Ames was president of The Johns Hopkins University in Baltimore from 1929 to 1935.

Anderson, William H.: State superintendent of the Anti-Saloon League of Maryland (1907–1914). Active in Anti-Saloon League affairs on a national scale, Anderson was indicted in 1923 and imprisoned in New York for alteration of the accounts of the Anti-Saloon League. In 1926 he originated a constitutional amendment to remove aliens from the population count in order to determine membership of the United States House of Representatives.

Anti-Saloon League: Founded in Ohio in 1893, the Anti-Saloon League was an organization opposed to the sale of alcoholic beverages. Drawing its membership from church and temperance societies, it conducted vigorous lobbying activities in 1919 at the time of the adoption of the Eighteenth Amendment to the Constitution.

Appleby, Samuel: Candidate for election to the United States House of Representatives from Maryland's second district (1920). Though nominally a Democrat, Appleby ran as an independent anti-prohibition candidate.

Armstrong, Alexander: Republican attorney-general of Maryland

(1919–1923). In 1923, Armstrong was the unsuccessful candidate for governor.

Atwood, William O.: Political and religious leader in Baltimore. Atwood was a Republican candidate for election to the United States House of Representatives in 1920. In the same year he refused nomination by prohibition elements as a candidate for the United States Senate.

Beach, Rex: Adventure story writer. Most of Beach's books appeared in the 1920's.

Becker, Charles: New York police lieutenant. Becker was indicted in 1916 for the murder of a leading gambling figure of the day and found guilty. He was prosecuted by Charles S. Whitman, later governor of New York.

Benjamin, Raymond: Lawyer and diplomat. From 1918 to 1936, Benjamin was assistant chairman of the Republican National Committee, and in 1930 he was rumoured to be slated for the chairmanship. This, however, never materialized.

Bennett, Jesse Lee: Journalist. From 1916 to 1926 Bennett contributed a column called *The Skeptics* to the Baltimore *Sun*.

Blease, Coleman L.: United States Senator (Dem.) from South Carolina (1925–1931). Blease was an unsuccessful candidate for renomination in 1930.

Bolton, Chester C.: Republican member of the United States House of Representatives from Ohio (1929–1937). Bolton was an unsuccessful candidate for re-election in 1936, but in the election of 1938 he was returned to the House. He died in 1939 and his wife was elected to succeed him.

Bonzano, John Cardinal: Apostolic Delegate of the Vatican to the United States in 1928.

Borah, William E.: United States Senator (Rep.) from Idaho (1907–1940). Borah formed part of the irreconcilable opposition to United States participation in the League of Nations. An ardent pacifist, he was one of the prime movers in having the United States call the Washington Conference for the Limitation of Armaments in 1921.

Bow, Clara: A motion-picture star, popular during the 1920's, who became known as the "It Girl."

Bowers, Claude G.: Diplomat and politician. Bowers was an editorial writer for the New York *World* (1923–1931). In 1928 he was chairman and keynote speaker of the Democratic National Convention. From 1933 to 1939, Bowers was Ambassador to Spain.

Brandeis, Louis D.: Outstanding jurist. Brandeis was appointed an associate justice of the Supreme Court (1916) by President Wilson. The Senate opposition to his nomination, largely based on religious prejudice, forms one of the less brilliant pages of senatorial history.

Brennan, George M.: Banker and government official. Brennan served with the War Finance Corporation (1923–1928). He campaigned vigorously for the nomination of Alfred E. Smith by the Democratic National Convention in 1928.

Brisbane, Arthur: Journalist and editor. Brisbane was influential during the 1920's as an editorial writer and columnist in leading Hearst newspapers such as the New York *Sun*, New York *Evening Journal,* and Chicago *Herald.*

"Brother Charley" (Bryan, Charles W.): Democratic governor of Nebraska (1923–1925 and 1931–1935). In 1924, Bryan was Democratic candidate for vice-president of the United States. Bryan was the brother of William Jennings Bryan.

Broun, Heywood: Journalist and author. With others in the literary world, Broun sponsored the Book-of-the-Month Club in 1927. He was a favorite journalist of the extreme liberal movement of the 1930's and very active in the Newspaper Guild.

Brown, Walter F.: Lawyer and politician. Brown was United States Postmaster-General from 1929 to 1933.

Burleson, Albert S.: Democratic member of the United States House of Representatives from Texas (1899–1913). Burleson was United States Postmaster-General from 1913 to 1921. He was an intimate friend and adviser of President Wilson.

Burns, William J.: Detective and politician. From 1921 to 1924, Burns was the director of the Bureau of Investigation of the United States Department of Justice. He resigned with Attorney-General Daugherty during the scandals involving the Department.

Butler, Nicholas Murray: President of Columbia University from 1902 to 1947. Butler was a perfunctory favorite-son candidate for the presidential nomination by the Republican party in 1920.

Butler, Pierce: Jurist. Butler was appointed to the United States Supreme Court by President Harding in 1922. An outspoken ultra-conservative, he was strenuously opposed to many of the early New Deal measures.

Candler, Asa G.: A manufacturer (1851–1929) who developed the production and marketing of Coca-Cola.

Candler, Warren A.: Methodist-Episcopal clergyman. Candler was president of Emory College, in Georgia, and a bishop of the Methodist-Episcopal Church of the South. His brother was the founder of the Coca-Cola Company.

Cannon, James, Jr.: Methodist-Episcopal clergyman. Cannon was chairman of the Anti-Saloon League of America and an active leader of the Southern Democrats opposed to Alfred E. Smith in the presidential campaign of 1928.

Cardozo, Benjamin N.: Jurist. Cardozo was an associate justice of the New York Supreme Court (1914–1928). In 1932, President Hoover appointed him an associate justice of the United States Supreme Court.

Cecil, Robert: British nobleman and statesman who participated in the drafting of the League of Nations Covenant. Lord Cecil was awarded the Nobel Peace Prize in 1937.

Christensen, Parley Parker: Lawyer and politician. In 1920, Christensen was a candidate of the Farmer-Labor party for the presidency of the United States. In 1926 he was the Progressive party candidate in Illinois for the United States Senate.

Colby, Bainbridge: Associated with the candidacy of Theodore Roosevelt for the presidential nomination in 1912. In 1920, when President Wilson asked for the resignation of Robert Lansing, because of his acts while Wilson was ill, Colby was appointed to succeed Lansing as Secretary of State.

Comstock Society: Better known as the Society for the Suppression of Vice. Founded by Anthony Comstock, the Society conducted spectacular raids on publishers and vendors during the early 1900's.

Coughlin, Charles Edward: Roman Catholic clergyman. Father Coughlin was the author of several controversial books and pamphlets in addition to a series of radio sermons. He was most active in the late 1920's and 1930's, ceasing his major activities of a non-ecclesiastical nature after the United States entered World War II.

Cox, James M.: Newspaperman and politician. Cox was a member of the United States House of Representatives (1909–1913) and Governor of Ohio (1913–1915 and 1917–1921). A strong advocate of United States participation in the League of Nations, Cox was the Democratic nominee for president in 1920.

Crain, Robert: Maryland lawyer and politician. A life-long Democrat, Crain was almost solely responsible for bringing the 1912 Democratic National Convention to Baltimore. He had been a delegate to all Democratic national conventions between 1908 and 1924.

Cram, Ralph Adams: A leading architect of principally university and college buildings which were constructed during the 1920's.

Crane, Frank: Methodist clergyman. During the 1920's, Crane was a widely read syndicated writer of a daily inspirational column for newspapers.

Creel Press Bureau: Officially known as the Committee on Public Information, it took the name of its chairman, George Creel. He was appointed by President Wilson to head the committee, under whose direction the government aimed propoganda at home and abroad.

Cummings, Homer S.: Lawyer and politician. Cummings was United States attorney-general from 1933 to 1939.

Curtis, Charles W.: United States Senator (Rep.) from Kansas (1907–1913 and 1915–1929). Curtis was an energetic and competent leader who early urged the selection of Warren Harding as the Republican presidential nominee in 1920. In 1928, Curtis was elected Vice-President of the United States.

Curtis, Cyrus H.: Publisher of magazines and newspapers. In 1876, Curtis founded the *Ladies' Home Journal*. He later established the Curtis Publishing Company, which, among other periodicals and journals, owned the New York *Evening Post*.

Daniels, Josephus: Journalist and statesman. Daniels served as United States Secretary of the Navy from 1913 to 1921.

Darrow, Clarence: Lawyer and writer. Darrow first achieved prominence as counsel for Eugene V. Debs when he was indicted in 1894. Further fame came as a result of several widely publicized trials, notably the Leopold-Loeb trial in 1924, the Scopes trial in 1925, and the Scottsboro case in 1932.

Daugherty, Harry M.: United States Attorney-General (1921–1924). Long desirous of making Warren Harding president, Daugherty was largely responsible for maneuvering Harding's nomination at the 1920 Republican National Convention. In

1927, Daugherty was tried and acquitted on charges of conspiracy to defraud the United States government.

Davis, James J.: United States Senator (Rep.) from Pennsylvania (1930–1945). From 1921 to 1930, Davis was United States Secretary of Labor, and in 1930, he was elected to fill the vacancy caused by the refusal of the Senate to seat William S. Vare.

Davis, John William: Lawyer and diplomat. In 1924, Davis and Charles W. Bryan were nominated for the presidency and the vice-presidency by the Democratic National Convention. On the 103rd ballot, Davis was selected as a compromise candidate to break the deadlock between William G. McAdoo and Alfred E. Smith.

Dawes, Charles G.: First director of the United States Bureau of the Budget (1921). Dawes was president of the commission to investigate possibilities of German reparations as a result of World War I. In 1924, he was elected Vice-President of the United States.

Debs, Eugene V.: Labor organizer and politician. Active in the railroad labor movement and a leader in the famous Pullman strike, Debs organized the Social Democratic party of America in 1897. He was the Socialist candidate for president five times between 1900 and 1920. In 1918 he was convicted of violation of the Espionage Act and sentenced to ten years imprisonment. He was pardoned by President Harding in 1921.

Denby, Edwin N.: United States Secretary of the Navy (1921–1924). Denby was criticized for allowing the transfer of naval oil reserves to the Department of the Interior from whence the lands were then leased to private firms. His signature on the leases of Teapot Dome oil lands involved him in the scandal, but he was never accused of corruption. He resigned in 1924 to lessen the embarrassment to President Coolidge.

Divine, Father: Father Divine (born George Baker) is an American negro leader of a religious cult. He moved north from Georgia in 1915, styling himself first as Major Divine, later becoming Father Divine. Many of his followers believe him a personification of the Deity. Mencken referred to Franklin Roosevelt as the Father Divine of the Democratic party.

Doheny, Edward L.: Oil producer and industrialist. Doheny was involved in the Teapot Dome oil scandals and in 1924 was accused of bribing Albert B. Fall, Secretary of the Interior, in order to obtain preferred treatment in the distribution of oil leases. He was indicted with Fall on charges of conspiracy and bribery.

Ebert, Friedrich: German politician. Ebert was the leader of the Social Democratic party and the first president of the German Reich (1919–1925). Ebert was one of the first Germans in a responsible position to attempt to suppress the rise of Hitler.

Evarts, William M.: Lawyer and reformer. Chief counsel for President Johnson in his impeachment proceedings and largely responsible for his acquittal, Evarts later led movements for law reform against the "Tweed Ring." In 1877, he was chief counsel for the Republican party in the Hayes-Tilden electoral vote dispute.

Fairbanks, Charles W.: United States Senator (Rep.) from Indiana (1897–1905). Fairbanks was elected Vice-President in 1904 with Theodore Roosevelt at the head of the Republican ticket. In 1916 he was an unsuccessful candidate for vice-president with Charles E. Hughes as the presidential candidate.

Fall, Albert B.: United States Senator (Rep.) from New Mexico (1912–1921). Fall was appointed Secretary of the Interior by President Harding and served from 1921 to 1923. Through investigation, Fall was disclosed to have secretly transferred government oil lands to private interests. In 1929 he was tried and convicted for defrauding the government and for accepting a bribe.

Farley, James A.: Politician. Farley was chairman of the Democratic National Committee from 1932 to 1940. Largely responsible for the organization and conduct of the presidential nomination and election campaigns of Franklin Roosevelt in 1932 and 1936, Farley broke with Roosevelt in 1940 over the third-term issue. He was United States Postmaster-General from 1933 to 1940.

Fess, Simeon D.: United States Senator (Rep.) from Ohio (1923–1935). Fess was an unsuccessful candidate for re-election in 1934. He had been a member of the group of intimates that surrounded President Harding.

Fish, Hamilton: Republican member of the United States House of Representatives from New York (1920–1945). An ultra-conservative, Fish was an unsuccessful candidate for re-election in 1944.

Fletcher, Henry P.: Chairman of the Republican National Committee (1934–1936).

Folk, Joseph Wingate: Lawyer and politician. Folk was a district

attorney at St. Louis in the early years of the 1900's who exposed
and prosecuted those responsible for municipal corruption. He
was governor of Missouri from 1905 to 1909 and was frequently
mentioned as a candidate for the presidential nomination.

Freeman, Douglas Southall: Editor and writer. From 1915, Freeman was the editor of the Richmond *News Leader*. A noted historian of the American South, Freeman was awarded the Pulitzer
Prize in 1939.

Freeman, Joseph: Journalist and writer. Freeman was the cofounder
of *New Masses* in 1926 and its editor from 1931 to 1937. Freeman has also published several books on the Soviet Union.

Garner, John Nance: Democratic member of the United States
House of Representatives from Texas (1903–1933). Garner was
elected Vice-President of the United States in 1932 and 1936.

Gary, Elbert H.: Industrialist. Gary was the chief organizer of the
United States Steel Corporation and served as its chairman from
1903 to 1927. In the great steel strike of 1919, Gary refused to
deal with the newly formed union of steel workers and in his determination to hold to an open shop policy brought the union to
defeat and caused the resignation of William Z. Foster as president of the union.

George, David Lloyd: Prime Minister of Great Britain during
World War I.

Gerard, James Watson: Diplomat and lawyer. Gerard was an associate justice of the New York Supreme Court (1908–1913). From
1913 to 1917 he served as ambassador to Germany. In 1914 he
was the Democratic Party candidate in New York for the United
States Senate.

Gibbons, James Cardinal: Roman Catholic clergyman and Archbishop of Baltimore in 1877. Elevated to the Cardinalate in 1886,
Cardinal Gibbons had long since gained the respect of all classes
by his judicious policies.

Glass, Carter: United States Senator (Dem.) from Virginia (1902–
1918). In 1918, Glass was appointed Secretary of the Treasury
in the Cabinet of President Wilson. He resigned from the Cabinet
in 1920, was elected to the Senate and served until 1946.

Goldsborough, Phillips Lee: Republican governor of Maryland
(1912–1915). In 1929, Goldsborough was elected to the United
States Senate and served until 1935. In 1934 he was an unsuccessful candidate for nomination as governor.

Goldsborough, T. Alan: Democratic member of the United States House of Representatives from Maryland (1921–1939). In 1939, Goldsborough was appointed associate justice of the District Court of the United States for the District of Columbia.

Gompers, Samuel: Labor leader and organizer. Gompers was one of the organizers and the first president of the American Federation of Labor (1886–1924). Ignoring formal alliances with or indorsements of particular political parties, Gompers led his union down the path which permitted him to take whatever advantages were available from either major party.

Green, William: Labor leader. Green succeeded Gompers as president of the American Federation of Labor. He kept the faith of Gompers and made no formal alliances with any political party. He brought to a stage of high development the practice of presenting his unions to businessmen as a bulwark against "radicals."

Gregory, Thomas Watt: Lawyer and politician. Gregory was Attorney-General of the United States from 1914 to 1919.

Grey, Edward: British nobleman and Secretary of State for Foreign Affairs (1905–1916). Grey served temporarily as British ambassador to the United States in connection with the German peace settlement following the First World War.

Guest, Edgar A.: Writer and poet. Guest was on the staff of the Detroit *Free Press* from 1895 until his death and conducted a column of verse and humorous sketches.

Hall, Grover Cleveland: Editor and writer. Hall was a liberal editor of several small Alabama newspapers and in 1928 was a Pulitzer Prize winner for his editorials against racial and religious intolerance.

Hamlin, Hannibal: United States Senator (Dem.) from Maine (1848–1857). Hamlin left the Democratic party in 1856 and was elected Republican governor of Maine, in which office he served for one year until his re-election to the United States Senate as a Republican. He served in the Senate from 1857 to 1861, when he was elected Vice-President of the United States. In 1869, Hamlin was re-elected to the United States Senate and served until 1881.

Harrington, Emerson C.: Democratic governor of Maryland (1916–1920).

Harris, William Julius: United States Senator (Dem.) from Georgia (1919–1932).

Harrison, Byron Patton: United States Senator (Dem.) from Mississippi (1919–1941). Harrison served as temporary chairman of the Democratic National Convention in 1924.

Hawkins, W. Ashbie: Lawyer and politician. Hawkins was the first Negro to be admitted to the Baltimore Bar. In 1920, he was a candidate for election to the United States Senate.

Hayes, Patrick Cardinal: Roman Catholic clergyman. Hayes, Archbishop of New York from 1919 until his death, was elevated to the Cardinalate in 1924.

Hays, Will H.: Politician. Chairman of the Republican National Committee (1919–1921), Hays was appointed Postmaster-General by President Harding. He subsequently became President of the Motion Picture Producers and Distributors of America.

Heflin, J. Thomas: United States Senator (Dem.) from Alabama (1920–1931). Prior to serving as a senator, Heflin was a member of the United States House of Representatives (1904-1920).

Heney, Francis Joseph: Lawyer and government official. Heney was employed by the United States attorney-general to prosecute land fraud cases at Portland, Oregon, in 1903. Heney secured the indictment of the United States attorney in Oregon and other prominent officials.

Herrick, Myron T.: Politician and diplomat. Herrick was active in aiding in the nomination and election of McKinley as President. He was Republican governor of Ohio (1903–1905) and United States ambassador to France (1912–1914; 1921–1929). Herrick played an active role in the nomination of Warren Harding in 1920.

Hobart, Garrett A.: Republican politician elected Vice-President of the United States in 1896.

Hog Island: A shipyard on the Delaware River built during the First World War by the Federal Emergency Fleet Corporation for the multiple fabrication of merchant ships. In its time it was probably the world's largest single-location industrial empire.

Hopkins, Harry: Government official. Hopkins was Director of the Works Progress Administration in the early years of the New Deal. He was appointed Secretary of Commerce in 1938 and served until his selection as head of the Lend-Lease Administration in 1941. During the Second World War, Hopkins served as personal envoy of President Roosevelt to Russia and Great Britain.

Hopkins, Richard J.: Associate justice of the Kansas Supreme Court (1923–1929). Hopkins was an active member of the executive committee of the Anti-Saloon League of America.

House, Edward M.: Friend and confidant of President Wilson. House was commissioned special representative of the United States at the interallied conference to effect co-ordination of military and naval action in World War I. In 1918 he was designated by the President to act for the United States in negotiating the armistice with the Central Powers.

House, Jay Elmer: Journalist and writer. In 1919, House was a columnist with the Philadelphia *Public Ledger* and the New York *Evening Post*. Between 1915 and 1919 he had been the Republican mayor of Topeka, Kansas.

Howell, Clark: Journalist and editor of the Atlanta *Constitution*. Howell was the director of the Associated Press from the date of its organization in 1900.

Hughes, Charles Evans: Republican governor of New York (1907–1910). In 1910 Hughes was appointed an associate justice of the United States Supreme Court. He resigned in 1916 and was the unsuccessful candidate for President. From 1921 to 1925 he was Secretary of State and in 1930 was appointed Chief Justice of the Supreme Court.

Huston, Claudius Hart: Businessman and politician. In 1920, Huston, a Republican, broke the so-called "Solid South" in Tennessee. From 1921 to 1923 he was Assistant Secretary of Commerce.

Hyde, Henry M.: Journalist and political reporter. Hyde was a star reporter on the Chicago *Tribune* and joined the Baltimore *Evening Sun* in 1920, his first assignment being to cover the 1920 conventions with Henry L. Mencken.

Ibsen, Henrik: Norwegian poet and dramatist of the late nineteenth century.

Ickes, Harold: Politician and government official. Ickes was prominent in Republican politics to about 1926. In 1932 he worked in the interest of the Roosevelt-Garner ticket and in 1933 he was appointed Secretary of the Interior and served until 1945.

Ireland, John: Roman Catholic prelate and archbishop of St. Paul, Minnesota. Archbishop Ireland was influential in founding the Catholic University in 1889.

Johnson, Hiram: United States Senator (Rep.) from California (1917–1945). Johnson was governor of California (1910–1917) and one of the founders of the Progressive party of the United States. He was that party's nominee for vice-president in 1912. A strong opponent of the League of Nations, Johnson sought the GOP presidential nomination in 1920, and several times during his career he was offered the vice-presidential nomination.

Johnson, Reverdy: United States Senator (Dem.) from Maryland (1845–1849; 1863–1868). Johnson first gained fame representing the defense in the Dred Scott case. He was United States Attorney-General (1849–1850). Unsuccessful in his vigorous attempts to avert the Civil War, he did manage to keep Maryland in the Union.

Kahn, Otto: Banker and financier. Kahn was also president and chairman of the board of the Metropolitan Opera Company of New York.

Kellogg, Frank B.: United States Senator (Rep.) from Minnesota (1917–1923). Kellogg was ambassador to Great Britain (1924–1925) and from 1925 to 1929 was Secretary of State, during which time he negotiated the Kellogg-Briand Pact with the foreign minister of France. In 1929 he was awarded the Nobel Peace Prize.

Kelly, Howard A.: Surgeon and professor of gynecology at The Johns Hopkins Hospital and School of Medicine (1889–1919). Kelley was the author of many books on medical and other subjects.

Kent, Frank R.: Journalist and author. Kent was managing editor of the Baltimore *Sun* (1911–1921) and since 1921 its vice-president. The writer of a column on politics syndicated in more than 100 newspapers, Kent was also the author of several books on politics and political behaviour.

Knickman, Walter E.: Physician. Though a Republican, in 1920 Knickman was the candidate of the independent anti-prohibition elements for election to the United States House of Representatives from Maryland.

Knox, W. Franklin: Newspaper publisher and politician. In 1936, Knox was the Republican nominee for vice-president. Though still a Republican, he was appointed Secretary of the Navy (1940) by President Franklin Roosevelt.

Landon, Alfred M.: Republican governor of Kansas (1933–1937).

In 1936, Landon was the Republican nominee for president of the United States.

Lane, William Preston: Lawyer and politician. Lane was attorney-general of Maryland (1930–1934). A Democrat, he was elected governor in 1947 and served until 1951.

Lansing, Robert: Secretary of State (1915–1920). Appointed by President Woodrow Wilson, Lansing's resignation was demanded by Wilson in 1920 because during Wilson's illness he committed acts which the President felt usurped his prerogatives.

Lewis, J. Hamilton: United States Senator (Dem.) from Illinois (1913–1919). Lewis was an unsuccessful candidate in 1918, but was a candidate again in 1930 and served until his death in 1939.

Lewis, John L.: Labor leader and president of the United Mine Workers since 1920. Lewis organized the Congress of Industrial Organizations and was its first president (1935–1941). He resigned in 1941 according to a promise he made if Franklin Roosevelt were elected for a third term, but he retained the presidency of the United Mine Workers.

Linthicum, J. Charles: Democratic member of the United States House of Representatives from Maryland (1911–1932).

Lodge, Henry Cabot: United States Senator (Rep.) from Massachusetts (1893–1924). Lodge was a delegate to every Republican national convention between 1884 and 1924, and served as chairman three times (1900, 1908, 1920). He lead the opposition to the League of Nations and was largely responsible for the Senate's refusal to ratify the Covenant.

Long, Huey P.: Democratic governor of Louisiana (1928–1931) and United States Senator (1931–1935). Noted for his demagoguery and for his dictatorial control over Louisiana, Long was assassinated in 1935. Prior to that he had presented a considerable potential threat to the renomination of Franklin Roosevelt by the Democratic party in 1936.

Lowden, Frank O.: Republican governor of Illinois (1917-1921). In 1920, Lowden was a leading candidate for the Republican presidential nomination, and the deadlock which ensued between him and General Leonard Wood made it possible for the nomination of Warren G. Harding as a "dark horse."

Lucas, Robert H.: Lawyer and politician. Lucas was the United States Commissioner of Internal Revenue (1929–1930) and was appointed executive director of the Republican National Committee in 1931.

Lusk, Clayton R.: New York State Senator and chairman of the New York State Legislative Committee investigating seditious activities in the state in the years following World War I. Lusk, desirous of establishing a State Sedition Bureau, was the World War I manifestation in New York of the hysteria which seems to follow every war.

McAdoo, William Gibbs: United States Secretary of the Treasury (1913–1918). McAdoo was a prominent candidate for the Democratic nomination for president in 1920, and in 1924 he lead the other candidates for nomination on more than 100 ballots, only to lose to John W. Davis on the 103rd. From 1933 to 1939 he was United States Senator (Dem.) from California.

McCormick, Anne O'Hare: Free-lance foreign correspondent of the New York *Times*. In 1937, Mrs. McCormick was awarded a Pulitzer Prize for European correspondence, the first woman to receive a major Pulitzer Prize in journalism.

McLean, Edward B.: A well known Washington figure of the 1920's, McLean, a multi-millionaire, was involved in the oil scandal arising from the fraud of Secretary of the Interior Albert Fall. At the subsequent hearings and trial, McLean contributed to the sordidness of the affair.

McPherson, Aimée Semple: Evangelist and religious leader. Miss McPherson began as an evangelist at 17 and traveled through the English speaking world. Most active in California, she built two large temples in the Los Angeles area and bought a radio station for her evangelistic work.

McReynolds, James Clark: United States Attorney-General (1913–1914). McReynolds was appointed an associate justice of the United States Supreme Court in 1914.

Maeterlinck, Maurice: Belgian poet, dramatist, and essayist. Maeterlinck wrote poignant articles about the German occupation of Belgium during World War I.

Mann, Edward Coke: Democratic member of the United States House of Representatives from South Carolina (1919–1921; 1927–1931).

Marburg, Theodore: Publicist and diplomat. A member of an old Maryland family, Marburg was United States Minister to Belgium (1912–1914) and an active supporter of United States participation in the League of Nations.

Marshall, Charles C.: Lawyer and writer. An authority on Catholic canon law and United States constitutional law, Marshall was the author of the famous "An Open Letter to the Hon. Alfred E. Smith," in which he requested Smith to state his position on possible conflicts between canon law and constitutional law should they arise while he was president.

Martin, Harry C.: Warden of the Baltimore City Jail during the 1920's. Martin retired from municipal service and entered private business with a fire insurance telegraph service.

Mellon, Andrew W.: Industrialist and diplomat. Mellon was United States Secretary of the Treasury (1921–1932) and ambassador to Great Britain from 1932–1933.

Michelson, Charles: Editor and writer. Michelson was publicity director of the Democratic National Committee from 1929 until 1940.

Moody, Dan: Democratic governor of Texas (1927–1931). Since 1931, Moody has been in the private practice of law.

More, Paul Elmer: Essayist and critic. More was editor of *The Nation* from 1909 to 1914.

Morgenthau, Henry, Jr.: United States Secretary of the Treasury (1934–1945).

Moronia Felix: Mencken's appelation for the South. Translated it means "Happy Land of Idiots."

Morrow, Dwight W.: Lawyer, banker, and diplomat. Morrow was a partner in the banking firm of J. P. Morgan and Company and ambassador to Mexico (1927–1930). In 1930 he was elected United States Senator (Rep.) from New Jersey and served until his death in 1931.

Moses, George: United States Senator (Rep.) from New Hampshire (1918–1933). Moses was president pro tempore of the Senate from 1925 to 1933.

Moskowitz, Belle: Social-service worker. Mrs. Moskowitz was active in New York City and New York State labor and social service work during the 1920's.

Most, John Joseph: German anarchist and editor of the latter half of the nineteenth century. Most had a long record of arrests and imprisonment in Germany, France, and England for anarchistic activities. On coming to the United States he resumed his operations and was imprisoned three times.

Mouzon, Edwin: Methodist-Episcopal bishop. A strong prohibitionist and an ardent conservative, Mouzon was nevertheless held in high esteem by people of all faiths and political persuasions because of his defense of minority groups.

Munsey, Frank A.: Publisher and owner of the New York *Evening Sun* and *Evening Telegram*. In 1912, Munsey became one of the chief financial supporters of the Progressive party.

Nation, Carry: Temperance agitator. Mrs. Nation went on wrecking expeditions through Kansas cities and towns in the early 1900's destroying saloons and other establishments selling intoxicants.

"Nebraska John the Baptist": Mencken's appelation for Charles W. Bryan, brother of William Jennings Bryan.

Newton, Louie D.: Baptist clergyman and journalist. Newton was the editor of *The Christian Index* (1920–1929) and a contributor to other Baptist periodicals. He had a column in some sixty Georgia weekly newspapers in addition to a daily column in the Atlanta *Constitution*, the Savannah *Morning News,* and the Columbia *Ledger.*

Norris, John Franklyn ("Two-Gun"): Baptist clergyman and educator. President of the Bible Baptist Seminary in Fort Worth, Texas, Norris was a leader in the fight for legislation against race track gambling and other forms of "vice." He was a radio pastor of three Texas radio stations and the editor of *The Fundamentalist.*

Noyes, Alfred: English poet and dramatist.

O'Connell, William Cardinal: Roman Catholic prelate. Cardinal O'Connell was bishop of Boston (1907) and elevated to the cardinalate in 1911.

O'Hare, Kate Richards: Socialist leader indicted and jailed in 1919 for a five-year term after having been found guilty together with Eugene V. Debs of violating the Espionage Act. In 1920, President Wilson commuted her sentence.

O'Leary, Jeremiah A.: Charged with conspiracy to obstruct the draft law through publication of a magazine in 1917, O'Leary was indicted in 1919, and his trial was one of the sensations of the day, involving long months of trial, hundreds of witnesses, and pages of newspaper publicity. He appealed to Irish-Americans on the basis of their antipathy to Great Britain.

Ohio Gang: The name applied to the group of intimate friends who followed President Harding to Washington after his inauguration in 1921. They included those politicians who, during and after Harding's administration, were found to have been involved in the corruption and scandals of that time.

Olney, Richard: United States Attorney-General (1893–1895). As Secretary of State (1895–1897), Olney directed United States policy in the settlement of the Venezuela bondary dispute with Great Britain.

Owens, John W.: Journalist and writer. Beginning newspaper work with the Baltimore *Evening Sun* in 1911, Owens became editor in 1927 and editor-in-chief of the combined *Sunpapers* in 1938.

Palmer, Mitchell: Democratic member of the United States House of Representatives (1909–1915) from New York. After serving as alien property custodian (1917–1919), Palmer was appointed attorney-general of the United States (1919–1921). In 1920, Palmer was a candidate for nomination by the Democratic party for president.

Parker, Alton B.: Chief justice of the New York Court of Appeals (1898-1904). In 1904, Parker was the candidate of the conservative wing of the Democratic party for the presidency.

Pater, Walter: British essayist and critic of the late nineteenth century.

Penrose, Boies: United States Senator (Rep.) from Pennsylvania (1897–1921). Penrose was identified with high protective tariffs and was opposed to prohibition, woman's suffrage, and measures regarded popularly as progressive. The Republican boss of Pennsylvania, Penrose was erroneously thought to have dictated the nomination of Harding in 1920.

Perkins, Frances: Social worker active in labor affairs. Miss Perkins was United States Secretary of Labor from 1933 to 1945.

Pinkey, William: United States Attorney-General (1811–1814).

Poincaré, Raymond: Prime Minister of France (1912–1913; 1926–1929).

Pound, Roscoe: Noted educator and lawyer. Pound was dean of the Harvard Law School from 1916 to 1936.

"Princess Alice" (Longworth, Alice Roosevelt): Daughter of President Theodore Roosevelt. Mrs. Longworth married Nicholas

Longworth, Republican member of the United States House of
Representatives from Ohio (1903–1913; 1915–1931).

Proskauer, Joseph M.: Lawyer and justice of the New York State
Supreme Court (1923–1930). Proskauer resigned from the bench
in 1930 and resumed the practice of law.

Pulitzer, Joseph II: Journalist and publisher. Pulitzer, the son of
Joseph Pulitzer founder of the Pulitzer Prize, succeeded his
father as publisher of the St. Louis *Post-Dispatch*.

Rainey, Henry Thomas: Democratic member of the United States
House of Representatives from Illinois (1903–1921). In 1920,
Rainey unsuccessfully contested his defeat at the hands of Guy
L. Shaw. He was re-elected in 1922 and served until his death in
1934. In 1933 he had been elected speaker of the House.

Ralston, Samuel M.: United States Senator (Dem.) from Indiana
(1923–1925). Prior to his election to the Senate, Ralston had
been governor of Indiana from 1913 to 1917.

Raskob, John J.: Financier and politician. Raskob was an officer
of the General Motors Corporation but resigned in 1928 to become chairman of the Democratic National Committee. He conducted the campaign of Alfred E. Smith in 1928 and following
the election entered into business with Smith.

Reed, James A.: United States Senator (Dem.) from Missouri
(1911–1929). Reed was a delegate at five Democratic national
conventions between 1908 and 1924.

Reid, Ogden Mills: Newspaper editor and publisher. Reid became
editor of the New York *Tribune* in 1913.

Ritchie, Albert C.: Democratic governor of Maryland (1920–1935).
Ritchie was a candidate for the nomination for the presidency by
the Democratic National Convention in 1924 and again in 1932.

Robinson, Joseph: United States Senator (Dem.) from Arkansas
(1913–1937). Robinson was chairman of the Democratic national
conventions in 1920, 1928, and 1936. In 1928 he was the unsuccessful candidate for vice-president on the ticket with Alfred E.
Smith.

Robison, John K.: Naval officer and engineer. Robison was appointed
chief of the Naval Bureau of Engineering and in this capacity
designed the Pearl Harbor Naval base. Upon retirement, Robison
was a consultant engineer for the Sinclair Oil Company.

Rolph, James, Jr.: Mayor of San Francisco (1911–1932). From
1931 to 1934, Rolph was governor of California.

Roosevelt, Theodore, Jr. (Teddy Roosevelt II): Son of President Theodore Roosevelt. Roosevelt was Assistant Secretary of the Navy (1921–1924) and in 1924 was an unsuccessful candidate for governor of New York. While Assistant Secretary of the Navy, he sent a detachment of Marines to protect the Sinclair Company in developing the Teapot Dome oil field.

Root, Elihu: United States Senator (Rep.) from New York (1909–1915). Root was United States Secretary of War (1899–1904) and Secretary of State (1905–1909). Chairman of the Republican national conventions in 1904 and 1912, Root was also active in international affairs and was awarded the Nobel Peace Prize in 1912.

Shuler, Robert P.: Clergyman and lecturer. In 1932 Shuler was a candidate of the Prohibition party for senator from California, and he polled 564,000 votes.

Simmons, William J.: Organizer and Imperial Wizard of the Ku Klux Klan in 1920. Simmons was for many years a circuit-rider of the Methodist-Episcopal Church and later became a professor of history at Lanier University, in Atlanta.

Sinclair, Harry F.: Businessman and oil producer. Leasing government oil lands through Albert B. Fall, Secretary of the Interior, Sinclair was found guilty of contempt of Congress in the subsequent investigation and imprisoned.

Sinclair, Upton: Writer and politician. Sinclair was a socialist candidate for United States House of Representatives from New Jersey in 1906. In 1920 he was a socialist candidate in California for the House, and for the Senate in 1922. In 1926 and 1934 he was socialist candidate for governor of California. The author of several novels, Sinclair won the Pulitzer Prize in 1934.

Slemp, C. Bascom: Republican member of the United States House of Representatives from Virginia (1907–1923). Slemp was appointed secretary to President Coolidge in 1923.

Smith, Frank H. ("Hard-Boiled"): A lieutenant in the United States Army, Smith was given the sobriquet "Hard-Boiled" by his men while he was in command of a prison camp in France during the First World War. In 1919 his command of the camp was investigated by Congress as a result of mismanagement and brutality.

Smith, Gypsy Rodney: English evangelist and writer. Smith was engaged in evangelistic work throughout the world and made some sixty-five trips to the United States.

Smith, Jesse: Confidant of Attorney-General (1921–1924) Harry M. Daugherty and one of the group of men involved in the fraud and duplicity of the Harding administration. Smith was revealed as having accepted a $50,000 bribe to facilitate a case before the Alien Property Custodian. In anticipation of exposure, he committed suicide.

Smith, John Walter: United States Senator (Dem.) from Maryland (1908–1921). Smith had previously been governor of Maryland (1900–1904). He was an unsuccessful candidate for re-election to the United States Senate in 1920.

Smoot, Reed: United States Senator (Rep.) from Utah (1903–1933). Active in the 1920 Republican National Convention and the ensuing presidential campaign, Smoot was appointed to the World War Foreign Debt Commission by President Harding.

Snell, Bertrand Hollis: Republican member of the United States House of Representatives from New York (1915–1939). Republican minority leader from 1931 to 1937, Snell was also chairman of the Republican national conventions in 1932 and 1936.

Straton, John Roach: Baptist clergyman. Straton was pastor of a church in New York City and became renowned as a religious zealot, denouncing vice from his pulpit.

Sulgrave Foundation: A historical and patriotic society which took its name from Sulgrave Manor, the ancestral home in England of George Washington.

Sullens, Frederick: Editor of the Jackson (Mississippi) *Daily News* since 1905.

Sullivan, Mark: Journalist, columnist, and commentator. Sullivan wrote in the New York *Herald Tribune* and was also the author of the invaluable American historical commentary *Our Times*.

Sumner, William Graham: Economist and sociologist. Sumner was a Protestant Episcopal clergyman and a professor of political science at Yale (1872–1910).

Sunday, William ("Billy"): Evangelist and professional baseball player. Sunday was ordained in the Presbyterian ministry in 1909, but was active in evangelistic work until his death in 1935.

Taggart, Thomas: United States Senator (Dem.) from Indiana (1916). Taggart was Democratic national committeeman from

1904 to 1916 and was instrumental in securing the nomination of Woodrow Wilson for the presidency in 1912.

Taney, Roger B.: United States Attorney-General (1831–1833). Taney was Chief Justice of the United States Supreme Court from 1835 to 1864.

Thaw, Harry Kendall: Murderer of Stanford White, noted American architect of the early twentieth century.

Townsend, Francis E.: Originator and head of the Townsend Recovery Plan. Dr. Townsend's proposal was for a monthly pension of $200 to all United States citizens over 60, the funds to be provided by a 2 per cent transaction tax.

Tugwell, Rexford Guy: Economist and teacher. Tugwell was one of the group of "Brain Trusters" called into consultation by President Franklin Roosevelt.

Tuttle, Charles H.: United States attorney for New York. Tuttle was a vigilant prosecutor of commercial frauds in New York in 1927 and 1928.

Tydings, Millard E.: United States Senator (Dem.) from Maryland (1927–1951). Tydings was one of the conservative senators who withstood the Roosevelt "purge" in 1938.

Tyler, Wat: Leader of the Peasant's Revolt in England in 1381.

Vandenberg, Arthur H.: United States Senator (Rep.) from Michigan (1928–1951). Vandenberg, prior to 1945 a conservative and an isolationist, was considered for the presidential nomination by the Republican National Convention in 1936.

Vare, William Scott: Republican member of the United States House of Representatives from Pennsylvania (1912–1927). In 1926 Vare was elected to the United States Senate, but an investigation of campaign expenditures in the primary in which he defeated Gifford Pinchot resulted in the Senate's refusal to seat Vare even though he defeated the Democratic nominee in the ensuing election.

Villard, Oswald Garrison: Journalist and editor. Villard was editor of the New York *Evening Post* (1897–1918) and owner and editor of *The Nation* (1918–1932).

Volstead Act: The name of the act authored by Andrew J. Volstead, Republican member of the United States House of Representatives (1903–1923), which enforced the prohibition of manufacture, sale, and transport of intoxicating liquors under the Eighteenth Amendment to the Constitution.

Wadsworth, James Wolcott, Jr.: United States Senator (Rep.) from New York (1915–1927). Wadsworth was an unsuccessful candidate for re-election in 1926, but in 1933 was elected to the United States House of Representatives and served until 1951.

Walker, James J.: Democratic mayor of New York (1925–1932). Walker, involved by a state legislative investigation of corruption in New York's municipal government, resigned in 1932 rather than answer charges before Governor Franklin Roosevelt.

Wallace, Henry A.: United States Secretary of Agriculture (1933–1940). The object of much criticism for his radical farm policies, Wallace was nonetheless the nominee of the Democratic party in 1940 for Vice President. Elected with Franklin Roosevelt, he served until 1944 when, having lost the confidence of the party leaders, he was denied renomination.

Walsh, Thomas J.: United States Senator (Dem.) from Montana (1913–1933). Walsh was permanent chairman of the Democratic national conventions in 1924 and 1932. In charge of the investigation of the leasing of naval oil reserves, Walsh uncovered the Teapot Dome scandals in 1923.

Walter, John: See Smith, John Walter

Watson, James E.: United States Senator (Rep.) from Indiana (1916–1933). Watson was a delegate at large to nine Republican conventions and in the 1920 convention was chairman of the committee on resolutions.

Weller, Ovington Eugene: United States Senator (Rep.) from Maryland (1921–1927). Weller, unsuccessful in his attempt for re-election in 1926, had been delegate at large and chairman of the Maryland delegation to the Republican national conventions in 1916 and 1924.

Wheeler, Burton K.: United States Senator (Dem.) from Montana (1923–1947). In 1924, Wheeler was the Progressive party candidate for vice-president on the ticket headed by Robert M. La-Follette. It was Wheeler who, in 1924, instigated the investigation of the attorney-general and the Department of Justice.

Wheeler, Wayne B.: General counsel of the Anti-Saloon League of America, 1915–1927. Wheeler, who reached success in the passage and ratification of the Eighteenth Amendment to the Constitution, was advisor to President Harding on matters of prohibition enforcement.

White, William Allen: Editor and proprietor of the Emporia (Kansas) *Gazette*. White developed his paper into one of the most notable small papers of the country, distinguished for its editorials and policies.

Whitman, Charles Seymour: Republican governor of New York (1914–1918). Formerly a district attorney and a judge, Whitman was a zealous law enforcement officer and reformer.

Wickersham, George W.: Attorney-general of the United States (1909–1913). Wickersham was one of a group of leading Republicans that were for the League of Nations.

Willard, Daniel: Railroad executive. Willard, president of the Baltimore and Ohio Railroad, was noted for his policies which avoided labor strife in an era of labor strikes and agitation.

Willebrandt, Mabel: Assistant Attorney-General of the United States (1921–1929). Mrs. Willebrandt was, among other things, in charge of cases arising out of federal tax laws and prohibition violations.

Winebrenner, David C.: Democratic Secretary of State of Maryland (1925–1935).

Wirt, William: United States Attorney-General (1817–1829). In 1832, Wirt was the Antimasonic candidate for president of the United States.

Wood, Leonard: Chief of Staff of the United States Army (1910–1914). General Wood was a prominent candidate for the Republican nomination for president in 1916 and in 1920, when the deadlock between him and Frank Lowden made it possible for Warren Harding to succeed as the compromise candidate.

Woodin, William H.: Industrialist and financier. In 1933, Franklin Roosevelt appointed Woodin secretary of the Treasury.

Young, Owen D.: Lawyer and corporation executive. Young was associated with Charles G. Dawes as American representative to the reparations conference (1924).

Zihlman, Frederick N.: Republican member of the United States House of Representatives from Maryland (1917–1931).

Index

Rogers, Will: 127
Rolph, James, Jr.: 286
Roosevelt, Franklin D.: 138, 219,
  222, 226, 233, 235, 240, 254–55, 256–
  60, 261–64, 271–75, 284–89, 291–93,
  295–313, 315–16, 318–22, 323, 326,
  328–29, 331–36; appointments by,
  283; and Hoover, comparison of,
  285–86; inaugural address, 270–71;
  as a monarch, 280–84
Roosevelt, Theodore: 4, 13, 16–17,
  22, 31, 32, 45, 53, 67, 69, 74, 114,
  117, 157, 210, 219, 221, 226, 232,
  237, 241, 245, 247, 248–49, 254, 295,
  303, 333
Roosevelt, Theodore, Jr.: 108, 122
Root, Elihu: 26
Routh, E. C.: 178
Russell, Lillian: 301
Russia: 31, 48, 326; doctrine of conformity in, 17
Ruth, Babe: 137, 241, 266

St. Louis Post-Dispatch: 127
San Francisco, and 1920 Democratic
  National Convention: 75–76
Saturday Evening Post: 11, 25, 114,
  176
Scandals: *see* airship, Alien Property
  Custodian, Daugherty, Denby,
  Doheny, Fall, Hog Island, oil, Vet-
  erans' Bureau
Scarboro, J. A.: 182
Scopes trial: 200
Sectionalism: 58–60
Shakespeare, William: 128
Shuler, Robert: 180
Simmons, William J.: 227
Sinclair, Harry F.: 122, 174, 177, 189
Sinclair, Upton: 319
Slemp, C. Bascom: 65, 66, 68, 109
Smith, Alfred E.: 58, 71, 76, 77, 78,
  103, 114, 122, 137–39, 141–45, 147,
  175, 187–92, 196, 198, 199, 214, 220–
  21, 226, 237, 239, 255, 257–59, 261,
  297, 298, 299, 303; defeat of, 209–
  13; and Hoover, comparison of,
  184–87, 201–203; and the issue of
  religion, 138, 141–42, 144, 147–48;

155–58; and Prohibition, 143–44;
  qualifications of, 200–205; and
  Southern denominational papers,
  168–72, 177–83, 192–93; Southern
  support of, 139, 143, 148, 150–52,
  154; speech before the Liberty
  League, 300
Smith, Frank H. ("Hard-Boiled"):
  27, 29
Smith, Gypsy: 43
Smith, Jesse: 183
Smith, John Walter: 32
Smoot, Reed: 75
Snell, Bertrand Hollis: 274
Socialism: 50, 89, 106
Socialist party: 21–22, 36
South, the: 113, 116, 155; clerical
  domination, breakdown of, 198–
  200; cultural growth of, 193–94;
  denominational papers in, 168–72,
  177–83, 192–93; party alignment in,
  97; processes of change in, 163–67,
  191–92; and Prohibition, 71–72,
  104–105, 195–96; Republicans in,
  151; and Roosevelt, Franklin D.,
  240; and Smith, support of, 139,
  143, 148, 150–52, 154; vote-getting
  in, 65–67
Southern Baptist Theological Semi-
  nary: 170, 179
Southern Christian Advocate (Co-
  lumbia, S.C.): 170, 177
Southwestern Christian Advocate
  (Cincinnati, Ohio): 178
Standard Oil Company: 56–57
Star (Marion, Ohio): 43
States' Rights: 149, 240
Stock market crash, 1929: 137
Straton, John Roach: 144, 200, 202,
  207
Sulgrave Foundation: 90, 168, 169
Sullens, Frederick: 168, 169
Sullivan, Mark: 276
Sumner, William Graham: 312
Sunday, Billy: 43, 52, 73, 119, 168,
  200, 207
Sunpapers: 78, 79, 80, 98, 155
Supreme Court: 102–103, 123, 146,
  153, 280, 314, 319